MACQUEEN'S LEGACY

SHIPS OF
THE ROYAL MAIL LINE
VOLUME TWO

Conventions of Style

The title of the Royal Mail company had two forms – Royal Mail Steam Packet Co. until the 1930s and Royal Mail Lines, Ltd thereafter. At times in this book their initials are used for simplicity – RMSP and RML. The sub-title of the book – *Ships of the Royal Mail Line* – encompasses both titles, for the phrase 'the Royal Mail Line' was commonly used under both regimes. A firm with which Royal Mail had long and close associations, The Pacific Steam Navigation Co., is also sometimes referred to by its initials – PSN.

The titles 'Commodore' and 'Senior Captain' (both carrying the same status) are used where appropriate. 'Commodore' was not officially adopted until the twentieth century but was used earlier as a courtesy title.

Measurements and monetary systems used are those existing at the time. Dimensions are generally in feet and inches and distances in miles; tonnages are imperial gross measurement unless stated otherwise (a unit of cubic capacity, 1 ton = 100 cu.ft). Monetary values are mostly in pounds sterling (£); where dollar values ($) are quoted they are US dollars unless specified otherwise.

Place names use the version in use at the time (e.g. Ceylon, not Sri Lanka).

There are many instances of ship names being used for more than one vessel. The relevant numbers (I, II, III and IV) are not given in the main body of text – that detail can be identified from the Contents pages or Index.

Cover Pictures

Front cover: View from the port bridge wing of *Amazon* (III) as she negotiates the bends of the River Thames above Gravesend during the 1960s at the end of a voyage from Buenos Aires. (Author's photograph)

Back cover: Portion of the cover from a booklet issued in 1959 for *Amazon* (III), *Aragon* (II) and *Arlanza* (II), before the ships entered service. This introductory guide to Royal Mail's last passenger liners was the work of artist Howard Jarvis.

MACQUEEN'S LEGACY

SHIPS OF
THE ROYAL MAIL LINE
VOLUME TWO

Stuart Nicol

TEMPUS

First published 2001

PUBLISHED IN THE UNITED KINGDOM BY:

Tempus Publishing Ltd
The Mill, Brimscombe Port
Stroud, Gloucestershire GL5 2QG
www.tempus-publishing.com

PUBLISHED IN THE UNITED STATES OF AMERICA BY:

Tempus Publishing Inc.
2 Cumberland Street
Charleston, SC 29401
(Tel: 1-888-313-2665)
www.arcadiapublishing.com

Tempus books are available in France and Germany from the following addresses:

Tempus Publishing Group
21 Avenue de la République
37300 Joué-lès-Tours
FRANCE

Tempus Publishing Group
Gustav-Adolf-Straße 3
99084 Erfurt
GERMANY

British Library Cataloguing in Publication Data.
A catalogue record for this book is available from the British Library.

ISBN 0 7524 2119 0

Typesetting and origination by Tempus Publishing.
PRINTED AND BOUND IN GREAT BRITAIN.

Contents

Other ships

Acknowledgements

Firstly I must roll back the clock more than thirty years, to Royal Mail's management who sanctioned the research work which provided so much valuable data, and to the people and companies, too numerous to list, who willingly responded to my requests for information.

More recently, I have received unstinting support from members of the Royal Mail Association (RMA); Bob Forrester and Geoff and Clive Penny, in particular, have been in regular touch with me on the other side of the world, and we have engaged in a stimulating exchange of ideas and material. The following members have permitted me to quote from stories they have written for the RMA's Newsletter (which also provided further information): Geoff Penny, Philip Smith, Capts Douglas Brookfield and Michael Mortimer. Capt. Sir Miles Wingate did likewise for a story in Royal Mail's house magazine in the 1960s, to which he has now added extra information. Pat and June Bushell gave their blessing to items quoted from those invaluable Company history books *Royal Mail 1839-1939* and *Eight Bells*, written by their father T.A. Bushell.

Terry Lilley, whose special role in the initiation of the publication of this book was referred to in Volume 1, also provided some invaluable last-minute material. Thanks also go to Campbell McCutcheon of Tempus Publishing for so promptly following up Terry's initial contact, and for being so supportive throughout the book's gestation.

Permission for further quotations was provided by A.P. Watt & Co. on behalf of the National Trust for Places of Historic Interest or Natural Beauty, for an extract from *Just So Stories* by Rudyard Kipling; Sampson, Low Ltd, for extracts from Capt. W.H. Parker's autobiography, *Leaves from an Unwritten Log-book*.

A number of further quotations have been used from material still in copyright, some from publications and publishers either unknown or no longer existing, for which I have been unable to track down copyright holders. I apologise for not being able to acknowledge them, but I hope that the value of those references will see them taken in the spirit of an attempt to provide the best possible coverage of the Royal Mail story.

Stuart Nicol
Adelaide, South Australia
June 2001

Preface

The place held by ships in the story of a shipping company has always seemed a little enigmatic. They are part of a shipowner's infrastructure: an essential piece of equipment. Yet anyone who has been closely associated with ships knows they are much more than that. They possess character; they build reputations as happy ships or unhappy ships. Navigating officers, engineers and deck crews alike will brand them as good or bad – because of the way they handle or the idiosyncracies of the machinery.

Joseph Conrad once wrote of the great clipper ship *Torrens*, of which he was chief officer:

> *...Apart from her more brilliant qualities, such as her speed and her celebrated good looks (which by themselves go a long way with a sailor), she was regarded as a 'comfortable ship' in a strictly professional sense, which means that she was known to handle easily and to be a good sea-boat in heavy weather.*

This is the intangible quality which sailors have long experienced – a sense, almost, that their ship was a living being, perhaps a gentle giant or maybe a cantankerous handful. Walter Parker, commanding Royal Mail's first *Andes* in the 1920s, caught that flavour when he wrote that she was 'a beautiful ship, and most comfortable. I was proud to command her, but while I was in her she was suffering with a bout of laziness, as ships do sometimes...'

There is, then, more to ships than statistics. This volume looks at more than 150 vessels – not overtly in search of their characters but that is an aspect which appears from time to time. Character defines a ship's individuality more than anything else, but it is one of many ingredients. They can include milestones like the first screw ship in a fleet, the first of steel construction, the last with square rig, the pioneer of a new service. Perhaps the passenger spaces were special, the speed particularly significant. Accidents and incidents were part of it – a collision, a grounding, a fire; wartime passages and U-boat torpedoes; wine barrels smuggled in passenger baggage and a gun-toting secret agent.

Because of the quantity of material, this volume concentrates on the ships involved in the South America services, to complement Volume 1 of *Macqueen's Legacy*. That first volume deals with various aspects of the history of the Royal Mail Steam Packet Co. and Royal Mail Lines, with the story of South America services as its core. The ships travel through those pages, but by the nature of such a broad subject matter, they are often tantalisingly on the horizon.

This volume has entries at two levels – a method which has allowed considerable detail for many South America service ships, while still acknowledging the freighters and some others that played supporting roles. Among the major entries, one aim was to provide a sense of progressive development through the principal mail ships. Therefore, there is increased detail for vessels which formed particular milestones – the first fleet, the *Orinoco* class from the 1850s, the *Thames* class from about 1890, the first group of 'A' ships built prior to the First World War and the Company's largest liner – *Andes* of 1939 – are examples.

Piecing together these ship biographies was an absorbing task, for it brought to light numerous facts, tales and pictures which had rarely or never seen the light of day. The first fleet exemplified this: for their construction period, most of the material I have used came from the directors' minute books. In their pages were so many aspects of the creation of a vast new fleet – interspersed with unexpected moments of drama – that this period of genesis could have filled a book on its own.

I would like to mention, particularly, the sources of the illustrations used in this book. Nearly all of them came from Royal Mail's official files, which we managed to preserve when so much material was disposed of after the takeover by Furness, Withy & Co. I was continually amazed at the pictures that turned up in the ubiquitous brown envelopes, many of them stored for a very long time – a richness of paddle steamers and early screw ships from the 1860s and 1870s, little-known intercolonial steamers from the late nineteenth century, torpedoed ships in two world wars, non-trading craft like launches and tenders, and pictures of people, from rigidly-posed third-class passengers to the last photograph ever taken of Sir Ernest Shackleton, courtesy of an RMSP ship's photographer.

All of this, spread between the two volumes, has provided an invaluable dimension to complement the text. I hope that the words and the pictures go some way to bring alive these ships and their careers; they are well worthy of their place in history.

Finally, a word about James Macqueen. The ships and voyages which feature in this volume were the legacy of his determined efforts in the 1830s to develop a plan for a mail steamer company and to nurse it through Parliament to its incorporation in 1839. He was then at the heart of the nitty-gritty of organisation which turned theory into reality. Macqueen's story is covered in some detail in Volume 1. In this volume his influence is felt only with the first fleet, but the debt which Royal Mail owed to this puzzling Scot is the reason for the book's title – *Macqueen's Legacy*.

Aragon (II) here represents one of the pinnacles of Royal Mail's life – she is seen in London's Royal Victoria Dock, dressed overall, on the afternoon of 28 September 1964, prior to hosting a special dinner to celebrate the Company's 125th anniversary.

The First Fleet

The germination of the Royal Mail Steam Packet Co. (RMSP), and its first fleet, was an astonishing affair. This was a special time in the maritime world, for RMSP was building a fleet of ships which were to be among the largest steamers in the world. No less than fourteen were built (and three smaller vessels too) before a single service voyage took place. The Company existed from September 1839 until January 1842 before it could earn so much as a penny.

That period is generally regarded as an orderly progression, as the wisdom of the decision-makers patiently pieced together the elements which would create a company whose future loomed very rosy indeed. There were certainly many pieces to the jigsaw, but the manner of its gestation and birth was, in several ways, so flawed that it is a wonder that some of its ships ever went to sea. Initially the problems were caused by the absence of someone to oversee design and construction. Once services were operating, there were difficulties with unworkable schedules.

The seed for the first fleet was sown on 3 October 1839, a week after the Company's incorporation. On that day the directors approved letters to four people, asking 'their opinions on ideal tonnage and dimensions'. The chosen four were Oliver Lang of Woolwich, Charles Wood of Greenock, Thomas Wilson of Liverpool and Edye of Somerset House. From their responses, the specifications of Oliver Lang were selected.

Lang was asked to produce complete plans of his design; in the meantime the specifications were sent to the builders invited to tender. In some cases the tenderer was an engine-builder who sub-contracted the hulls. This happened with Caird's of Greenock, whose ships were sub-contracted to Robert Duncan, Robert Thompson and Charles Wood, and with Acraman Morgan & Co. – their hulls were built by William Patterson.

Those invited to tender were: Wigram & Green; Curlings & Young; William Pitcher (all on the Thames); Thomas Wilson of Liverpool; Charles Wood of Glasgow; Caird & Co. of Greenock; Scott Sinclair of Greenock.

Tenders for engines were sought from Miller, Ravenhill & Co.; Seaward & Capel; Maudslay, Sons & Field (all of London); Farcett & Preston of Liverpool; Scott Sinclair of Greenock, Caird & Co. of Greenock; Robert Napier of Greenock.

While that was the original list, others were added later. The following tenders were initially accepted:

1) William Pitcher, Northfleet – three ships at £22 per ton.
2) Caird & Co. Greenock – four ships at £49,000 each, including engines.
3) George Taylor, Barking – one ship at £21 15s per ton.
4) T.& J. White, Cowes – one ship at £22 per ton, including delivery at London or Liverpool.

5) Robert Menzies, Leith – one ship at £22 per ton, including masts and delivery at London or Liverpool.

6) Robert Sinclair, Greenock – two ships at £21 10s per ton including masts and boats.

7) Acraman Morgan & Co., Bristol – two ships. Hull of each, including copper and joiners work £27,300; engines, each pair £18,300. The remainder of the outfit except cabin furniture, plate etc., £4,900. Duplicates, tools and extras, £3,053.

Engines (apart from the six with Caird's and Acraman Morgan):

1) Maudslay, Sons & Field – two at £22,000 per pair.
2) Miller & Ravenhill – two at £22,000 per pair.
3) Robert Sinclair – two at £20,000 per pair.
4) Edward Bury, Liverpool – two at £17,000 per pair.

Not all of those initial acceptances worked to plan. Part of the contract required builders to take part payment in the form of RMSP shares. For each ship £2,750 was to be paid out, of which the deposit of £5 per share on 150 shares had to be paid to the bankers. George Taylor refused to take a full quota of shares and his tender was therefore rejected. P. Chaloner Sons & Co. had tendered £21 per ton and were given Taylor's order, but they didn't like the idea of taking shares either, and so William Pitcher took on this ship in addition to the three already placed with him.

Some months later, the Secretary of the Admiralty advised that a clause in the mail contract would authorise the Admiralty to employ the ships as vessels of war should the need arise. The need never *did* arise, except to carry troops, but designs had to be amended to permit strengthening to support heavy guns. Other structural alterations were needed to meet the Admiralty's demands as well. Thus, after construction of most ships had already begun, significant changes had to be made.

By then the summer of 1840 was approaching. During July the directors sifted through tenders for ships' fittings. J. Robertson & Co. of Limehouse Hole were asked to supply cordage for the London ships, while Quintin Leitch & Co. of Greenock received a similar order for the Clyde and Leith vessels. Another Limehouse firm, Hall & Ranney, made the sails for the London ships and Fish Brown & Co. supplied them for the Greenock ones. Anchors came from John Scott & Sons and Acraman Morgan. C.A. & T. Ferguson supplied the London and Cowes vessels with masts, yards and blocks. And the redoubtable Mr Snow Harris of Plymouth supplied lightning conductors for the entire fleet. These and many other orders were dealt with directly by RMSP rather than through the builders.

The first constructional setback appeared in August 1840, when Lt Kendall RN (who was assistant to the firm's founder, James Macqueen, but was virtually – and, one suspects, without significant experience – filling the role of marine superintendent) was told by John Scott Russell, manager of Caird & Co's yard, that his firm proposed placing the boilers abaft the engines in its four vessels.

RMSP was annoyed – the specification instructed that they should be forward of the engines. No reason for the change was revealed, but more than likely Scott Russell was

Launch of the first fleet ship Forth *at Leith in May 1841, reportedly in front of 60,000 spectators.*

concerned that the centre of gravity would be too far forward. It had been the Company's intention that all fourteen ships would be identical, and for this reason Lt Kendall asked Caird's to conform. Russell replied that construction was too far advanced to make any change. Thus we find the origin of that odd phenomenon in the first fleet – the placing of the funnel abaft the paddles in some ships and forward in others, when all were built to a common design.

Early in September Lt Kendall suggested fitting a roundhouse or poopdeck. The builders unanimously opposed the idea as it would create a dangerously top-heavy element. The idea was abandoned but they later approved the addition of a light spardeck, which accounts for the high-sided appearance of the hulls.

Next the Building Committee approved Oliver Lang's plans for the interior layout, with cabins on the main deck (10ft above water), each lit by a scuttle. The saloons, on the lower deck, would be moderately lit and ventilated and had the advantage of being shielded from the hot tropical sun. Further cabins opened off the saloon.

By October work was progressing well on the Thames and Clyde, and at Cowes and Leith. Those at Bristol were proceeding more slowly. Then the directors discovered that without their permission, or even their knowledge, more than one builder had taken it into his head to reduce the beam by one foot.

Hot on the heels of that revelation came another. This one was frightening, for it concerned a design flaw so serious that the entire fleet was in danger of losing a significant part of its structural strength. Originally the Company had specified dimensions for the ships, but they were changed after Lang's specifications were received. Among other things, Lang's new figures reduced the height of the Upper Deck by 18in. Now that construction was well under way, builders were discovering that the main shaft would cut through the upper deck – they were at precisely the same height. Without an RMSP representative to keep an eye on things, the builders had a field day choosing how to overcome the problem. One even invented an ingenious method of bending the deck around the shaft.

The Company remained ignorant until one of the builders thought to let them know. He was John Scott Russell, perhaps attempting to make amends for the wrath he had incurred by re-locating the engines. At that stage he was manager of Caird & Co., but was close to parting company with them, prior to embarking on a successful career as a shipbuilder on the Thames. Russell told the directors that he had spotted the problem early enough to raise the height of the deck so that it would pass over the shaft. In view of that seemingly logical solution, the directors – clearly out of their depth – asked him to help the Company by negotiating with the other builders. The Upper Deck must now pass over the shaft, so as to be about 22ft 6in above the upper side of the floor at the shelf and 23ft in the middle. The Main Deck was to be placed 8ft below the upper deck, and the Platform Deck was to be 5ft 6in below that. At the same time they authorized a light spardeck seven feet above the Upper Deck.

Demanding such drastic changes at so advanced a stage was a tall order, but Scott Russell agreed to take it on. His two reports were delivered with remarkable speed:

I went down the river to Northfleet to communicate with Mr Pitcher for the purpose of determining with him the mode to be adopted in raising the ships and for agreeing with him upon the plan of midship section with which to furnish the other builders. I found him, as formerly, most confident that the plan proposed, of returning back to the original dimensions, was the best possible mode of proceeding, and that he was delighted at the prospect of having permission to adopt it, without making any additional charge to the company.

Next day I had an interview with Mr White of Cowes, with whom I entered fully into the subject. Mr White was of opinion that the expense of the change would amount, in his ship, to upwards of £1,000. Being desirous, however, to promote the object in view, he has agreed to be himself at part of the expense, and ask from the Company only the sum of £750…

On Saturday night I set out for Scotland and reached Greenock on Monday morning. All that day and Tuesday were occupied in repeated interviews with Messrs Scott & McMillan. On Wednesday and Thursday I went to Leith and arranged with Mr Menzies.

My interview with Mr Menzies was quite satisfactory, but owing to certain circumstances… his position is considerably different from that of the other builders and the alteration will be to him much more expensive. He had for a considerable time entertained the expectation that the ships would have to be raised to about 23 feet, and had therefore proceeded on that supposition, keeping up his top timbers sufficiently long to admit of this increased height. When, however, he received orders from the Committee to place his decks at the height last determined on by Mr Lang, viz 21 feet, it happened that his men were out of work and to give them employment he at once ordered them to saw off all the top timbers to suit this new height of 21 feet 3 inches at the shelf and 21 feet 9 inches at the centre, and he instantly set about planking the upper part of the ship, proceeding with great rapidity. He

13

The 1,856-ton Trent *(I), a unit of RMSP's first fleet built in 1841. She was broken up at Woolwich in 1865, the last survivor of the original fourteen ships.*

was, however, suddenly brought to a stop by finding that this height would entirely cut away all the strength and fastening of the ship in the middle inasmuch as the shaft of the engine would pass right through the centre of the deck; and therefore, seeing the impossibility of proceeding at this height, he at once stopped short, otherwise I should have found the whole of his ship entirely planked.

I also found that he had received the order to raise the ship to 21 feet, without any condition in regard to expense, and had accordingly run up a large bill for expense so incurred, which must necessarily be thrown away as the ship cannot be retained at its present height of 21 feet, but must either be raised 12 inches or lowered 18 inches. The alterations thus made increase likewise the difficulty of the change to 23 feet, as the work thus done will have to be entirely undone, before it can proceed. Mr Menzies, it will thus be seen, labours under double disadvantages, but nevertheless he consents to make the proposed change for the sum of £1,285, a sum which, under all the circumstances, may be considered sufficiently reasonable.

It thus appears that out of the whole fleet, the Company may now have 10 ships alike, in general dimensions, for the aggregate sum of £2,035. There only remain four others to be dealt with, viz: two with Scott & McMillan and Acramans & Morgan's two.

I regret to state that although I found Messrs Scott & McMillan quite willing to make the proposed change, I found them quite impracticable as regards doing so at a moderate sum. They seem quite determined to insist upon the large sum already named by them, and although I endeavoured to show them the unreasonableness of this demand, and used every argument to induce them to assist the directors out of their present dilemma, I failed entirely in obtaining any abatement of this charge except with Mr McMillan, who agreed to deduct 3/- per ton from his former charge.

In these circumstances I felt myself at a loss how to proceed. I consulted eminent builders, who are well acquainted with the state of these ships and begged of them an estimate of the real cost of the alteration required by the Company. I have thus obtained detailed estimates on which I can place implicit reliance. The estimates are made in the most expansive manner and charge for at the high rates of profit usually [existing] in doing ships' repairs – and this ample estimate amounts to £846 3s. The charge which Messrs Scott & McMillan propose to make, for the same work, is £1,734 15s on each ship. It remains for the directors to consider how this claim should be dealt with.

About the Bristol ships there can be no difficulty as their frames are not yet in such an advanced state as to make it necessary for the builders to incur any considerable expense in placing the decks at the same height as the others. In that point they may possibly imitate the readiness of Mr Pitcher to meet the views of the directors, at all events something like £500 a ship would probably cover the amount of their claim.

In conclusion I beg to add that although I feel most deeply the responsibility of the position in which the directors have placed me, and although it would be a matter of sincere satisfaction to myself as an individual to have altogether abstained from mixing myself up in this matter, in a way more likely to make me enemies than to gain me friends; yet I do not after the most mature and, I may say, painful consideration of the subject over and over again, and after consultation with those practical men whose past success renders their opinions most worthy of respect, perceive the slightest cause for entertaining a doubt as to the sound practical expediency of the conclusion at which the directors arrived at their late meeting. I find it a matter of deep regret with the owners of the Halifax ships [Samuel Cunard's recently-completed first ships, of about 1,100 tons] that their capacity was not made greater than it is. I also find from the builders of one of these ships that he would have had no hesitation, even with their beam three feet less than ours, in raising up a poop and forecastle deck upon her to the same height as our own, in perfect confidence of her stability. I am confident, therefore, that all this discussion and delay, however disagreeable, has been attended with most valuable results to the future mercantile success of the Company.

The Court of Directors approved all of those amounts, except that Scott & McMillan were offered £1,000 per ship.

On 26 November came Scott Russell's second report, dealing with the ships at Bristol:

Gentlemen, I have this morning returned from Bristol after having visited the ships there, building for this Company under the contract of Messrs Acramans & Morgan; and having had an interview with Mr Morgan, and with Mr Patterson the builder of the ships, I am happy to be able to state that the result of this interview is highly satisfactory. After going with them most thoroughly into the examination of the whole subject, Mr Patterson, having before him the experience of the Great Western of which he was the builder, gives it as his decided opinion that the dimensions originally intended for the ships, and to which it is now intended to return, are, in every respect, preferable to Mr Lang's dimensions, and Mr Morgan coincides entirely with him on the expediency of having the deck raised to pass over the shaft; which will require a depth of 22 feet 9 inches at the shelf and 23 feet 3 inches at the centre.

Mr Patterson is quite satisfied of the stability of the ships. He further states that the iron ballast carried in the Great Western was not for the purpose of correcting any deficiency in her stability, but for the purpose of correcting her trim which had been greatly deranged by Messrs Maudslay's new plan of putting the boiler before the engines.

Messrs Acramans & Morgan, if permitted to raise their decks over their shafts as now proposed, will be happy to do so at their own expense, with the proviso only, that they be permitted to do it in the way which Mr Patterson considers most beneficial to the strength of the ship. If, however, they are compelled to follow up the letter of their specification the Company will be required to pay on each vessel the sum of £500.

Thus then, Gentlemen, I have completed the mission with which I have been entrusted by the Court, and in such a manner as I hope is to their satisfaction.

The aggregate tonnage of your fleet will now be increased by 3,000 tons. Its nominal value increased by £60,000 and the whole of the vessels rendered capable of performing, in the best possible manner, the duties expected of them and for the performance of which they would, on their old dimensions, have been quite incapable. For this change the Company will only have to pay the sum of £4,035…

The crisis, then, had been averted, but the nearness to a calamity had shocked the Court. Lt Kendall resigned almost at once, and Capt. Edward Chappell RN was appointed Marine Superintendent. There were many matters which desperately needed the expertise of such a person, and Capt. Chappell proved more valuable than anyone else to RMSP during the next year or two.

His first major task was to report on the rig for the ships. His recommendations were based on fourteen years in sailing ships as well as consultations with the captains of three transatlantic steamers, the *Great Western* among them. Chappell's principal concern was to keep top hamper to a minimum, which would save money and improve their seagoing qualities. He proposed eliminating main yards, main topsail yards, flying jib-booms, lower studdingsail booms, topmast studdingsail booms, topgallant mast studdingsail booms, flying jibs, main courses, main half topsails, main topmast staysails, lower studdingsails, topmast studdingsails and topgallant studdingsails – a comprehensive culling of canvas power.

An idea of the scale of the rig may be gained from the following dimensions:

Foremast, 80ft high by 2ft diameter; fore topmast, 36ft by 1ft; yards, 70ft by 1ft 3in, 52ft by 10½in, 34ft by 6½in, and 28ft by 4in; gaff, 36ft by 10in. Main mast, 88ft by 2ft; main topmast, 55ft by 10½in; gaff, 36ft by 10in. Mizen mast 60ft by 1ft 3in; mizen topmast, 40ft by 7in; gaff, 27ft by 6 inches; spanker boom, 42ft by 1ft. The bowsprit (outside knight heads) was 24ft by 1ft 10in, and the jibboom 36ft by 11in.

Next to gain Capt. Chappell's attention were the ships' boats. His report was presented to the Court during the first few days of 1841 – this was what the directors were asked to consider:

Establishment of boats

This matter appears to have been frequently considered, but has not yet been fully determined. The subject presents some difficulty, as no trans-Atlantic steamer yet built carries boats adequate to save the lives of passengers and crew, even should the ship catch fire and be burnt in a dead calm; nor have any of them a boat capable to carry out a bower anchor, to heave the ship off should she ground in the finest weather. This last point is not perhaps of such great importance where the vessels proceed straight across the Atlantic from one port to another, without touching at intermediate bays or roadsteads; but where it is necessary to perform coasting voyages among islands and shoals as in the West Indies, the want of a good large boat may occasion the entire loss of a ship.

The reason why steamships are not fitted with launches or long boats like all other vessels, is that the space on deck is occupied so entirely for other purposes, with engine hatches, cabins, stock pens etc, that room cannot be afforded for placing large boats; and to hoist them outside the ship would occasion injurious straining upon the upperworks, cause heavy rolling in a sea etc.

All projectors of ocean steamers have felt the difficulties here described. In the Great Western they had at first a long boat stowed before the crank hatches – two cutters, one on each quarter, a gig and a jolly boat. The two last, being stowed on the sponson grating, abaft the paddle boxes, were washed away in the first gale of wind and never replaced. One of the quarter cutters afterwards filled and broke her back, and a lifeboat built at New York was substituted, but which it is openly admitted they carry more for show than for use. The long boat was subsequently left on shore altogether and the remaining large cutter is so fixed bottom up amidships, that it is doubtful if she could be got out even in harbour without considerable difficulty. This detail has been furnished to the Marine Superintendent by the Managing Director of the Great Western, who concludes by saying 'You would do well to think of Smith's paddle box boats'.

In the Halifax steamers [i.e. Cunard] they seem to have evaded this question, and to have discarded all hope of saving lives etc by merely supplying the ships with four small boats, which are stowed two on each quarter; but the Marine Superintendent is informed that the Government are not inattentive to this deficiency, and it is not unlikely but it may ultimately interfere to compel a greater attention to public security.

Mr Kendall seems to have contemplated for the Company's ships an establishment of boats similar to that of the Halifax steamers, but he was also strongly in favour of Smith's paddle box boats.

The plain matter which the Court will have to decide, therefore, is whether the Royal Mail Company's ships shall be sent to sea, like other transatlantic steamers, without boats capable of saving all hands, or of carrying out a bower anchor; or whether the directors will incur the expense of Smith's paddle box boats, by which such objects may be obtained.

This very important subject had occupied much consideration of the Marine Superintendent previous to his undertaking the duties of his present office. In a report made by order of the Admiralty to the Parliamentary Committee in May 1839, he gave a decided opinion in favour of Smith's boats, which judgement has since been confirmed by the unanimous testimony of every person who has either seen boats so fitted, or made trial of them afterwards.

As relates to their adoption by the Royal Mail Co., the question seems to resolve itself under three heads: weight, space, expense.

1) Weight. These boats would be about 30 feet long, 10 feet 8 inches wide and 3 feet deep – calculated to carry about one hundred persons each. They should be built with diagonal double planking, filled between timbers – so that they would prove tight and durable in a tropical climate and be considerably lighter in proportion to their size than ships' long boats usually are, independent of which there will be some diminution of weight from part of the paddle box being removed...

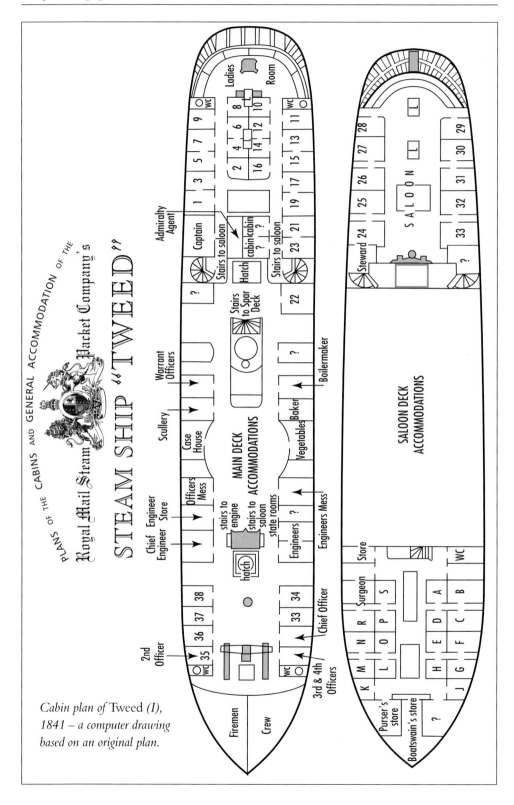

PLANS OF THE CABINS AND GENERAL ACCOMMODATION OF THE

Royal Mail Steam Packet Company's

STEAM SHIP "TWEED"

Cabin plan of Tweed *(I),
1841 – a computer drawing
based on an original plan.*

2) *Space. A paddle box fitted to be covered with a boat of this description will be no higher than the common paddle box, while the form of a boat's bottom certainly offers less resistance to the wind.*

3) *Expense. Captain Smith calculates the whole cost of such boats, with all the iron davits etc complete at £200 each vessel. He states also that he shall make no charge for his patent right but as he must necessarily incur expense in superintending their fitment and preparing drawings etc, he would have to leave it to the Court to make such reasonable compensation as it may deem proper and just.*

Should the Court decide upon the adoption of these boats, no time must be lost in apprising the builders of the situation in order that the paddle boxes may be constructed accordingly, and it may occur that one or two ships will be found too far advanced to admit of it.

As relates to the ordinary working boats of the ships, the Marine Superintendent respectfully recommends the adoption of the scale establishments in the Halifax steamers as follows:

1 – Pinnace   25 feet long; 7 feet beam moulded; 2 ft 9 in deep
2 – Pinnace   22 ft 6 in long; 6 ft 3 in beam moulded; 2 ft 6 in deep
3 – Cutter   20 ft 6 in long; 5 ft 6 in beam moulded; 2 ft 6 in deep
4 – Gig   24 ft long; 4 ft 10 in beam moulded; 2 ft deep

These four boats to be carried as quarter boats, two on each side, abaft the paddle boxes.

Resolved: Captain Chappell's recommendations be adopted, including the adoption of the paddle box boats.

Chappell's next report concerned names for the steamers, which he said was a matter of some urgency, not least as a guide to the figurehead carvers. 'It is presumed,' he told the Court, 'that you desire the fleet to be named as a class. I first considered rivers as the theme, but there are so many steamers with such names that it appears the most common of all'. In view of that, Capt. Chappell provided alternative ideas, but the directors nevertheless decided on river names. It started a tradition which was strongly, though not exclusively, adhered to throughout the Company's life. Though it *was* a commonly used theme, in time these names became particularly associated with Royal Mail. The names put forward on 14 January were: *Thames, Medway, Isis, Trent, Clyde, Tweed, Tay, Teviot, Dee, Yarrow, Severn, Avon, Medina, Forth*. Of those, only *Yarrow* was not approved – it was changed to *Solway*. That was to allow Caird's four ships to bear Scottish names – *Tay, Teviot, Dee* and *Solway*. In fact, as far as practicable, all of the names were of rivers in the vicinity of their respective builders.

The final subject broached during the marathon meeting of 14 January returned to less aesthetic matters. Chappell reported: 'It is customary to keep a skilful naval architect making drawings of various fitments required. Continual references are now being made by builders for such information and I am at a loss to whom I should apply on the subject. As the ships seem to be building upon a plan of Mr Pitcher's, should he be asked to supply all the drawings? Or will the Court employ a marine draughtsman, to consult with Mr Pitcher, and prepare what is required under his instructions?'

That, too, seemed an amazing oversight. The Court selected the latter course.

Getting Ready For Sea

By the winter of 1840/41 the more significant matters of design and construction had been dealt with, and the focal point came closer. Which chronometers should be ordered? Two-day ones, the Court decided. How can they be accurately checked? Capt. Chappell talked to the Hydrographer to the Navy, Capt. Beaufort, and was recommended to Mr Fisher, chaplain of Greenwich Hospital and a first-rate astronomer who lived within sight of the signal ball on Greenwich Observatory. The Rev. Mr Fisher agreed to take on the job. After six months he announced that four were faulty and the rest in good working order.

Should cabin stoves be fitted? Surprisingly, that question caused some discussion, seemingly on the basis that some directors felt that, as services mostly would be concentrated around the Caribbean, heating would not be needed. Common sense prevailed – early parts of voyages would, for much of the year, be in cooler climates and it was intended to extend services to New York and Halifax, NS. Anyone who has voyaged in winter along the American coast northwards from the Caribbean will know that there is a region where the hot, tropical air abruptly changes as you approach the Grand Banks – within two days temperatures of 80°F can plummet to freezing point.

A week later, the directors tackled the question of china. For the 'first table', they decided, the china would bear a design with oak wreaths. The 'second table' would have the same china but without wreaths! Innumerable matters of that kind occupied the people during the winter. As the brighter days of spring appeared there were reports of construction proceeding in earnest. Those reports generally came from Capt. Chappell, who now really began to show his worth. Had some of the workmanship gone unheeded, there would have been unpleasant – and quite possibly dangerous – consequences.

On 18 March he reported on the vessels in Scotland. *Forth*, *Tweed* and *Tay* were generally of 'very fair workmanship except where *Tay* has no stop for oakum and some trusses made from Quebec oak instead of the African or English as per contract'. In Scott & Sons yard, *Dee* was the victim of some rough work and two breast hooks, found to be sappy and defective, were condemned. Of *Teviot*, which Duncans were building on behalf of Caird's, the Marine Superintendent wrote:

> *She is all in frame but I am sorry to add that the timbers are not so well squared as they ought to have been, the sap having been left on in many places, the joints of the frames and fillings have been caulked instead of being fitted as per specification. I had also to complain of the unfairness of the bottom and of the defective manner in which the bottom plank was worked, the timbers being badly trimmed, and rendered it impossible for the plank to touch them but at intervals.*

Solway (which would be lost less than two years after entering service) drew this comment: 'Materials and workmanship in this ship are very good and I consider the *Solway* one of the most substantial ships in the fleet'. *Clyde* was 'to all appearances faithfully built, her materials and workmanship being good where visible'.

Over in Bristol he reported that in *Avon* 'three main deck strakes are entirely in Dantzic pine instead of English oak as in contract. The lower timbers comprising the frame of the ship show a good deal of heart shake, and much sap has been left on the angles; and of the oak timbers aloft several were so defective that three long timbers in the larboard quarter, one in the starboard bow, one hawse timber and one piece of the main keelson were condemned…' Sap had also been left on in many parts of *Severn*, but the frame was better, the timbers having been selected earlier.

Capt. Chappell next went to Cowes and found *Medina* making slow headway, though the timber seemed sound and workmanship good. Because of their close proximity, William Pitcher's four ships on the Thames were not included in the reports. There was, in fact, no reference to them in the minutes, from which it may be assumed there were no serious problems.

After a two-month gap, Chappell re-visited the ships in Scotland. He dealt first with *Dee* and *Solway*:

> *The holding down bolts of the engines were driven through the bottom planking in a most objectionable manner, being countersunk at unequal distances. In both the* Dee *and* Solway *the main deck (instead of being raised fairly over the paddle shaft as per agreement to be paid for by the Company) has been bent, so as to give it an unsightly appearance, though it may not be weaker on that account. On examination of the* Solway's *rudder, the main piece, from not being properly constructed, was discovered to be notched so deeply for the rule joint as to cut away all but five inches of solid wood. The Marine Superintendent is convinced that such a rudder would scarcely have carried the ship safely out of the Clyde. It was consequently condemned.*

Tay was in no better shape and her rudder was condemned for the same reason – she had eight inches of wood where the thickness should have been eighteen. Much more workmanship warranted complaint – weak knees, bad bolting and so on. *Tweed* had to be examined in drydock because she had become leaky after launching.

Ships were often run aground to take in their engines, to which Capt. Chappell objected strongly. Samuel Cunard's ships had survived that treatment, but he pointed out that they had already been strengthened by doubling. Now he stressed the point again, for *Clyde* had strained badly while taking in her engines.

Caird's vessels were more advanced than the others and, at the beginning of June 1841, RMSP wrote to them enquiring if three would be ready to take the sailings on 1 August, 15 August and 1 September. Such optimism! Services did not begin until months later.

The initial crewing arrangements were decided in June, and though slight modifications occurred, the basic crew structure was as overleaf.

It was later decided that two midshipmen would be employed on each ship 'to be not younger than 14 nor older than 16, unless they have been to sea, and in no case older than 18'.

Though the Admiralty had insisted on the ships being able to carry heavy ordnance, they refused to supply any portion of the vessels' armament, even though the Company's security for their safe custody was promised. Only small arms were taken on board: two 6lb signal cannon and thirty each of muskets or carbines, pistols, cutlasses and pikes. A 32lb gun was to have been placed on the foredeck, but the Admiralty's reaction to the supply of guns caused a change of heart. 'The question of heavy ordnance', a minute on 29 July recorded, 'shall be left for future consideration'. They were never fitted.

Proposed Establishment of Officers and Men & Scale of Pay

No.	Ship's crew	rate of pay
	Deck	
1	Captain (p.a)	£500
	remainder per month	
1	Chief Officer	£15
1	Second Officer	£8
1	Third Officer	£6
1	Surgeon	£6
1	Purser	£10
1	Boatswain	£5
1	Gunner	£5
1	Carpenter	£6
1	Carpenter's mate	£5
1	Ship's Cook	£4
12	Able Seamen	£3
6	Ordinary Seamen	£2 10s
2	Boys	£1
1	Captain's Servant	£2
1	Officers' Servant	£2
33	**TOTAL** (p.a)	**£2,024**
	Engine Room	
1	Chief Engineer (p.a)	£250
	remainder are per month	
1	Second Engineer	£14
1	Third Engineer	£13
1	Fourth Engineer	£12
1	Smith & Armourer	£4
12	Firemen	£4
1	Chief Coal Trimmer	£4
8	Coal Trimmers	£3
1	Engineer's Apprentice	£1
27	**Total** (p.a)	**£1,690**

No.	Ship's crew	rate of pay
	Stewards' Department	
1	Head Steward (monthly)	£8
1	Head Waiter	£5
5	Waiters	£2 10s
1	Pantryman	£4
1	Head Porter	£2 10s
1	Second Porter	£2
1	Storekeeper	£4
1	Storeroom Man	£1 10s
1	Butcher & Stock keeper	£3
1	Stewards' Boy	£1
1	Baker & Pastry Cook	£5
	Females	
1	Dish Washer	£2
1	Head Cook	£8
1	Second Cook	£4
1	Third Cook	£3
1	Stewardess	£4
1	Second Stewardess	£2
21	**Total** (p.a)	**£858**

Total per ship of £4,572 per annum for wages

By the autumn of 1841 several vessels were completed, and others nearly so. At Cowes, *Medina* was taking on a ballast cargo of pipe clay, specially shipped across from Poole, for the tow north to Liverpool where she was to receive her engines. Early in October *Tweed* made trials on the Clyde but bad luck remained with her – a man fell overboard and a valve became choked.

The following month Capt. Chappell was on board *Forth* for her trials, out through the Rock Channel and returning to the Mersey through the Victoria Channel, a circular voyage of thirty-five miles. She reached $10\frac{3}{4}$ knots, averaging 10. The engines worked up to $16\frac{1}{2}$ strokes per minute. Chappell wrote of the engines: 'There certainly cannot be a finer piece of workmanship – they worked as smoothly as the machinery of a watch and were the admiration of every person... Mr Menzies has completed the hull in the most satisfactory manner'.

There the compliments stopped, for during the trials another major blunder became apparent. Chappell was alarmed at the violent and constant vibration. The skylights, cabin doors and after capstan shook incessantly, he said. There was also a constant cloud of spray abaft the paddle boxes which kept the decks permanently wet.

His deduction was that the clearance between the paddles and paddle-box casing was not great enough to allow free movement of the lifted water. The builders and engineers, it transpired, were worried that the vessel's centre of gravity would be too far forward; without a word to the Company they had shifted the shaft, paddles and the entire body of machinery one foot further aft. The paddles thus came so close to the after paddle beam that part of the beam was whittled away to allow a bare inch of space between the two. Measures were quickly taken to rectify matters.

While the fleet was nearing completion, James Macqueen returned from a marathon stint across the Atlantic to arrange the Caribbean end of the operations, and while he continued refining the schedules, he now also worked out the initial appropriation of steamers, based on a first departure on 15 December – four and a half months later than planned. Scheduling was not completed until 25 November, and there were numerous last minute arrangements to be made.

An important matter, of course, was food, and in addition to the usual provedore it was decided to carry live animals for slaughter during the voyage. An extensive farmyard was listed for purchase: ten cows and calves at £15 each; 180 Southdown sheep at £2 10s each; 120 pigs at £1 7s 6d each – a total of £915. Quantities of hay, oil cake, peas, oats and barley were purchased for fodder. The animals were purchased for cash at the Salisbury livestock market and the crops from the Southampton Corn Exchange.

Passage rates, again drawn up by James Macqueen, were printed during the month before operations began. The Court now began to express concerns about *Avon* and *Severn*, which were making laboriously slow progress at Bristol. The problem emanated from Acraman, Morgan, which went into liquidation before the ships were completed. Royal Mail's directors consequently authorized the purchase of two Glasgow ships. The deal was completed on 15 December 1841. J. Martin and G. & J. Burns were paid £23,599 11s for *Actaeon* and Thomson & McConnell received £11,800 10s for *City of Glasgow*. It will come as little surprise to learn that their purchase in Glasgow was handled by John Scott Russell.

As the final arrangements were sorted out, ships sailed from all parts of the coast round to Southampton, where they congregated in a show of mercantile strength which must have given new heart to the people who had endured such a roller coaster ride for the past two years.

Across the Atlantic

What manner of ships were these great steamers awaiting the moment of departure? In his Royal Mail centenary book, T.A. Bushell described the fourteen mail steamers thus:

> *The best cabins were right aft, opening out of the main saloon and with large windows set in the stern and counters. The square sterns of these early ships, with their gilded ornamental scroll-work surrounding two tiers of windows, were somewhat akin to the galleons of earlier times, although they did not rise so high out of the water. Above was the quarter-deck, with wheel and compasses, from which the ship was navigated. Most contemporary vessels had an open deck between forecastle and poop, but the Royal Mail company filled in the intervening space with a light spar deck. This provided a continuous promenade for the passengers and a drier ship in heavy weather.*
>
> *The bottoms of all the vessels had to be sheathed in copper to protect them against the ravages of the toredo worm in tropical waters. This was costly. Many alternatives seem to have been tried, but apparently without success. All the vessels were originally fitted with three masts and rigged as barquentines, i.e. with yards on the foremast only, but in later years many had their mizens removed to reduce the top weight. Later still, yards were added to the mainmast in an attempt to give increased speed and the resulting brig rig remained in vogue for many years.*
>
> *Not a great deal is known about the engines of these early ships. They appear to have been of the side lever type, giving a service speed of 8 to 9 knots on a nominal horsepower of 400. The boilers were of cast iron, with brick flues, and the steam pressure did not exceed 6 lbs per square inch. The paddle floats were of birch wood. Those of the Clyde were 8ft 8in long, 3 feet wide and $2\frac{1}{2}$ inches thick. Considering the early character of these engines, they gave surprisingly little trouble and proved very reliable. There were no engine-room telegraphs, the orders were passed verbally through the gratings or through a voice pipe to the engineers below.*

They were certainly built with barquentine rig, and some had the mizen removed several years later, as Bushell stated; a general change was apparently also made to add yards and square sails to the mainmast, producing brig rig. Accurate detailing of the changes, however, is practically impossible. For instance, two illustrations of the incident on board *Trent* in 1861, when two officials during the American Civil War were taken from the ship by force, show *Trent* still with three masts (long after the mizen would have been removed if that had been the case). One shows square rig on the mainmast while the other has no yards.

The first steamer to sail was *Forth*, which departed on the morning of 17 December 1841. Next day three more left Southampton. After more than two years of sweat and toil, of problems, solutions and more problems, this giant enterprise was on its way, though those first Southampton departures were placement voyages and the mail service officially began only when *Thames* and *Tay* left Falmouth in the early days of the New Year. The operation was not the smooth slipping into gear that has sometimes been portrayed – RMSP simply swapped one set of problems for another. In one sense the new ones were worse, for at least while the ships were building, embarrassing matters could be kept reasonably within the family. Once the ships were at sea there was no secrecy – they could expect public criticism if things didn't go right.

They *didn't* go right. By 1843 forthright attacks on management appeared in newspapers after announcements of repeated losses, and much of the reason for that could be traced back to the inadequacies and immense complexity of the schedules.

It is important to keep matters in perspective. Many a business enterprise was started by people who, had they known what they faced, would probably never have contemplated the proposition. They pulled through by their faith in a vision, sheer hard work and, probably, a little luck. That was the way of it for Royal Mail; in time, as it grew and prospered, it left behind the gloomy days when the directors met at number 55 Moorgate Street once a week and read the reports – a litany of vessels stranding, misconduct by officers, complaints from passengers, financial claims from all quarters. There were, of course, good items, too – often letters of testimonial to captains.

Extracts from captains' reports provide a stark picture of the first tentative fingers of steam navigation probing across the ocean to the tropical waters of the Caribbean. One of the biggest problems to overcome was the metamorphosis from the days of sail. These ships were a giant advance on the barques and brigs of the day; they were run differently and that was where officers, engineers and crews alike had to make significant adjustments. Many did, but enough found the transition difficult to explain some of the reports which follow. Seamen were grasping, perhaps a little blindly, at something new and strange. Ocean-going steamships were so much in their infancy that the halcyon era of the clipper ship still had not arrived.

In short, the period of a single lifetime had wrought changes to the maritime world of such immense proportions that it is hardly surprising that many took time to adjust to the new world of steamers, and to the distinctly more civilised environment expected by passengers. The problems experienced during RMSP's early operations not only reflected that, but also the intricately-geared mechanism of Macqueen's complicated schedule. These are snatches based on 1842 captain's reports received in London:

Actaeon – *Reached Grenada 21 January 1842; sailed 23 January and returned from Curaçao on the 30th. During her return passage the ship passed Puerto Cabello and the Purser accordingly wants to know how to charge fares.*

Clyde – *At Nassau on 19 February, having left the Jamaica mails behind. Running nine days behind schedule.*

Forth – *At Havana on 14 February, having completed her second voyage round the Gulf of Mexico. Havana authorities complaining of crew's rowdyism; they want a stone wall built around the depot to keep them in.*

Solway – *At Havana 14 February. A strong 'norther' forced her to omit Tampico. Delayed off the Mississippi awaiting a tug.*

Tay – *At Havana 15 February. Coaltrimmers were up before the magistrate at Belize. Strong 'norther' and haze delayed voyage from Belize by 36 hours; leaving harbour here the ship grounded but sustained no injury.*

Dee – *At Barbados 3 February after voyage of 16 days 22 hours from Southampton. Sighted* Medina *during voyage. Crew all well and no complaints.*

City of Glasgow – *First voyage out. Scarcely any trade wind. Negroes were on strike in Demerara which made coaling difficult – took 24 hours to ship 52 tons, which was all that was available. Chief Engineer and a coaltrimmer suspended for 'misbehaviour'. Did not call at Surinam (Dutch Guiana) or Tobago, though ordered to do so.*

City of Glasgow – *March 1842. The surgeon was sent home because he was insane. Ship's crew described by Captain Boxer as 'absolutely very little short of savages'. The third engineer was imprisoned at Barbados for attacking the saloon cook – 'he is a notorious character having been flogged and dismissed Her Majesty's service'.*

Clyde – *April 1842. After an investigation into the conduct of Captain Woodruff, he was suspended and later dismissed.*

City of Glasgow – *At Barbados 23 March. Captain Boxer reports he learns a passenger is to complain about lack of attention; he will take legal action against the passenger if it becomes necessary. Three pieces of iron have been found in the valves – put down to foul play by the chief engineer who was dismissed for misconduct. Also reports a broken side-beam; has been recommended not to go to sea on one engine.*

A report from Capt. Hast at St Thomas, dated 9 April, mirrored the complexity of schedules: *Thames* arrived Barbados 4 April after a very favourable passage – eleven days from Madeira. As *Trent* was waiting to convey the mails to Trinidad etc, Capt. Hast was unable to carry out his instructions any further. Since *Actaeon* had not arrived, and as she had six days' coal left, *Thames* sailed through the northern islands to St Thomas where she arrived on 8 April:

Thames – *Having taken on 100 tons of coal here, and transferred quicksilver to* Medway, *she leaves St Thomas today (9 April) for Grenada to complete coaling, the stock at St Thomas being low, so that she will be in time to receive the Trinidad mails from the next outward Packet.* Thames *will have to call at Barbados as* Actaeon *left for there on 9 April. This is fortunate as* Thames *has a crack in the engine framing which is becoming worse and the mail agent is protesting against the vessel continuing in service until it is strengthened. The vessel will go to Grenada to coal and strengthen the cracked casing.*

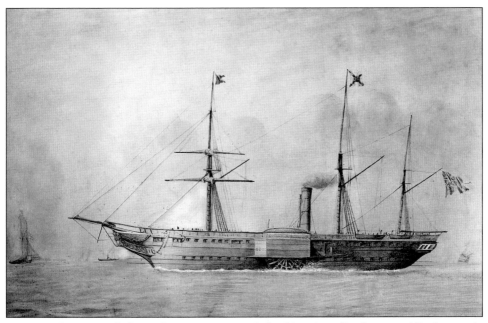

Drawing of Dee *(I) which may be contemporary with the ship – its earliest known publication was in a brochure in 1906. Note that, compared with illustrations of other ships from the group, her funnel is abaft the paddles. This occurred in the four ships contracted to Caird & Co., and is explained in the story.*

Trent – *At Barbados 23 April. Captain Miller reports that ship and engine logs prove that none of the Company's fleet could perform Table 3 within the allotted time.* Trent *has just completed the voyage laid out in Table 3 and is the first vessel to do so on schedule, but she only managed it by omitting six ports. Complains that a coaling hulk at Demerara with 1,200 tons on board should remain there when other ports have nearly run out. Captain Miller writes forcibly on the Company's arrangements in the West Indies, claiming that agents of 'active, energetic, decisive habits, wholly and entirely devoted to the Company's service' should be sent out from England to superintend the native labour forces.*

That suggests there was an inefficiency in operations and that, without some control, the Company was paying more for goods and services than it should. Captain Miller also criticised, as others had done, the complicated schedules which were making a mockery of timetables. That, in turn, was having an adverse effect on passenger bookings. He stated that sailing ships were leaving for England overflowing with passengers while RMSP's ships were attracting little support.

Thames – *23 April. Captain Hast will attempt to complete Table 3 on schedule but doubts it will be possible – if it becomes evident the ship is falling behind, they will return via Trinidad, coal at Grenada and thus be ready to receive the mails for the western area. If* City of Glasgow *is still disabled he will take the mails for Guyana.*

Loss of Isis, *October 1842.* Isis *is the more distant vessel – the dominant ship to the right is* Medway *(I), which was escorting her. Painted by 'Mr Higgins from a sketch made at the time by Mr J. Johnston, Surgeon of the* Medway'.

Isis – *23 April. Captain Liot reports he had received no orders on leaving England. The vessel ran out of coal three days short of West Indies – completed voyage under sail only.*

City of Glasgow – *Needs a new side lever. Trinidad say they can probably have one cast there. The ship's company is against sailing on one engine.*

Actaeon – *27 April. Starboard 'pedestal or plumber block' broken. Government engineer at Antigua is making a model of it. When it is completed,* Actaeon *will sail for Trinidad or elsewhere to get one made.*

Tweed – *Strained badly during heavy weather en route for Chagres – deck seams wide open.*

Trent – *At Halifax 18 May. In letting go the bower anchor at New York it broke off at the shank, both flukes being lost.*

Medway – *Report from Halifax agents: 'The* Medway's *linen was left here in a most filthy state, and some parts almost destroyed by mildew and iron rust. It was shameful such valuable property should have so little care taken of it'.*

Dee – *Captain Owen wrote to the directors to explain why he had pulled down cabins on board the ship. At the same time the Court was asked how the ship should dispose of some turtle on board: 'To be delivered to the Company's office'.*

From those reports it is clear that RMSP had miscalculated in many matters. It wasn't alone in this, for other firms were also pioneering a radically different shipping world, but RMSP's difficulties were exacerbated by the sheer scale of the operation and the interdependence of each of the eleven schedules on the others. If one route suffered delays, it impacted on the others in a domino effect.

The situation became so critical that there was a real risk during late 1842 and early 1843 that the Company would collapse. This was starkly shown in the directors' report at a General Meeting in March 1843:

It is now generally, if not universally, admitted, that the original project of the Company embraced too extensive a sphere of operation; that its calculations, whether as related to the number of ships required, to the work they could perform, to the practicability of their visiting all the specified places, to the adequate security of the ports of assemblage, to the cost of building, outfit and maintenance of the ships, and to the amount of revenue likely to be realised, – were all of too sanguine a character; and that the receipts, in particular, were dependent more on eventual than immediate results.

In this position the Directors, as stated in their first Report, brought the matter under consideration of Her Majesty's Government, with a view to obtain, either an additional grant of money, or such a reduction of the steaming, and consequently of the expense, as might afford a reasonable prospect of making the contract remunerative. Convinced from the accounts furnished by other steam associations, that the Company could not proceed without assistance, the Government permitted such curtailment of its operations, as encouraged the Directors to propose, and the Proprietors to acquiesce in, a perseverance with the undertaking.

A Decade Down the Track

The fleet sailed through those rather dismal early days, and while there would be many more problems and setbacks, within a decade the Company was in a much less precarious position. By the New Year of 1851 the RMSP fleet looked very different. Seven vessels had been lost in a little under a decade (*Tweed, Forth, Solway, Medina, Isis, Actaeon* and *Lee*), while two more – *City of Glasgow* and the schooner *Liffey* – had left the fleet with less drama. A number of extra ships had replaced them – all but one were less than 1,000 tons, reflecting the fact that the 1,800 to 1,900 tons of the original vessels was unnecessarily large for some of the intercolonial schedules.

How easy it is to record the loss of ships as an academic record. This account of the loss of *Tweed*, which ran aground on the Alecranes Reef off Mexico in 1847, acknowledges the human side of the disasters of that first decade. Almost half of the people on board – seventy-two – perished. The following are snippets from a long letter written by a survivor, a Liverpool merchant, to his mother, from Yucatan on 20 February 1847:

As I am incapable of moving about just now, in consequence of the soles of my feet being so much cut up owing to having had to work for some days up to the middle in water, with naked feet on coral rock, I may as well give you some account of my almost miraculous escape from the shipwreck of the steamer Tweed, *in which I left Havana for Vera Cruz on the evening of 9 February…*

It was blowing rather fresh about 3 a.m. on the 12th inst when I was awoke by the vessel striking. The first thing I could hear was the roaring of the waves over the vessel and a cry of the stewardess that we were all lost. With each wave the water came pouring into my cabin, which was on the main deck on the starboard side, through the ports which were open.

I was not long in getting out of it and going forward to the centre of the vessel where the companion stairs led up to the spar deck. There a solitary lamp, for it was a pitch dark morning, allowed me to see the horror of our situation; the vessel rolling from side to side, with each roll the water rushing through it, and the timbers creaking as if at each moment those above and those below would separate. Being only in my shirt I felt it cold.

I returned to my cabin to try and get some clothing. The seas had washed my trunks and the furniture against the inside of the cabin door and only by making a great effort could I force it open, and then it was impossible to remain there for a minute as each wave appeared sufficient to drown me… I returned to the space at the bottom of the companion stairs and held on there to an iron stanchion. At this time two persons I knew, in the endeavour to reach the bottom of the companion stairs, fell down and were washed away.

The deck above my head now began to fall in, and I rushed on deck. The vessel was now on her beam ends, the larboard side out of the water and the starboard side buried in it. I got out onto the larboard side of the vessel and clung to the lower part of the main shrouds. In some minutes these began to give way and fearing to be precipitated with them and the mast into the roaring waves, I crept onto the mizen shrouds and held on by the davits from which a boat with a number of sailors in was suspended, now immersed in the water, now lying dry on the side of the vessel… The funnel now went over the side, and with a hideous crash the vessel broke up in three parts, the fore and aft parts separating from the centre…

We were now evidently drifting through the breakers, and when day began to dawn we were in comparatively smooth water… The view was anything but cheering – a desert isle would in comparison have appeared a paradise. As far as the eye could reach in one direction was evidently a coral reef, covered with water except in one or two small spaces of some yards square in our immediate neighbourhood; in the other direction, the broad ocean, with separate pieces of our noble vessel at about 100 or 200 yards distance.

…As [the tide] rose it floated towards us planks, spars, casks etc, which we collected together and with which we formed a sort of raft about four feet high, the tide rising gradually but evidently, and we watching it with intense anxiety… Two of the boats were in sight of us, though drifted considerably to leeward. As our only chance of salvation now appeared to depend upon them, parties were sent off to examine them. One, a large lifeboat, was found completely broken in two; the other, a small one, the Admiralty Agent's, was brought in, the bows completely staved in and the seams open. The boatswain and others set to work on it; with nails torn out of the planks by our hands they patched it up with canvas and clothes as well as could be done under the circumstances. When finished, nobody would have liked to venture on a pond in it… It was decided that ten persons should commit themselves to the deep in this frail bark, and endeavour either to reach land or fall in with some vessel…

They left us about 4 p.m. with a handkerchief full of dry flour, one of oatmeal and 10 or 11 bottles of wine. Not a drop of water had we, nor could we hope to have any as the water in the steamers is kept in tanks, not in casks…. This night we lay down as we could on our uneven planks in our wet clothes, with the water moistening our backs as we lay…

We suffered so much from thirst that we made several endeavours to distil fresh from salt water, but did not succeed. We had a barrel of vinegar on the raft, and every now and then a little was served round to each in a small stopper of a scent bottle: part of my small lucifer box served as a cup for some brandy which had also been saved, but the want of water was more dreadfully felt than our hunger. With what avidity we swallowed on Sunday morning some very small cakes we had baked, made of flour, butter and salt water. How delicious they were...

I must return to the boat which left us on Friday afternoon. All that night it was wending its way through the shoal water, now and then touching the rocks, and only next morning did they get into deep water. It was impossible to carry sail on her for she would have filled immediately. Two men were constantly occupied baling out the water which poured in at the bows and in all directions; four rowed, and this all that day and all the next night, when on Sunday morning (when nearly sinking from exhaustion – for they had not been able to swallow the dry flour) they espied a sail which proved to be the Spanish brig Emilio. *They were taken aboard with their tongues swelled and nearly dead and they begged them to come to our succour. Not a moment was lost, the brig went to Sisal, took in tow a large canoe and favoured by the winds flew to our rescue.*

About noon on Monday we espied a sail, but I thought it impossible we could be succoured before Wednesday, even had the boat succeeded in its perilous attempt... To accomplish this, however, was still a difficult matter. The brig was compelled to remain at some distance from the reefs, as she was to windward and the surf through which the canoe had to pass was very dangerous. The canoe, however, passed through it in safety and brought to us the Spanish captain, who insisted on remaining on the raft...

There were further hardships to be endured, but the worst was over. While the fleet had changed because of those losses, services had also been modified – in fact James Macqueen had been reorganising the schedules when the reports quoted earlier were coming in, and more changes had occurred since then.

There were still attacks on the Company, though; it seemed there were people intent simply on bringing down tall poppies. In April 1852 the directors alluded to some of them, and while admitting that there had been problems, added that:

for the last ten years there has not been a single instance wherein the provisions of its Contract with the Government has been violated; and at the moment when an outcry is raised against them, the Directors are engaged in expending at least £650,000 in the construction of the most powerful steam ships in the world in order to improve transatlantic communication, and to accelerate the conveyance of the public mails.

The feeling behind that statement hardly needs amplification.

Of the nine survivors from those initial fourteen steamers, six were subsequently used on the South America route which opened in January 1851. They were *Teviot*, *Tay*, *Medway*, *Severn*, *Thames* and *Avon*. *Teviot* made the historic first voyage to Brazil, while *Avon* didn't see South America until the 107th Brazil voyage, departing from Southampton in December 1859. By then *Avon* was bigger than when she was built, for in 1852/53 she was lengthened, increasing her tonnage by almost 200 tons. Both of those voyages were commanded by Capt. Richard Revett, who was thirty-seven years old when he took *Teviot* across in 1851. He was later Senior Captain and by 1860 was receiving a salary of £1,200 per year. After his retirement he was elected as a director and remained so almost until his death in the 1890s.

New ships entered the fleet during the 1850s and as a consequence RMSP attempted to sell some older ones. In November 1853 they asked £30,000 for *Severn*. A joint offer for *Severn*, *Medway* and *Great Western* was made three months later by a Mr Raydon, but was not accepted; the Company fixed £70,000 as the unrealistic figure for the three ships. In the event, none departed during the next two years, principally because of the Crimean War. The Comptroller of Transport Service hired ships as troop carriers from May 1854. According to the period of hire, the asking rate was between £2 2s and £2 10s per ton. Then, on 16 November 1854, *Thames* received orders for a voyage via Toulon and Marseilles (embarking French troops) to the Black Sea. Because of the short notice, her 9 December sailing to South America was cancelled – the first gap in the schedule since the service had begun. On her previous voyage *Thames* had escorted the King of Portugal from Southampton to Lisbon.

Thames was also Royal Mail's first cruise ship, for a 'pleasure voyage' of a few days in August 1853 had, as a highlight, attendance at a Royal Naval Review at Spithead. She was also the first steamer to cross the Atlantic using feathering paddles, which were fitted in 1850. That innovation was not always beneficial and at least one ship reverted to ordinary ones. *Thames* was eventually broken up in the West Indies. Her ship's bell was rescued and came back to Royal Mail as a prize exhibit in the head office museum in the 1960s.

The Admiralty wanted to convert *Severn* into a hospital ship in the Crimea, but the idea came to nothing and she, too, was eventually used for trooping. RMSP was now faced with a problem, for *Thames* and *Severn* were among the three vessels then operating the Brazil run. Among the ships used to fill the gap was the newer *Solent*. *Severn* was finally sold, together with *Great Western*, for breaking up on the Thames at Vauxhall. Together they fetched £11,500 – a stunning reduction from the £30,000 asked for the *Severn* alone a couple of years earlier.

Steam superheating machinery was sufficiently established early in 1857 for RMSP to consider trying it. Ever cautious about such innovations, they refused at first a request for the equipment to be fitted in *Avon* until learning the results of experiments by William Denny at Dumbarton. When it was clear that superheating was beneficial, approval was given and it was fitted in a number of vessels during the following year.

The first fleet units employed on the South America run (apart from *Severn*) left the fleet as follows: *Teviot*, sold 1864; *Tay*, lost 1856; *Medway*, sold 1861; *Thames*, sold 1865; *Avon*, lost 1862. Neither of the two losses occurred on the Brazil service – *Tay* ran ashore on the coast of Mexico through a navigational error and *Avon* was caught by a 'norther' at Colon, was torn from her moorings and flung onto the rocks.

Great Western

The first ship on the transatlantic service to South America other than units of the first fleet was *Great Western*, which RMSP purchased in 1847. Her Brazil debut, under Capt. C.H. Onslow, was the 9 July departure of 1853.

Great Western, *which joined the Royal Mail fleet in 1847.*

A West Country ship through and through, *Great Western* was built to Isambard Kingdom Brunel's design for the Great Western Steamship Co's service between Bristol and New York. The order went to Bristol shipbuilder William Patterson. Her keel was laid in June 1836 and on 19 July 1837 she was launched before 50,000 spectators. She was towed round to London to receive her engines, which were built by Maudslay, Sons & Field.

Among her notable features was the first recorded use of bilge keels, fitted to alleviate rolling caused by the weight of structures on the sponsons. A record credited to *Great Western* was the extent of her saloon, whose 75ft by 21ft size was reported to be the largest room in any ship up to that time.

Maudslay, Sons & Field erred in positioning the engines, deciding to place the boilers forward of the engines instead of abaft, which upset the vessel's trim. That explains why the funnel was so far forward, and also the presence, for her entire life, of a large quantity of iron ballast aft to correct the trim. She was described as a wooden-hulled paddle steamer, four-masted and schooner-rigged. Length: 212ft bp, 236ft oa. Beam: 35ft 6in. Beam over paddle boxes: 59ft 8in. Depth: 25ft 6in. Depth of hold: 23ft 2in. Mean laden draft: 16ft. Displacement tonnage 1,320 and gross tonnage 1,775.

Designed for the North Atlantic, she was given great longitudinal strength. The ribs were of oak, with scantling equal to contemporary line-of-battle ships. Staggered rows of bolts $1\frac{1}{2}$ inches in diameter and 24ft long, ran longitudinally through the bottom frames. She was closely trussed with iron and wooden diagonals and shelf-pieces which, with the whole of her upperworks, were fastened with bolts and nuts to a much greater extent than had formerly been the practice. The hull was sheathed with copper below the waterline.

There was stowage for 800 tons of coal, or coal and cargo combined, without encroaching on provision and water rooms. She accommodated 148 passengers, though an extra 100 sleeping berths could be provided. The crew list totalled sixty.

Paddle wheels were of the cycloidal form introduced by Joshua Field in 1833, with the shafts fixed to the hub in the curve of a cycloid so that they caused little resistance to the engine on entering the water. Paddle dimensions were 28.75ft diameter, with fixed floats 10ft wide. The paddle shafts, forged at Acraman's Ironworks in Bristol, weighed 6.5 tons each. The paddles were driven at about 15rpm by side-lever engines of 450 collective nominal horsepower. The engines had two cylinders, 73.5in diameter by seven-foot stroke, which gave 750 total horsepower. Coal consumption was about thirty tons per day; the bunkers held 800 tons, estimated as sufficient for twenty-five days at full steam. On trials the engines reached 19 strokes per minute, the speed 'nearly 17 miles per hour'.

The style and lavishness of passenger spaces were the focal point of *Great Western's* reputation, the genesis of philosophies which would blossom in later decades. The style of the great saloon was Louis XIV:

> *The ornamental work is very judiciously arranged… At the end of the recesses are large pier glasses fitted in richly ornamental frames, in imitation of Dresden china. The panels are tastefully decorated by no less an artist than Edward Thomas Parris, RA, an historical painter to Her Majesty… The prevailing colour of the apartment, pilasters etc, is a light flesh or salmon colour, with rich gold ornaments and decorations. The cushions of the settees are covered with a new article composed of horse hair and American grass, said to be of greater durability than silk, of which it has much the appearance…*
>
> *At the lower end of this saloon, on the right, is a small apartment elegantly fitted up with sofas and draperies, as a withdrawing room, exclusively for the use of lady passengers.*
>
> *…The small cabins on each side, communicating with the saloon, each contain two sleeping berths, so arranged that in the daytime they may be turned up against the side of the vessel and conceal the bedding, thereby forming a small sitting-room seven feet by eight.*
>
> *The figurehead of the vessel is a demi-figure of Neptune, with his trident admirably carved and gilded; and on each side are dolphins, finished in imitation of bronze. The mouldings are also gilded.*

Among her innovations was an elaborate system for calling the steward. Mahogany boxes in the steward's room contained a bell connected by wires to each cabin in the section. When the bell-rope in the cabin was pulled, and jangled the bell, it also forced out of the box-top a piece of tin with the cabin number painted on it.

After her machinery had been installed on the Thames, *Great Western* left for Bristol. Material surrounding the boilers caught fire and as a precaution the ship was run onto the soft mud of Chapman Sands, off Canvey Island. When the fire was extinguished, the ship was refloated and continued to Bristol. From there, on 8 April 1838, she left for her first voyage across the North Atlantic.

Her years on this run, operating later in conjunction with *Great Britain*, enjoyed mixed success. In 1841, for instance, she only carried more than 100 passengers on two occasions.

There were four voyages that year in which she had only between 30 and 44. She was employed on Atlantic voyages until the end of 1843, except during the winter closed-navigation season. From 1843 until her sale to Royal Mail in 1847 for £24,750 she made further voyages but for a period was laid-up. Contrary to some reports she was operating still in October 1846 – and having a rough time of it during a passage to New York, as this extract from her log shows:

> *A heavy sea broke over the fore-part of the starboard wheelhouse, which started the ice-house etc, washing all to leeward. Attempted to wear ship; lowered the after-gaffs down; manned the fore-rigging and loosened the weather yard-arm for the foresail to pay her off, but of no effect, and the sails blew away from the yards; the lee-quarter boats torn from the davits by the heavy lee-lurches.*

When *Great Britain* stranded in 1846, the Great Western Co., already in some difficulty, found it uneconomical to operate the smaller ship on her own. At that time Royal Mail was also in trouble, having lost several of its first fleet; *Great Western* was exactly what was needed. It wasn't the first time they had had their eye on her, for as early as March 1842 George Mills, RMSP's Superintending Engineer, was instructed to arrange for the vessel's purchase 'at a price not exceeding £36,750'. GWS was already suffering financial problems, which doubtless explains RMSP's offer; it wasn't accepted and in 1843 she was put up for auction but was passed in at £40,000 and remained on the North Atlantic run.

Once in the Royal Mail fleet she was used on both Brazil and West Indies services. An unsuccessful attempt was made to sell her in 1854 as part of the £70,000 package with

Engraving of Great Western *battling a North Atlantic gale in 1846, from* Illustrated London News.

Severn and *Medway*. During September that year she collided with a Brazilian schooner – on the day the Court of Enquiry report was delivered to the directors, they were also asked by a manufacturer if a new helmsman's telegraph could be fitted to a mail ship as a trial. They selected *Great Western*, perhaps imagining her people needed a little help. A couple of months later Capt. Bevis and his officers were the subjects of a complaint from the Admiralty – they had been less than civil, it was reported, to the Health and Port officers at Madeira.

The ship now remained permanently on the sale market until she left the fleet. In September 1855 she was definitely no longer wanted, and great efforts were made to sell or charter her. With the need for troop transports for the Crimea she attracted the interest of the Government, but they declined to take her at a rate of £2 2s per ton, which was 3s a ton less than most other units were attracting. Not until February 1856 did the Transport Board agree to hire her – and then there was a dispute about pay for the crew and another about fitting the vessel for the carriage of horses. Finally, though, she sailed for the Black Sea, though the rudder and a boiler were damaged and she put in at Gibraltar for repairs.

In July she was again advertised for sale; now in an embarrassing position, the Company couldn't get rid of her and decided to sell her by auction. However, that stage was not reached, for a Vauxhall shipbreaker bought her, together with *Severn*, for £11,500, the contract being signed on 31 July 1856.

Tyne (I) and *Tamar* (I)

Though *Tamar* had a wooden hull and *Tyne* an iron one, they were essentially built to a common design. Both ships were ordered in 1852, *Tamar* being the last wooden ship built for RMSP (though one was acquired second-hand later) and William Pitcher's swan-song for the Company. Those two factors were linked, for Thames shipbuilders constructed only limited numbers of large iron ships, especially steamers. The combination of a crippling strike at around this period – which sent many of the best artisans to yards in the north – and the advent of steamships and iron hulls (with London far from raw materials and the developing industrial centres) were hurdles which Thames builders couldn't overcome.

It was a pity to see the relationship between builder and owner fade away like that, for William Pitcher had been strongly involved with RMSP since the Company's inception, providing much of the early design work in addition to building ships. He was even, for a time, secretary to RMSP's directors and then the Company's accountant. Pitcher was also given a contract, in July 1844, 'for the future repair of all the Company's transatlantic steam ships' – within four months *Thames*, *Forth*, *Medway*, *Dee* and *Tay* had been 'docked, stripped, caulked, felted, wood-sheathed, re-coppered, repaired and painted throughout' at his renowned Northfleet complex just upstream from Gravesend.

Pitcher's tender for *Tamar* was approved in September and, as was usual, there were no recorded snags accompanying her construction.

The 1,603-ton Tyne *(I), built in 1854, pictured ashore off the Dorset coast in 1857. She was refloated without damage.*

With *Tyne* the story was a little different. William Patterson's tender was accepted in July, but this veteran builder of many famous ships was in the process of being ruined through no fault of his own – that story appears shortly and relates to RMSP's *Demerara*. With Patterson unable to overcome the financial setback, the Company had to withdraw the order for *Tyne*. Miller and Ravenhill had already been contracted to build the engines and now they were offered the hull as well, which they accepted. Though both ships were paddle steamers, and remained so all their lives, the Court considered in 1856 converting *Tyne* to screw propulsion. However common screw steamers were becoming generally, they were still rare for Royal Mail.

Tyne and *Tamar* entered service in 1854. *Tamar* did a trooping stint to the Black Sea, and then both were employed on the Caribbean routes for which they had principally been built. *Tamar* switched to the Brazil run late in 1855, where she was joined by her iron consort almost a year later. They made many voyages to Brazil, mostly incident-free journeys. Superheating machinery was fitted about 1859. While *Tamar* was at Colon in 1866, her crew helped the victims of an explosion and fire on board the steamer *European* (formerly a running-mate of *Tasmanian*, which had since entered the RMSP fleet). Capt. Moir of *Tamar* received a gold chronometer for his part in the proceedings.

In addition to operating Caribbean and Brazil services, both ships were involved with one of the Company's early Australian ventures, operating the Southampton – Alexandria leg of the Australia mail service. *Tyne* later survived the St Thomas hurricane of 1867 and was sold in 1875. *Tamar* was sold in 1871.

The only serious accident to befall either of them – with the exception of the hurricane – involved *Tyne* one foggy January day in 1857. Returning from Brazil, she grounded on rocks off the Dorset coast. The accident happened off St Alban's Head, near Kimmerridge. Afterwards, in his efforts to save people, a local coastguard was drowned, but otherwise the rescue went off smoothly.

A passenger wrote a few days later:

> *So much stress is now laid on expedition in all steam transit by sea or land that hours are more often valued than lives. Speed is attained by increased risks and by increased expenditure of various kinds. The faster the public choose to go, the more lives will from time to time be lost; and though we may, when accidents occur, throw back the responsibility on the professional men who have been thus goaded on, still our impatience of delay is at the bottom of the mischief in a great number of cases.*
>
> *Everything might have been much worse had the officers, crew and servants, instead of being affable, self-possessed and communicative, and like brave men who knew their risk, and met it, might have made our situation much more hard to bear. Captain Valler, as a man of sound judgement, encouraged us by procuring our usual food, in going where we would in the ship, and in possessing ourselves of such information as we chose.*

Although *Tyne* remained firmly grounded for some weeks, she was successfully refloated, 'with her form unaltered', and returned to service.

Tasmanian and *Oneida*

Australian Origins

In the mid-19th century there was no shortage of companies seeking to establish steamer services to Australia. The combination of advancing steamer technology and the burgeoning growth of Australia (especially during the gold rush) was irresistible and it took some years for shipowners to realise that, however beneficial the new technology was for European and Atlantic routes, it still had a long way to go before it would be viable for the long haul to Australia.

RMSP was inordinately anxious to join the bandwagon as a mail ship operator, making three forays in the 19th century and a fourth just after 1900. Its first attempt was particularly interesting, for it displayed the Company's expansion philosophy in the early 1850s, which seemed to have in mind something of the global aspect originally espoused by James Macqueen. One of RMSP's resident superintendents in the Caribbean suggested in January 1852 a service extension from Savannah, Georgia to Chagres on the Panama isthmus. With the American West opening up, travellers from the east coast had either to travel overland or by sea around Cape Horn. Southerners generally travelled to New York before using either route.

What Royal Mail wanted to do (in co-operation with The Pacific Steam Navigation Co., which operated steamers on the west coast of South America) was forge a link across the isthmus of Panama to connect Atlantic and Pacific services. 'If we do anything in this matter', the superintendent pointed out, 'we should lose no time, but forestall Cunard and not seem to take our measures as a check upon his movements'.

Then came the punchline:

> *The establishment of steam communication between Australia, New Zealand and Panama is anxiously desired, not only on the isthmus of Panama, but in the United States likewise. A similar feeling was strongly manifested by several gentlemen from Sydney and Port Phillip, who came home in the* Avon *on her late trip from Chagres, after finding their way to Callao in a sailing vessel and thence to Panama by one of the British Pacific mail steamers.*

The outcome, at the end of April 1852, was the formation of the Australasian Pacific Mail Steam Packet Co., a joint venture between RMSP and PSN. The new company applied for a Royal charter and mail contract – and without waiting to learn the outcome of either, placed orders for five large screw steamers at a cost of £200,000. The charter was duly granted, but the mail contract wasn't. No mail subsidy would be forthcoming until the Panama route had been tested – and no wonder. The isthmus was a mass of jungle-clad hills, rivers and stagnant waters, mosquitoes which spread yellow fever and malaria, and reptiles which 'render walking across next to impossible'. Henry Wells, co-founder of the Wells Fargo coaching service, made the crossing in the year RMSP was preparing to start its service, and commented: 'Thank God the isthmus is passed and I am alive and kicking, but awful sore and tired.'

Construction of the steamers nevertheless continued – *Kangaroo, Emeu, Black Swan* and *Dinornis* on the Clyde and *Menura* on the Thames. They were delivered early in

A ship with a varied history, Oneida *was used in the Crimean War, on the Australian mail service and then in RMSP's South America and West Indies trades. She is pictured after her sale by RMSP, when she had been converted to a sailing ship.*

39

1854 and *Emeu* was advertised to sail that February, but before her departure date the company was summarily wound up – presumably due to cold feet at the absence of a mail subsidy. *Black Swan*, *Dinornis* and *Menura* were sold and the others were chartered for trooping duties in the Crimean War. Then *Emeu* was sold to Cunard Line and in 1855 *Kangaroo* went to Inman Line.

So ended RMSP's first attempt to enter the Australian trade. When the Crimean War ended, the return of steamer mail services to Australia received high priority, for the demand on steamers for war service had forced Australia to revert to sailing ships. Several companies tendered for a new mail contract, while a separate bid came from an irrepressible James Macqueen, RMSP's founder, who was now in his seventies. His submission failed because he had no ships with which to commence the service, while RMSP's bid for a service via Panama was probably again rejected because of the untried nature of the Panama route.

The firm with which Australia found itself linked bore an unfamiliar name – the European and Australian Royal Mail Co. (E&A). Not only did E&A not have enough ships ready, its knowledge and experience east of Suez was poor and arrangements totally inadequate. As 1857 progressed, ships were not sailing on time, let alone arriving on schedule. Arrangements for the two halves of the service – England to Alexandria and Australia to Suez – did not coincide, which left passengers stranded for long periods awaiting a connecting ship.

The 2,285-ton *Oneida* began her part of the service that January, leaving the eastern colonies with the homeward mail. After a brief stop at King George's Sound she sailed for Galle. From then on there was silence and *Oneida* was eventually reported missing.

Out of the blue, one day she limped back into King George's Sound. The problem had come at three o'clock one morning, when:

> *...the passengers were all alarmed by a terrific vibration, as if the ship had got on some rocks. The majority of the passengers rushed out of their cabins to ascertain the cause of the shock, when it was discovered that, in consequence of the breaking, in several parts, of the bedplates forming the foundation of the engine, the crankpin had snapped asunder.*

There was nothing but praise for Capt. Hyde's seamanship in getting the crippled ship back to Western Australia and then to Sydney for repairs. *Oneida* was going to be out of commission for some time and E&A needed a temporary replacement. They selected *Emeu*, a remnant from RMSP's early venture and now owned by Cunard. Sailing from Liverpool in June 1857, she reached Melbourne in fifty-eight days to start a twelve-month charter. She had hardly started her task when she grounded on a reef, ploughed five metres along it and ripped open her hull.

Like *Oneida*, the *Emeu* was rescued, repaired and eventually returned to service. Before the end of 1857, though, E&A was in serious trouble and had to sub-contract the UK – Alexandria portion of the service. The firm which took it up was RMSP – which thus gained the foothold it had been seeking in the Antipodean trade. *Tamar*, with Capt. Jellicoe, commenced the operation, and *Teviot* took the Alexandria sailings for most of 1858.

Royal Mail operated the service under increasing tension as 1858 progressed. Even earlier, late in 1857, a boardroom disagreement surrounded a proposal to buy *Oneida* for £50,000 as part of an agreement to bail out E&A. The deal went through, with E&A's *Tasmanian* being used as security. If RMSP hoped that this and later financial arrangements would keep it clear of losses, it was sadly mistaken. It became more deeply entrenched in E&A's affairs as the months passed – and when it was too involved to pull out, it discovered that the deficit was not £40,000, as it had been led to believe, but something of the order of £200,000.

In dire trouble now, with confidence in E&A at rock bottom, the two companies went cap-in-hand to the Admiralty to stop the operation collapsing altogether. Unfortunately, that coincided with E&A being declared 'irretrievably insolvent' and the Admiralty refused to deal with them. Royal Mail was left on its own – now the owner of *Oneida* and, by default, *Tasmanian* (neither of which it really wanted) and having inherited a gigantic headache. It made the best of a bad job by negotiating a tough short-term contract to operate the entire service, which cost the Admiralty dearly to cover the period until a new long-term contract could be implemented.

Into the RMSP Fleet

Tasmanian was an iron screw steamer built by Hill at Port Glasgow. Her entry into the Royal Mail fleet was a maze of legal technicalities. In July 1858, for example, before E&A's liquidation, RMSP was negotiating with the East India Co. for the hire of *Tasmanian* as a troop carrier; it seems she was not suitable, but *Oneida* was chartered instead, at £27 4s 10d per man. *Tasmanian* thus appears to have been under Royal Mail's control well before she entered the fleet.

On 1 September 1858 (when E&A was placed in liquidation) *Tasmanian* was put up for sale by RMSP. *Oneida* was still operating in eastern waters – October 1858, for instance, saw her at Bombay. By the end of the year RMSP was trying to find a buyer or charterer for her, too. There were hints of desperation in March 1859 with further attempts to sell *Tasmanian*, dropping the price by £5,000 each time.

Then came the confusing part. On 24 May 1859 the directors' minutes read: 'Respecting sale of *Tasmanian* – £60,000 to be given provided no-one bids up to that amount'. Clearly, then, Royal Mail did not own the ship. All previous matters had been on behalf of E&A and then of their creditors. The Company *did* buy the ship now, the purchase being completed in June. On 9 July, retaining her old name, she took the Brazil sailing under the command of Capt. Jellicoe. There were complaints about the food and accommodation, and the homeward mails were 'wetted' while being landed at Southampton. To top things off, the ship unwittingly conveyed a runaway slave to England from Rio de Janeiro.

After that she was transferred to other routes and returned for only a single voyage to Brazil. In 1860 she brought home from the Caribbean a consignment of 2,124 packages of specie – valued at well over £1 million. This astonishing cargo needed thirty-six waggons with 113 horses to carry it to the Bank of England.

Over the years she underwent two upgrades. In 1864/65 bilge pieces were fitted and her poop extended. The latter operation greatly improved her accommodation, which emerged almost unrecognisable. Her machinery was altered to compound engines in

Tasmanian was built to operate an Australian mail service in which RMSP gained an interest. She entered Royal Mail's fleet in 1859 after the collapse of the Australia service.

1872, after which she spent a further six years in the fleet before being lost off Puerto Rico. Those upgrades, incidentally, significantly increased her gross tonnage, from an original 2,253 to 2,445 and finally 2,956. During 1872 – possibly her first voyage with compound engines – she broke the record for a Barbados-Plymouth passage with a run of eleven days, eighteen hours.

After *Tasmanian* had completed her first Brazil voyage her place was taken by *Oneida*. She, too, was an iron screw vessel but, unlike *Tasmanian*, had not been built for E&A; she was laid down in 1855 for Canadian owners but was quickly taken up for trooping duties in the Crimea before E&A bought her. She was a regular on the Brazil run for most of her largely uneventful RMSP years. After her sale in 1874 her new owners, H. Ellis & Sons, took out the engines and she operated as a sailing vessel until the late 1890s. She was seen in various corners of the world, her holds filled with freights like timber and Australian wheat.

She earned a moment of glory in October 1865 for rescuing the entire complement of passengers and crew (well over 100) from Gellatly Hankey's stranded 1,400-ton clipper ship *Duncan Dunbar*. *Oneida* was bound home from Brazil when *Duncan Dunbar's* captain, who had put to sea in a boat after despairing of being found on a spit of land which the survivors had reached, was sighted by *Oneida's* crew. The sailing ship had been wrecked on Las Rocas reef, off the north-east coast of Brazil. *Oneida* was taken close to the reef, a manoeuvre so potentially dangerous that her captain insisted she should not remain after dark. The last of the stranded people were taken on board as the sun set.

Amazon (I); *Demerara* (I); *Magdalena* (I); *Orinoco* (I) and *Parana* (I)

After ten years of operation, RMSP's reputation had improved – in spite of losing several ships – and its financial position was much healthier. A promising development was the mail contract of 1850 for a service to Brazil and the River Plate.

Orders were placed for five wooden paddle steamers – not for the new service but for the then more important West Indies mail route; their presence would allow older units to operate to South America. Their gross tonnages were just over 2,900. William Pitcher built *Orinoco* and *Magdalena* at Northfleet, R. & H. Green built *Amazon* at Blackwall, M. Wigram built *Parana* at Southampton and William Patterson built *Demerara* at Bristol. Though all were generally similar, there were a number of differences. Machinery varied between side-lever and direct-acting engines, for instance, and design improvements included changes to bulkheads after the loss of *Amazon*.

The Company looked forward to their prestige value as much as anything; they were much larger than their predecessors, the machinery more powerful and the passenger accommodation more extensive. They were, in other words, just what one would expect after a gap of ten years.

Loss One: *Demerara*

The first of two devastating accidents involved *Demerara*, which left her builder's yard at Bristol in November 1851 in tow for the Clyde, where her engines were to be installed. During the passage of the narrow and winding River Avon she failed to take a tight bend. Her bow embedded itself in the Gloucestershire bank of the river, then she slewed round and her stern jammed against the Somerset bank. The tide went out and left the ship bridging the river, with space under her keel.

Since there was ballast to the tune of 1,200 tons in the engine-room spaces, the result was fairly predictable, although, in fact, this wooden ship did not break her back but merely changed shape.

William Patterson, her builder, must have despaired of human logic. Caird's had built the engines and so the Glasgow paddle tug *Independence* had been sent down for the tow to Greenock. The pilot was apparently quite happy watching the tug hauling her charge along at some 4 or 5mph, despite the tug crew's lack of knowledge of the Avon. Patterson and Capt. Hast (*Demerara's* captain-designate) were, by contrast, far from happy, but their advice to lower the speed went unheeded.

Of the hours which followed the bizarre accident, the *Illustrated London News* had this to say:

All day a crowd of men were engaged in lightening her by getting out a quantity of ballast and making other preparations with a view to enabling her to float with the next tide. As night came on, a number of tar barrels and torches cast a most unearthly glare over the busy multitude, who were making the air ring with the noise of their labours.

> *The scene, viewed from the top of St Vincent's Rocks, was very exciting; the numerous small craft that kept plying about the* Demerara, *conveying ropes from shore to shore, and carrying out other necessary arrangements, looking like a multitude of ants round the carcase of a prostrate giant.*

She eventually returned to Bristol and was placed in drydock, but so severe was the structural damage that Royal Mail immediately gave notice that 'the ship *Demerara* was abandoned as a total wreck'. Now in the literal sense that was not true, though in the immediate aftermath the possibility of breaking her up was not ruled out. 'Constructive total loss' was a term not used before and so the ship's insurance of £48,000 was not easy to claim; legal argument hampered progress for a long time.

Who owned her during the long period of wrangling? Probably it was whichever of the three parties involved – RMSP, Patterson and the underwriters – possessed the least proportion of the monies due at any one time. During construction Royal Mail paid instalments to Patterson, but as soon as the vessel stranded, payments were stopped. The building contract stated that she would be handed over to RMSP on the Clyde, after her engines were installed and she was ready for sea.

William Patterson was clearly in no way to blame for the accident and in an effort to alleviate his financial problems and show continued faith in a very skilled shipbuilder, he was offered a contract three months after the stranding for a replacement ship. He did not build the ship; the chances are he could not raise sufficient money for materials and labour, and he was later declared bankrupt. The replacement was built by Caird's, who still had *Demerara's* engines awaiting a hull. With the exception of the boilers, the machinery was used in an improved and enlarged version of *Demerara*, an iron ship which was christened *Atrato*.

The dramatic scene depicting Demerara *(I) wedged between the banks of the River Avon in November 1851. She became the first recorded constructive total loss.*

Once *Demerara* had been drydocked, RMSP had her examined. They reached the conclusion that repairs would not be worth the expense. In March 1852 a loan of £9,000 was made to Patterson, using vessels in his yard as security, until the insurance was paid. During that summer a number of payments varying from £700 to £2,000 came trickling in from underwriters. Patterson was still asking for more money, and although Caird's were now building *Atrato*, the Bristol builder's tender for 'a *Demerara* replacement' was still being considered. His worsening financial situation continued to stand in the way. That August he was advanced £5,000, using the hull of *Demerara* as surety. That must have been unique – a company using as surety a ship it had abandoned. The directors would advance a further £4,000 to kick-start the new ship, providing Patterson could find security for his part of the contract. Presumably he could not, for the ship was never built.

A potential buyer in May the following year was told that negotiations must be postponed – clearly RMSP had not relinquished all interest. That autumn William Patterson proposed terms for the purchase of *Demerara*, and desultory correspondence continued through 1854, 1855 and 1856. Patterson's persistant demands for money eventually led to a strongly-worded letter, drafted by the solicitors, from RMSP. There is no record of its contents, just a suggestive entry in the minute book a little later: '2 October 1856 – Letter received from Mr Patterson expressing surprise at the views of the directors respecting his claims on account of the *Demerara*.'

In time she was extricated from the maze of legalities, underwent repairs and was sold. No engines were placed in her and she emerged as – reputedly – the world's largest sailing ship, named *British Empire*. She operated successfully for some years, reportedly often in the Australian trade. As she was never listed in *Lloyd's Register*, tracking down her later ownership is not easy, but she was most likely the 2,680-ton ship-rigged vessel owned in the 1860s by Joshua Bros of London. In 1867 she was in the Caribbean and was among numerous ships lost (including RMSP steamers) in a hurricane at St Thomas, her holds filled with coal consigned for the bunkers of Royal Mail steamers.

Demerara had been given a large figurehead comprising (as described in the Royal Mail house magazine years later) a full length figure of a South American Indian with 'feathered head-dress, upraised spear and an outstretched hand that once held a bunch of grapes'. Her new owners did not want an Indian for a figurehead and it was therefore removed and installed on the frontage of Demerara House in Bristol, where it remained until the building was demolished in 1930. It survived for a short while longer, 'but he proved too large an ornament and so was finally broken up'.

Loss Two: *Amazon*

Though the saga of *Demerara* dragged on for years, the Company knew as soon as the accident happened late in 1851 that it had lost one of its five new ships. If they had been told then that another would be gone, in far more frightful circumstances, less than two months later, it is doubtful that they would have entertained such a notion. That, though, was the story with *Amazon*.

She was the first of the group to enter service, arriving at Southampton during December 1851. Imagine the scene as this showpiece of British shipping prepared for her first haul across the Atlantic. Admiring eyes gazed at the 300ft-long hull, at the giant paddle boxes and the great wheels they encased, each 40ft across. Equally impressive were the three masts towering over the quayside. Almost 3,000 tons of ship – larger than anything most people had ever seen, for she was then second only in size to *Great Britain*.

Southampton welcomed in the New Year, then preparations for the voyage drew to a climax. During Friday, 2 January the mails were placed on board, bound for islands in the Caribbean, for Mexico and the Spanish Main. Several hundred tons of freight were packed into the space left vacant after 1,000 tons of coal had been shipped. More than £20,000-worth of specie and 500 bottles of quicksilver were escorted on board and locked in the specie room. The quicksilver was for blasting purposes at Mexican mines.

During the course of the day fifty passengers climbed on board. They marvelled at the splendid new ship; at her elegant fittings, her spaciousness. Discussions turned to the coming voyage. *Amazon* possessed engines of much higher power than those in the ships she was replacing. Eight-hundred horsepower, the knowledgeable were saying; and she will reach a speed of 15 knots. There was talk of a record passage to the West Indies.

As the blustery day drew to a close, she moved slowly down Southampton Water. Soon her bows reached out into the Channel and the passengers suddenly felt uncomfortable as *Amazon* turned into strong head winds and rain squalls. During the next twenty-four hours the ship was hove-to twice; those powerful engines, stiff and taut in their newness, were stopped because of overheated bearings. The second halt was called at 9.30 p.m. on Saturday the 3rd. She must have been turning off Ushant. After two hours the engines were restarted, and once more the steady thumping of machinery was heard. She worked up to $8\frac{1}{2}$ knots, but conditions were worsening as she entered the Bay of Biscay. A few souls held tight to the rails, but many of the 161 men, women and children lay below in resigned discomfort.

Midnight passed. Forty minutes later, someone saw smoke escaping from a hatchway ahead of the forward funnel. Almost at once flames burst through the hatchway. An alarm bell rang and Capt. Symons ran on deck. The Chief Officer, Mr Roberts, joined him. Water buckets were brought into use and a hose was quickly run out.

Several men attempted to clear bales of hay, food for animals which were now panicking. Only two bales were dislodged before the whole lot crackled into fire. As the sleeping passengers and off-duty crew awoke and realised that this giant ship was on fire, there was panic. Engineers, under instructions from Capt. Symons, tried to stop the engines, while more and more people surged onto the decks and started to lower the boats. The mail boat, with twenty-five people, was the first to reach the water; high seas and the velocity of *Amazon's* progress were enough to swamp the boat. All twenty-five died. A woman cried out for someone to take care of her child. Seamen attempted to keep panicking passengers below decks while the firemen struggled up to reach fresh air. Some time passed before Capt. Symons knew that the engines could not be stopped – it was impossible to get into the engineroom.

By heading into the wind she would perhaps travel slowly enough for boats to get away, but in doing so the fire would quickly be driven aft where the remaining boats lay. If he turned her stern to the wind and ran before it, more time would be granted to man the boats, but the risk from putting them in the water as *Amazon* scudded along would be far greater. Who could say which course would be the least disastrous? Capt. Symons chose to turn his ship to hold the fire off the stern.

The pinnace was lowered; it sheered across the sea before the people in it could unhook the forward tackle. Passengers were tossed into the water and the boat swung briefly by the bow. A large wave crashed over the second cutter as it was being lowered and all but two of its occupants were washed away. Sixteen managed to get away in the starboard lifeboat. The ship was now blazing furiously, spreading rapidly to the hencoops and paddle boxes. Many people were trapped in their cabins; some burned to death and others suffocated.

A midshipman, the chief steward, two seamen and a passenger got the dinghy away and shortly afterwards were picked up by the starboard lifeboat. One passenger, while attempting to reach this boat, injured a foot when it broke through the blazing deck. Others reached the boat at the third attempt by climbing through flames and acrid smoke onto the top of the starboard paddle box and sliding down to the sponson.

The starboard boat was rowed towards *Amazon*, hoping to pick up other survivors, but abandoned the attempt when they were threatened with being swamped. So they sat and clung to their frail craft, shivering and saturated in the January night. They gazed at the uncanny sight of *Amazon*, blazing like a torch, rolling in the heavy seas, and still rushing through the water with paddles thrashing at full speed. Silhouetted men and women were seen on board, kneeling in prayer. Others ran about screaming. Capt. Symons and his officers remained at their posts, keeping the ship on course and as stable as possible.

The wooden steamer Amazon *(I) on fire in January 1852, early in her maiden voyage. The horror of this disaster caused the Admiralty to allow future mail ships to be built of iron.*

A barque, under close-reefed topsails, was sighted. How she missed seeing the blazing inferno remains a mystery, but she quickly slipped from view. By four in the morning the fore and main masts had come crashing down in showers of sparks and tangled rigging, one on the starboard side and one on the port. The mizen remained standing but the ship was now blazing from stem to stern. At five o'clock the night shook as the powder magazine exploded. The mizen fell. The funnels glowed red hot. She lurched, and with a great sizzling and spattering *Amazon* slid beneath the waves.

The surviving boats were pulled towards the French coast. Dawn rose over a grey sea and at half-past ten that morning the people in the starboard boat were picked up by the London brig *Marsden*. Another twenty-five were rescued by a Dutch ship. The number of lives lost has been put at various figures between 105 and 115, out of 161 who sailed from Southampton.

In April the Company reported that:

> *from the searching investigations made by this Company and by the Board of Trade, it would appear that the cause of the fire will never be ascertained. If anything could console the Directors under this terrible disaster, it would be in the reflection that, of the nine boats with which the ship was provided, seven escaped conflagration, and six of those seven are now at England or in Brest, having each saved a number of human lives.*

That tally does not seem to match the description above, which was garnered from contemporary accounts. Furthermore, while the enquiry didn't deduce a cause for the fire, the evidence suggests it might well have started in the engineroom.

The horrific nature of the event precipitated a spontaneous national appeal for widows, orphans and survivors, spearheaded by Queen Victoria, Prince Albert and other members of the Royal Family.

Three Surviving Ships

Three-fifths of the much-vaunted new ships remained. The greater amount of surviving information deals with *Orinoco*. Her length, from figurehead to taffrail, was 301ft, but between perpendiculars was 269 feet $2\frac{1}{2}$ inches. Her breadth was 41ft 10in, and from outside to outside of the paddle boxes 71ft 10in. Her burthen tonnage (the most precise figure which survives for a Royal Mail ship) was $2,245\frac{31}{94}$. Double-cylinder engines developed 800hp. The paddle wheels, 40ft in diameter, were fitted with feathering floats.

The Times provided a description which emphasised her size and the ability to carry heavy armament – that she had been 'pronounced capable of being armed with 26 guns', a mixture of Paixhan long-range guns, 24- and 32-pounders, even a 68-pounder on a traversing slide carriage if the spar deck was strengthened.

Of the machinery it said:

> *The engines are on the patent double-cylinder direct-acting principle, and embrace all the most recent improvements applied to marine steam machinery. Each of the four cylinders are of 68*

inches diameter, equal to two 98-inch cylinders such as are supplied to the ordinary side-lever marine engines; and the boilers are eight in number, each boiler having three furnaces, and possess an aggregate evaporating power of 9,000 gallons of water per hour.

A more personal view of the ship came at about the same time from *Household Words*, a journal edited by no less than Charles Dickens:

I should probably have arrived a little earlier, but for the trivial accident of my having been taken to Fenchurch Street by the railway, instead of to Blackwall; but at last I found myself there – peering out from the banks of the river on the damp shipping – and speedily fixing my eyes on the vessel I wanted, namely, the West India Mail Company's Orinoco *– the sister-ship of the unfortunate* Amazon...*

'A massive hull, that of the* Orinoco *– taffrail thirty feet above the water, I dare say. What two huge black columns these funnels are! Really, she is as big as a line-of-battle ship,' I remark (with a slight professional chagrin); her engines are eight hundred horse-power; her crew numbers one hundred and ten men; her length is three hundred feet.*

Blackwall is not a lively place in winter. The river looks muddy and sullen, and seems, in the distance, to be emptying itself into a sea of mist. The rigging of the ships looks flabby and dirty; the smoke clings to everything. The hotels are deserted. If you enter one of them, you find the stairs ghastly and uncarpeted, and a general air of an impending funeral on the first floor. There were no temptations to look about, so I was glad enough to find myself on the main-deck of the Orinoco. *The smart noise of hammers, the smell of fresh paint, loose ropes lying about, and bustling mechanics running backwards and forwards, showed the activity with which preparations were going forward.*

I instinctively remark, in the first place, the height of the deck; that is always the first thing which attracts my attention. I have served in 'Symondites', where the loftiness of the deck is always a characteristic, and where you will never break your head, as you do in old-fashioned craft. I note that the Orinoco's *main-deck is as high as the* Vanguard's, *in which remark the chief officer very cordially acquiesces. And now I go aft, to glance at the cabins, and see the arrangements in progress for the comfort of those ladies and gentlemen who are now, in various parts of the country, bidding good-bye to friends and relations, and getting ready for the passage out.*

The Orinoco, *one learns, to begin with, has sleeping accommodations for about a hundred and fifty-six passengers. You pass a row of them, neatly painted white, with gilt mouldings, and fitted with ornamental glass. Each cabin is arranged, as a general principle, to accommodate two; one of the beds being triced up during the day, and lowered down at right-angles across the end of the other when wanted. A particularly admirable arrangement prevents gentlemen from having any control over their lights at night; the light is placed in a little triangular nook, in perfect safety, communicating through ground glass all the benefit that the inhabitant can possibly require, and being ready for snug removal from the deck outside. Abaft are the ladies' private cabins, for their own drawing-room purposes.*

Descending to the saloon deck, we find ourselves in the dining saloon, where a hundred and twenty persons 'dine' (it does not become me, as a nautical man, to grin sardonically here, but I do). There are sixteen cabins, and here are two fireplaces. The mahogony tables are screwed into the deck. Here you observe the steward's cabin, whence (in the hot latitudes) so much consolation may be expected to flow. In this excellent establishment, there are arrangements for the stowage of sixty dozen bottles; and there is a patent filter (a work of great genius); and exquisite conveniences protect the plates…

From the dining saloon let us descend to the orlop deck where cabins of interest are to be seen. In these, in the very heart of the vessel, on either side of the narrow passage, through which we go, preceded by a lantern, lie the bullion cabin and the mail rooms. The mail rooms are lined with zinc, to protect the huge bagfuls of letters, which the steamer carries for all parts of the West Indies. In this region, too, are rooms for passengers' baggage; and down below is the magazine. For the steamer carries two twenty-four pounders, and small arms for a hundred and twenty men. Meanwhile we see near us racks laden with cheeses; and observe likewise two wine-racks to hold a snug fifty dozen of wine.

Feeling tolerably secure that all will go well in the eating and drinking department, I now descend to visit the engine-room. I find myself in the centre of the massive iron-work of machinery in an engine-room seventy feet long. To supply the mighty life that is to make all this throb gigantically – tolerable provision is made – in five hundred and fifty tons of coal – aft; in five hundred and fifty ditto, in the bunkers. There are eight boilers, fore and aft – four for each funnel. And no wonder. The paddle wheels are forty feet in diameter, with floats ('feathering' floats) eleven feet six inches long, and four feet six broad; – and how these must go!

…In looking at the galleys, we must notice that the Amazon's galley was on the side, while that of the present vessel is amidships. And the arrangement of the engineer's store-room is different likewise from that of the lost vessel. The Engineer's store-room in the Amazon was over the boilers; between the boilers and the ship. That of the Orinoco is alongside the engine, between that and the ship's side; built sound- and air-tight. This difference of position will doubtless receive the attention of professional men in the enquiry concerning the fatal fire.

There is a hollow clanging and hammering resounding for ever in that engine-room. Nevertheless, it must not altogether quash our little experiment with those gutta percha tubes – long flexible tubes dangling down from the deck above, to communicate orders through. The courteous Captain Allan calls out 'Ease her', through one of them, and you hear it distinctly. And now we ascend up the neat iron ladder to the air.

Arrived on the upper deck – the spar deck they call it – I had occasion to admire afresh the bulk and symmetry of this fine vessel, from another point of view. She is perfectly rigged, and could spread an immense surface of canvas to a fair wind. Wind being foul – down, of course, come topsail yards, topmasts and lower yards, and away she thunders in the teeth of it – giving as little surface aloft to it as she can. Pacing about, fore and aft, you see pens and coops, for flesh and fowl – admirable conveniences to keep pig comfortable till his hour is come, and he is wanted in the saloon. All the paddle-box region is made useful; among other purposes, for baths…

Of course, I turned a very attentive eye to the boats. The Orinoco's boats are nine in number. The two chief 'life boats' are before the paddle boxes, hanging to davits, but resting on 'chocks' – the after-part, at least – on the wooden platform there. I must try to make the reader understand the arrangement; these 'chocks' are important items; for most people are agreed that the Amazon was unfortunate in having her boats resting on 'cranks' i.e. a kind of iron stanchions projecting from the sides. The 'chocks' are made of wood – the lower one is square, the upper shaped like a wedge, and ready to be drawn out. Thus, the wedge drawn – and the davits, which are iron (and made to swing) being swung – the boat glides bodily out from her seat, and hangs clear of the ship, ready to lower, with much facility.

Whereas, according to the 'crank' arrangement, it would be necessary – and in the Amazon *was necessary – to hoist at the tackles, before lowering could take place. I saw the 'chock' system tried, and though at the time there were only 'lumpers' on board to go through the manoeuvres, its performance seemed to be very satisfactory. Let us hope that these boats would be successfully worked. But you may be sure, reader, that when I came fresh from the huge engine-room, and the decks, and the cabins, and the galley – with all the scenery of the* Amazon *stamped on my imagination – and the thought of the dark, stormy night, and the sudden springing fire, and the wild wind, and the terror – I was in no humour to be critical…*

Despite such appreciative descriptions, *Orinoco, Magdalena* and *Parana* were not really a great success, though the Company was initially well pleased when *Orinoco* averaged 10 knots on her maiden voyage and *Parana* averaged $12\frac{1}{2}$ knots on trials. They were overburdened with top-hamper – a lesson the Company might have learned ten years earlier – and the upper yards were soon removed. After *Amazon's* fire, bulkhead alterations were carried out in the remaining three.

The Admiralty's opposition to iron hulls meant that these ships were at a disadvantage from the start. *Demerara* 'bent' after her stranding, principally because she was built of wood. *Amazon's* fire was made all the more frightful because of her totality of timber. The

A fine painting of the barque-rigged Magdalena (I). *Despite the aesthetic appeal of such a vessel, she and her sister-ships were too heavily rigged and the sail plan was cut down after a while.*

other three ships suffered a much slower disease because of their wooden hulls – dry rot. After seven or eight years *Orinoco* had to be broken up, so bad was the infestation.

Magdalena and *Parana* lasted much longer, thanks to extensive refitting and the replacement of affected timbers. *Parana* was also soon found to be in need of strengthening – that was revealed early in 1854, after she had undergone a special survey by William Patterson. While the directors announced in April that the strengthening would take place, and that at the same time she would be lengthened by 25ft in the fore-body to increase her capacity, it is not certain whether all or any of the work was carried out. Most likely, the strengthening was but the lengthening wasn't. It was also decided that the feathered paddles in *Magdalena* were not successful and in November 1852 the order was given to replace them with ordinary ones.

Capt. Chappell's daughter launched *Magdalena* at Northfleet at noon on 12 July 1851. Five days later her masts were in place, and a month further on she entered drydock to be coppered. That took almost two months, and it was on 20 October that she left the Thames, in tow of the steamers *Londonderry* and *Perseverence*, for the Clyde. There she took in her engines, built by Robert Napier.

During trials she reached almost 13 knots and averaged $11\frac{1}{2}$ The cost of her hull was reported as £44,869 and the engines £29,500. By the time a long list of fixtures and fittings were added, her total cost exceeded £100,000.

Three days after *Magdalena's* launching, *Parana* entered the water from Wigram's yard at Southampton. She took in her engines on the Clyde as well, for they were built by Caird's. Problems were evident almost at once and the engines had to be extensively overhauled after a year. She returned to the Clyde in the autumn of 1852 to have new paddle wheels fitted. During 1853/54, repairs were carried out to her timbers, on which a fungus growth had begun.

The ships were initially placed on the Chagres route. By 1854 the convulsions in the Crimea led to *Orinoco* and *Magdalena* being chartered for Admiralty trooping; *Parana* was hired the following year to carry French troops to the Black Sea. When the war was over they returned to the Chagres route, having fired not a single broadside between them, in spite of the lengths to which the Government had gone to cater for just that kind of situation. They remained on Caribbean routes for the remainder of the 1850s. One of the few events of note was an explosion on board *Parana* in November 1856 which killed three men and injured nearly a dozen; the stokehold area was left in a terrible mess. In addition, in April 1857, *Magdalena*, under the command of Capt. Abbot, staggered through appalling weather, in which the third officer and three crew members were lost overboard.

When this group of five ships was ordered as the Company's first major newbuildings, the directors would have had great expectations for them. After the two early losses, their misery became complete as the others displayed their inadequacies during the 1850s. As early as January 1854 only essential repairs were being given to *Orinoco*, RMSP having decided to sell her if they could. She was reprieved by the Crimean War, but during August 1858 both *Orinoco* and *Magdalena* were in a bad enough state for the Court to again consider their sale. How intent they were on getting rid of them may be gathered by the fact that two new ships had already been laid down at the Thames Ironworks, Blackwall – their names earmarked to be *Orinoco* and *Magdalena*. The two original ships would be sold for scrap but their engines would be placed in the new ships, for they, at least, were now working well.

Orinoco was put on the sale market for £10,000; ultimately she went to Thames shipbreakers at Vauxhall for little more than £5,000 – one of the largest steamers of her day and only eight years old! Her engines were duly placed in the new ship (which, in the event, was given the name *Parramatta*). The directors had second thoughts about doing the same with *Magdalena*, deciding to keep her and hinting that a transfer to the Brazil service might occur. The decision to keep *Magdalena* had already been taken when *Parramatta* entered service, and the directors must have heaved a sigh of relief, for *Parramatta* was lost on her maiden voyage. It was that event which caused *Tasmanian* to be withdrawn from the Brazil route after a single voyage, for she was hurriedly transferred to take *Parramatta's* place on the Caribbean run.

A further year passed before *Magdalena* was switched to the Brazil route, and in the meantime she and *Parana* carried more troops, this time to a bitterly cold Canada. Once *Magdalena* had joined the South America service, replacing the ageing *Avon* in March 1860, she remained on the route for the remainder of her career. By the mid-1860s, though, she had become unseaworthy and was sold for breaking up on the Thames.

Parana was a regular on the Brazil service from 1862 to 1865. During her final South America voyage she picked up survivors from a wrecked steamer belonging to RMSP's French rival, Cie Messageries Imperiales. *Parana* brought the survivors to Europe and the Company graciously allowed a 25% discount on their fares!

Her withdrawal from the service was made possible by the advent of *Rhone* and *Douro*. While *Parana* suffered under the same kind of problems as the other two she somehow struggled on. Her time in the fleet seems quite exceptionally long under the circumstances, for she remained with RMSP until 1876; however, her active life ended in 1868, after which, engines removed, she became a coal hulk for the Company at St Thomas, replacing coaling facilities which had been lost in the hurricane of 1867.

La Plata (I)

Amazon burned during the early hours of 4 January 1852. Ten days later, Capt. Chappell, RMSP's Secretary, was negotiating with Samuel Cunard for a replacement. About three weeks earlier, on Christmas Eve, the wooden paddle steamer *Arabia* had been launched for Cunard from the Glasgow yard of Robert Steele. Cunard agreed to sell *Arabia* to RMSP – whose need was now desperate after the loss of both *Demerara* and *Amazon* – for £125,000, which was over £10,000 more than Cunard was paying for her.

RMSP decided to rename her *Maranon* (after a tributary of the River Amazon). After a week or two they had second thoughts and opted instead for *La Plata*. She was the first of four RMSP ships over the years to bear the name of the river on which Buenos Aires stands.

As she had been designed for the express North Atlantic service, *La Plata* did not conform to RMSP's needs in some respects, but as she was at an early stage of fitting out, some changes were able to be made. Late in January Capt. Chappell travelled to Scotland to examine her. The layout of her accommodation differed from other ships in the fleet, particularly regarding the spaciousness and ventilation which were so important in the tropics. It was decided, though, that ventilation was adequate. The spar deck, a standard fitting in Royal Mail's ships, was not incorporated. The dining saloon amidships gave somewhat cramped seating for 140 – some passengers had to put up with being handed their food over the shoulders of others. Equally cramped were the cabin arrangements, with a capacity of 180. Lounges fitted out below included a separate saloon for the ladies.

There were other differences from the Royal Mail style. To reduce weight there was less coppering and much greater distances between beams. She had less freeboard and a lighter brig rig. Although her fine lines made her sleek and a fast mover, she tended to bury herself in heavy weather. Her speed capabilities meant that fuel consumption was exceptionally high. Cunard had allowed bunker spaces for 1,200 tons. Now that her routes would often be longer, Royal Mail added an extra 200 tons, which reduced cargo spaces to 800 tons.

English and African oak, teak, pitch pine and rock elm were used in the hull, which also incorporated small amounts of iron. Her overall length was 314ft, breadth 41ft and diameter of paddles 36ft 10in. With recent RMSP ships the best average speed was expected to be around 11 knots; *La Plata* averaged $14\frac{1}{2}$ knots during her voyage from Greenock to the Mersey, en route to Southampton – an unprecedented performance for a Royal Mail ship.

Her engines were of the old-fashioned side-lever type, constructed by Robert Napier. They had two simple cylinders, each about 8ft 6in bore by 9ft stroke, mounted vertically side by side on huge timber baulks laid fore-and-aft along the ship's bottom. A cross-head on each piston rod was connected to a pair of beams which rocked about a fulcrum on the bedplate. A second cross-head, linked to the free end of the beams, drove a crank on the paddle shaft through a connecting rod. Two sets of tubular boilers, with a working pressure of about 20lb per square inch, were fitted forward and abaft the engines, using the condensation from sea-water jet condensers. These boilers required constant blowing down and frequent scaling for a life of about ten years – the vessel herself lasted almost twice as long. The machinery filled the entire beam and depth of the ship amidships, and a considerable part of the length as well.

During 1852 she was placed on the Southampton – St Thomas mail run. That November she became a hot-bed of yellow fever; epidemics of this dreaded disease regularly swept St Thomas, and on this occasion succeeded in finding its way onto *La Plata*. In the space of thirteen days – the period of her passage to Southampton – seven crew members died, including her master, Capt. Allan (the same 'courteous Captain Allan' who had featured in *Household Words* earlier in the year, as master then of *Orinoco*). When the ship reached England, twenty-one people were ill from the disease, including the ship's doctor. *La Plata* was placed in quarantine and some time passed before the mails were brought ashore, followed by a full-scale fumigation.

Perhaps because of the high coal consumption, her voyage earnings varied enormously. Sometimes only a couple of dozen passengers travelled in her, and that, combined with fuel costs and limited cargo space, equated to a loss. At other times she carried many passengers and might also have her specie room packed with £1 million-worth of bullion and other valuables.

In April 1856 she joined *Atrato* and *Tay* at Spithead for a naval review to mark the end of war in the Crimea. Her service continued without incident until November 1860, when she caught fire at Southampton. A watchman noticed 'a haze' along the foredeck at about one in

The sleek lines of La Plata *(I), purchased as a replacement for* Amazon *(I) while under construction for Cunard.*

the morning. Eight fire engines and two tugs, with the help of the ship's crew and seamen from a nearby P&O ship, fought the blaze until 7.30 a.m. Starting in the boatswain's store, the fire caused significant damage.

A year later *La Plata* played a central role in the last act of a story which had evolved as one of the most dramatic in the Company's history. The American Civil War was in progress. Two Commissioners for the Confederates, Messrs Slidell and Mason, together with Slidell's family and their secretaries, ran the Federal blockade from the southern States and safely reached Havana. They were anxious to cross the Atlantic, for they had despatches seeking the support of Britain and France for the Confederate cause.

In Havana they boarded RMSP's *Trent*, from which they would transfer to a transatlantic steamer at St Thomas. Shortly after leaving Havana, in a carefully-picked narrow channel, the Federal warship *San Jacinto* awaited them. As *Trent* approached, *San Jacinto* ran up the American flag and put a shot across *Trent's* bows. A further shot, from a large swivel gun, passed a few yards from the British ship, from which the man-of-war's open and fully-manned gun ports were only too obvious.

Trent came to a halt and a liberally-armed boarding party arrived. Capt. Moir, *Trent's* master, refused to hand over his passenger list or – when the Americans became more direct – Slidell and Mason. He was hardly, though, in a position to argue with the artillery facing him. The Commissioners themselves stepped forward – and then promptly placed themselves under the protection of Capt. Moir. Exactly what Moir was supposed to do wasn't revealed. He must have been angered by the extraordinary manoeuvre, especially when the men, as they were taken from his ship at gunpoint, placed all blame for their capture on Capt. Moir.

There were people who believed that Capt. Moir, in accepting his passengers, knew that 'if he violated the neutrality of England by carrying dispatches, military men, or otherwise serving either belligerent, North or South, in America, he was liable to seizure as a prize by the other'. In truth, of course, Royal Mail was given no choice but to lose Britain's neutrality, for accepting the passengers would favour the South and refusing them would favour the North. As far as Britain's Government was concerned, the case was clear-cut – a British mail ship had been stopped by force, boarded by armed men, and fare-paying passengers removed at gunpoint. The repercussions were swift and dramatic. Their immediate release was demanded; so was an apology, and a promise that they would be allowed unhindered passage to Europe. The alternative was a declaration of war against the Federal States.

The threat of war was not grandstanding. RMSP's *Magdalena* and *Parana* were quickly filled with British troops and on their way to Nova Scotia in readiness for hostilities. The arrival of these wooden ships, designed for voyaging in the tropics, in Canadian waters in the heart of winter was uncomfortable to say the least – but they made it through the ice where others failed. The powerbrokers of the North evidently decided that discretion was the better part of valour. Slidell and Mason were released and allowed to make their mission to Europe; *La Plata* closed the book on this bizarre matter by carrying the men to Southampton, where they arrived on 28 January 1862.

La Plata continued her West Indies voyages until taking the Brazil sailing on 9 May 1865 as a replacement for *Parana*. She was in fine fettle at this time, having just emerged from re-boilering and the installation of steam superheating equipment, as well as major improvements to her

The moment which brought Britain and America to the brink of war. The daughter of Confederate Commissioner Slidell stands between her father and attacking Federal troops on board Trent *(I). Slidell and his colleague Mason were taken from the ship at gunpoint.*

accommodation. She was used only as a stop-gap, though, until the new *Rhone* and *Douro* entered service. Thus she made two Brazil voyages before returning to the Caribbean; then, in July 1868, she returned to the Brazil run and remained on it until her sale three years later.

Among the ships which shared their service between the two regions, it is astonishing that so many had almost nothing of note to report from South America but all manner of events from the West Indies. This was the case with *La Plata*. Between her two spells on the Brazil line she was at St Thomas in January 1867 and suffered an almost exact repetition of the yellow fever voyage of 1852. The number of deaths and illnesses seems not have been recorded, but they were considerable. Eliza Stokes, the stewardess, worked tirelessly with the doctor. She looked after the sick and tried to stop the infection spreading, labouring day and night. Then a bombshell dropped: the ship's surgeon, Dr Young, contracted the disease and died well before Southampton was reached. Virtually all of the work then fell on Eliza's shoulders. A newspaper reported: 'It may be fairly inferred that but for her unwearied exertions many more would have fallen victim to the dreadful disease and the catalogue of deaths consequently largely increased'.

Those on board were so full of gratitude for Eliza's marathon efforts that the crew made a spontaneous collection for her at Southampton. There were seventy-six names on the list, with donations ranging from £2 from Capt. Jellicoe to florins and even single shillings by some of the Ordinary Seamen for whom such a sum was no mean amount. Capt. Jellicoe reported to the directors, of course, which resulted in the Company immediately authorising the payment of a further £20 to her. While the Post Office considered the Company's measures to stop this kind of disaster happening again, the Southampton Regatta Club put on a theatrical show to entertain the men from the ship who were still hospitalised.

If the people from *La Plata* imagined that troubles from the island of St Thomas had finished with them, they had not long to wait to discover otherwise. Later in 1867 she managed to avoid the devastating hurricane which caused such destruction and loss of life, only to be caught, less than a month later, by a tidal wave. This Virgin Islands harbour was first rocked by an earthquake. The water receded from the beaches and shortly returned with the speed of an express train in the form of a 30ft wave. In its path lay *La Plata*, riding at anchor off Water Island.

The wall of water struck her on the starboard quarter. She spun round and most of her fittings were ripped away. The starboard bulwarks were stove in, boats were lost overside and davits hung grotesquely. Unlike many vessels *inside* the harbour, she survived. A number of ships, borne up by the wave, were deposited on the main street of St Thomas.

When *La Plata* returned to the Brazil route in 1868 it was no doubt in the hope of a quieter life. She made more than a dozen more voyages across the South Atlantic and they were, indeed, largely uneventful, apart from an unexplained complaint from the Company's agent at Rio de Janeiro about a shot being fired over her from the fort at Rio in April 1869.

Her last voyage was in the summer of 1871, under Capt. W.W. Herbert. A lay-up then preceded her delivery, two days before Christmas, to Denny Bros at Dumbarton, in part-payment for the *Boyne*, a new ship for the Brazil and River Plate run. She was reported to have realised £7,600.

Rhone and *Douro* (I)

These two fine iron screw steamers were built for the Brazil service in the mid-1860s. Their specifications were approved by the Court of Directors on 22 May 1863; nineteen days later the contracts were given to Caird & Co. at Greenock (for the ship to be named *Douro*) and the Millwall Ironworks Co.

The common name theme of rivers was followed, but by this time the criteria being used seemed confusing. The first fleet used British rivers in the vicinity of the place of build. Many since then had used South American rivers, particularly in the northern regions not far removed from the Caribbean sphere of operations – *Magdalena*, *Atrato* and *Orinoco*, for instance. With *Seine*, a European river was used for the first time in 1860. This was followed by *Eider*, *Douro*, *Arno*, *Rhone* and *Danube*, seemingly random choices, for rivers in Italy and Schleswig-Holstein, for instance, had no apparent links for RMSP. Soon the names of the River Nile in Egypt and Leningrad's River Neva had been used. This was such a diverse collection that one is tempted to believe they were personal choices from the directors.

With *Rhone* and *Douro*, though, there were signs of diplomacy. The River Douro flows through northern Spain and Portugal, whose links with South America hardly need emphasis. The Rhone is in France and, while the ships were being built, negotiations were in progress with the French Post Office to rationalise mail services to South America – it was principally that matter which ultimately prompted the extension of the transatlantic service to the River Plate in 1869.

For all their impressive profiles, the two ships did not at first please the Admiralty or the Post Office. During building *Douro* was criticised by the Admiralty surveyor and as a result, in May 1864, plans for strengthening her were approved by the Post Office. Then they objected to the bulkheads and watertight compartments in *Rhone*. Eventually they were completed to everyone's satisfaction. With a length of 310ft and breadth of 40ft, they each accommodated 253 first, 30 second and 30 third class passengers.

While they were not the first screw steamers in the fleet, they were the first designed and built for Royal Mail. What a milestone that was – it seems extraordinary that a major mail ship company should continue building paddle steamers for ocean voyaging into the 1860s. As with the delay in introducing iron hulls, this has been blamed on constraints imposed by the Admiralty. However, Cunard and P&O, whose mail contracts presumably placed them in much the same position, were both building screw ships in the early 1850s.

Douro's gross tonnage was 2,824 and *Rhone's* 2,738. Their contracts (excluding machinery) were £23 10s per ton and £25 17s 8d respectively. While that amounted to a sizeable difference, the engines (also contracted to the hull builders) swung the balance the other way: *Douro's* engines cost £32,000 and *Rhone's* £24,500. Both ships reached about 14 knots on trials.

Their maiden voyages were in 1865, *Douro* completing hers before *Rhone* left Southampton for the first time on 9 October. After initial trouble through overheated bearings, *Rhone* settled down as a fast and comfortable ship. This was the period when her first master, Capt. Woolward, described the switch from *Magdalena* as being like moving from a cart-horse to a racer. So good were these ships, in fact, that it was inevitable they would not long remain on the Brazil run, for the Caribbean was still the more prestigious route. After six voyages across the South Atlantic the switch was made. Late October 1867 saw *Rhone* settling into her new duties. She was anchored, on her tenth voyage, away from the harbour of St Thomas in the Virgin Islands. As yellow fever at St Thomas was particularly bad, she had anchored by the little island of St Peter's, about 25 miles east of St Thomas. The view from her anchorage took in the picturesque islands of Tortola, St John's and St Peter's; the water was glass-smooth, and so clear that waving sea-ferns were seen seven fathoms down on the coral reef.

The morning of 29 October dawned clear and still. As the sun climbed into a cloudless sky, life stirred in the sixty ships crowding the harbour, and in others anchored nearby. Why would such a small port harbour so many ships? Geographically the Virgin Islands were perfectly situated as a central point along shipping routes between Panama, New York, the east coast of South America and Europe; it was like the hub of a great trading wheel.

A falling barometer hinted that the weather would worsen, but the sky remained blue and the sea calm. Late in the morning, the mercury dropped like a stone to 27.95in. With unnerving suddenness, day was transformed into semi-night as a hurricane tore into the island. The sea became a boiling death trap. Unprepared ships rolled and heaved, trying desperately to make their way out of harbour to the open sea.

Rhone lay at anchor by an island chain bounding the St Francis Drake Channel, where she was loading cargo and stores for England. The first onslaught snapped off a spar, which hit and killed the chief officer as it crashed to the deck. After blowing from the NNW, the wind lulled at 12.15 p.m. The ship's master, Capt. Woolley, was familiar

The 2,738-ton Rhone, *the finest ship in Royal Mail's fleet when she was built in 1865 for the South America mail service.*

enough with cyclonic systems to know they were in the eye of the hurricane and that a second blow would come from the opposite direction – onto the islands. So by 12.30 the ship was steaming south-eastwards, striving to gain sea room. The channel was narrow and rocky, but *Rhone* reached the last point of land without mishap. At that point the hurricane returned, as the ship was passing the tip of Salt Island. The sky darkened again and a 'fearful blast' threw *Rhone* onto the rocks. She broke in two amidships and sank immediately – it was as simple and instantaneous as that.

An Italian passenger and several crew members were washed onto a razor-sharp reef. Six men clung to a hammock bin and were eventually saved, while a fireman climbed to the foretopsail yard, where he stayed for seventeen hours awaiting rescue. Capt. Woolley was washed overside between his ship and the rocks and was never seen again. No boats were launched – the catastrophe was so sudden that those below decks perished as soon as the ship hit. Of the 145 people on board, fewer than two dozen survived.

So after only two years *Rhone* was brutally reduced to a battered wreck. She was not the only Royal Mail vessel in the area. *Derwent* and *Wye* were also lost. *Conway* was blown ashore, severely damaged, but in time was salvaged. *Solent* and *Tyne*, having been outside the harbour, survived, though largely dismasted. Of the sixty ships inside the harbour, only two survived. News of this sobering event was brought to England by *Douro*.

Douro, like *Rhone*, spent her first two years trading between Southampton and Rio de Janeiro. In February 1867 she, too, was sent to the West Indies, a move which upset the Post Office as she hadn't been surveyed for that service. In the following month, outward bound for St Thomas, her rudder was damaged. The ship's company had a long, hard task repairing it – in fact it was such a job that the Company paid a month's wages to every man involved and a piece of plate valued at 30 guineas was presented to Capt. Bevis.

Some time later she suffered damage in the English Channel after colliding with an unidentified barque. She was at that period principally used on the extended West Indies route to Colon, the Atlantic end of the Panama Railroad built over a decade earlier. Capt. Woolward had been around the traps long enough to remember the days when the Panama Railroad was being built – memories of swampy, fever-infested country which 'carried off thousands of labourers; it was said that a labourer was buried at the end of each sleeper'. Every Royal Mail ship on the Panama route at that time carried up to 300 labourers from Cartagena to Colon; often no more than twenty were on the return voyage.

Under Capt. Woolward, *Douro* returned to the Brazil route in April 1869. This was to be a crucial year for the service, for in October *Douro* made the first through-voyage to the River Plate. While new tonnage for the West Indies (*Neva*, *Nile* and *Elbe*) provided the logical reason for *Douro's* return to the South Atlantic, it is likely that RMSP was looking ahead to the prospect of the through-service and wanted to have good ships on the route. In 1868 *Oneida* was the only screw ship regularly operating the Brazil service; the paddlers *Seine*, *Shannon* and *La Plata* took most departures, while the August and December sailings were inexplicably given to *Danube*.

The contract ratifying the through service was signed with the Post Office on 9 June 1869 and it began with *Douro's* departure four months later. Her itinerary for that historic voyage was: Depart Southampton, 9 October 1869; Lisbon, 13 October; St Vincent, 19 October; Pernambuco, 25-26 October; Bahia, 28 October; Rio de Janeiro, 31 October-3 November;

Wreck of the Rhone, *destroyed by a hurricane in the West Indies only two years after being built. This picture from* Illustrated London News *was based on a sketch by Lionel Lee, chief officer of RMSP's* Tyne *(I).*

By the 1960s, commercial dive companies were operating underwater tours of wreck sites in the Virgin Islands. One of the operators took this photo of the bowsprit of Rhone, *after almost a century underwater.*

Montevideo, 7-8 November; Buenos Aires, 9-14 November; Montevideo, 15 November; Rio de Janeiro, 20-23 November; Bahia, 26 November; Pernambuco, 28 November; St Vincent, 5 December; Lisbon, 11 December; Southampton, arrive 1 a.m. 15 December. For the outward passage she embarked 120 passengers and shipped 631 tons of cargo at Southampton, in addition to the mails. Changeable weather characterised much of the passage, including fog which caused a delay of over eight hours reaching Lisbon. The homeward voyage began with strong winds but improved later. The total time for the round voyage was 66 days 10 hours 10 minutes, of which 51 days 3 hours 35 minutes were spent under steam.

Douro then remained on the South America run, except for a period from the end of 1876 until April 1879. During that break, in 1878, she underwent a thorough refit and was given compound engines from Day, Summers & Co. at Southampton. From the time of her resumption on the River Plate service in 1879 we find an early reference to the long-standing link between RMSP and its Vigo agents Eduardo Duran y Hijos. The Duran family began handling the Company's affairs in 1876, the first vessel to call being *Guadiana*. *Douro* became a regular visitor, and in 1879 a newspaper advertisement placed by Duran read: 'These steamers do not go into quarantine, and they offer the highest comfort to 3rd class passengers, giving them bed with bedding, fresh bread and wine with all meals. They carry Spanish cook and stewards'. Schedules at that time were greatly at the mercy of fever in South America and the consequent threat of quarantine.

Her 62nd voyage began at Southampton on 9 February 1882. It was uneventful until she was abreast of Finisterre northbound. She had nearly 140 people on board. The late evening of 1 April was clear as she began the Bay of Biscay crossing. About 50 miles north of Cape Finisterre she was in collision with the 2,197-ton Spanish steamer *Yrurac Bat*. The bow region of the Spanish ship, which rammed *Douro* on the starboard side, was badly crumpled, including the bulkhead of number one hold. From the speed with which she sank – about fifteen minutes – it seems likely that the force of the collision also breached other bulkheads. *Douro* had a large hole in her starboard side, both above and below the waterline. She sank in about thirty minutes. About thirty people were lost from *Yrurac Bat*, while the toll from *Douro* was five passengers, six officers and six crew.

Douro was either partly or wholly to blame. An action was taken against RMSP by the owners of *Yrurac Bat*, and an enigmatic Company report stated that 'a communication to the newspapers does not appear necessary in regard to letters and statements which have appeared therein'. First-hand accounts from *Douro's* passengers, published in the *Hull and Eastern Counties Herald* on 13 April did not greatly enhance the Company's position. (The interest for Hull was that *Hidalgo*, owned in Hull by Wilson Line, rescued all but two of the survivors.)

There were significant points about the collision in those reports. One account clearly stated that *Douro* was travelling from south to north and *Yrurac Bat* from east to west. 'Their lines of route formed really the two sides of a rectangle, and they were both tending towards a common point. Those on board the *Douro* could see the red light of the *Yrurac Bat*, while to the latter vessel the green light of the *Douro* was visible. So remote seemed the idea of a collision to those in charge of the vessels that some of the crew of each were actually standing on the bows, watching each other in the moonlight while they approached nearer and nearer... Suddenly seeing that a collision was inevitable, the *Yrurac*

Bat altered its course southwards, apparently with the view of endeavouring to pass by the stern of the *Douro*. It was too late to do that, and she went crashing into the side of the mail steamer with terrific violence'.

From that, *Douro* seems to have been in error, for the 'rule of the road' states that 'the vessel which has the other on her own starboard side shall keep out of the way of the other'. In other words, 'green keeps clear of red'. That, of course, doesn't negate the common obligation to take whatever measures are necessary to avoid a collision, and though the *Yrurac Bat* attempted to do so, it was clearly too late.

There were common themes among statements by passengers; the calmness and helpfulness of the officers was commended, but the crew panicked to an extent and seemed to have little idea what they should do, while the passengers were calm and enterprising. The rowlocks for the oars were stored in the boats instead of being fastened in position, and at least one boat did not have in it a single person who knew how to row – some were pushing while others were pulling, neither apparently understanding the stroke needed to get them away from the ship.

Another boat landed in the water, its ropes still attached – but there was no knife to be found to cut the ropes until a young boy passenger produced a penknife from his pocket. In another boat the bungs were missing and it instantly began to leak – buckets disintegrated the moment they were used. In the end it was being baled with shoes, hats and anything else people could find. Lifejackets were lashed in so well that they couldn't be released.

Very shortly they saw *Yrurac Bat* 'blow up' and disappear. Then *Douro* went, stern first. Just as the people on both ships did not become aware of the danger of collision until too late, so they didn't appreciate the extent of damage to their ships; that they would sink so

This is among the earlier surviving photos of RMSP ships – Douro *(I), sister-ship of* Rhone, *most likely photographed at Southampton during the 1870s.*

quickly. It was considered that this factor cost a good many lives, with people thinking they had longer to evacuate.

As for the rescue ship *Hidalgo*, Capt. Turner, there was nothing but praise. He took the shipwrecked people to nearby Coruña rather than to England, where his ship was headed, simply because well over 100 additional people meant that he had not enough provisions. When they reached Coruña matters approached the farcical, for this was the fever season in South America and the rescued people would have to wait eight days before the quarantine period was up. Capt. Turner was unimpressed and said that if necessary he would buy more stores and continue to England, but in the end the quarantine demands were waived.

That the officers of *Douro* did their utmost to maintain order and get passengers and crew into the boats there is no doubt. The sheer tragedy of the affair was encapsulated in a short comment from one passenger as he watched *Douro* from his lifeboat: 'The last that was seen of Capt. Kemp of the *Douro* he was standing weeping on the deck, and blowing out a lifebelt, but shortly after the ship went down, and he was never seen again'.

Shannon and *Seine*

The late 1850s was a logical time for Royal Mail to order new ships. The surviving units from the first fleet were utterly outdated and less than popular with the travelling public. With the restriction on iron hulls now lifted, this form of construction was in great demand. The Company was also seeking expansion and service improvements, and these ships were essentially ordered to fulfil a newly-signed two-year extension of its West Indies mail contract.

The earliest surviving reference to *Shannon* and *Seine* (and to their sister ship *Parramatta*, which was wrecked on her maiden voyage) appeared in the directors' minutes for 23 October 1857, when the Thames Ironworks Co. asked if they could tender for a new ship. On 4 November the managers submitted specifications for ships fitted with feathering paddles, and a week later their ideas were sent to Robert Napier for his views. The Glasgow builder approved the plans and the following January Napier was given the contract to build one of them, supply of ship and engines within sixteen months. This was *Shannon*. The Thames Ironworks Co. was contracted for *Parramatta* and *Seine*, though the latter ship was not begun until *Parramatta* was afloat. Day, Summers & Co. built *Seine's* engines.

The Thames Ironworks was located at one of the last bends of the tiny River Lea, shortly before it joined the Thames between Canning Town and Blackwall. The angle of the slip was crucial, for there was little room to spare for launching ships as large as these, a fact the shipbuilder knew well enough for a few years earlier the world's largest ship at the time – P&O's *Himalaya* – had entered the water there. An imbalance of drag chains was probably needed to keep ships in centre stream after launching, perhaps explaining the excitement when *Parramatta* was launched:

Immediately on the arrival of her forecradles at the bottom of the ways, the gigantic vessel gave a tremendous lurch to port, and impressed the breathless spectators with an idea that she must go over altogether, but after a few violent lists she righted herself…

The fact that *Parramatta* was quickly lost on the West Indies route explains why she does not feature greatly in this entry, but there is one matter in which she is relevant. While *Shannon* was intended to bear that name from the start, the other two were at one stage to have been named *Parramatta* and *Yarra*. The inference was that they were intended to join the new Australian venture in which RMSP was involving itself at that time. However, the first reference to them stated that all three were intended for the West Indies, so the compliment to Australia was rather oblique. Before the ships were completed the Australian service had folded, and the name *Yarra* was altered to *Seine*. *Parramatta* was retained, for she was by then already christened.

To complicate matters further, the names *Parramatta* and *Yarra* were not the original choices – even earlier they were to have been named *Orinoco* and *Magdalena*. The existing *Orinoco* and *Magdalena* – badly infested with dry rot – would be scrapped and their engines transferred to the replacement ships. *Parramatta* received *Orinoco's* engines, but *Magdalena* gained a reprieve for a few years, and so in January 1859 the Company hurriedly ordered new engines for *Seine*.

Shannon entered the water from Napier's slipway on 19 March 1859, and was damaged in the process. *Seine* emerged from the Thames in the summer of the following year. They were iron-hulled paddle steamers. The Napier ship was a little larger than the others at 3,609 gross tons; *Seine* was 3,440. The most obvious difference between these ships and the *Orinoco* class (apart from hull materials) was the use of straight stems rather than clipper bows. Having made this change earlier than many companies, Royal Mail reverted to the old style and was still building clipper-bowed ships in 1890.

Designed for the West Indies trade, *Seine* and *Shannon* did not join the Brazil run until *Rhone* and *Douro* were switched to the West Indies route early in 1867. It was a stopgap measure which lasted into 1868. From comments by a passenger in *Shannon* it is evident that forms and long tables were used in the saloon – the concept of individual chairs and smaller tables was still in the future. The low-ceilinged saloon served as both dining room and lounge. There is little more surviving descriptive material, but they would have been along similar lines to the *Orinoco* class.

Soon after entering service *Shannon* was in trouble. She made a westbound Atlantic crossing in 1860 under sail alone and also with steering problems after running into a storm while under tow by the ageing *Trent*. During 1864 she carried one of the most valuable consignments of specie yet found on board an RMSP ship, valued in its day at £1,500,000.

Seine also had some early troubles – exactly what happened in 1861 is unclear, but it resulted in her master, Capt. Revett (the Company's Senior Captain) having his certificate suspended for three months, and he was not to be placed in command again 'until he has been examined as to his knowledge of the pilotage of the English Channel and its ports'. The chief officer was reduced to an appointment in a smaller ship with the same qualification. How dramatically fortunes can swing – four years later, in August 1865,

A painting of Shannon *made while she was still a paddle steamer. The distant vessel towards the left is either* Parana *(I) or* Magdalena *(I).*

Seine suffered a serious fire shortly after leaving St Thomas. A potential disaster was kept to reasonable levels and the directors had 'much pleasure to present Capt. Revett, the officers, engineers and crew of the *Seine* each with a suitable testimonial or gratuity, as a recognition of their services'.

Apart from those incidents, little of note happened to *Seine* during her eleven-year life. It was a short allotment, for she was sold for demolition in 1871. Not for the first time Royal Mail came face to face with the backlash of its continuing policy of building paddle steamers when all around were switching to screw propulsion. *Shannon* was given a reprieve, rather on the basis of 'if you can't beat 'em, join 'em', for her machinery and paddles were removed and she was given Maudslay, Sons & Field compound engines and a large two-bladed screw. That was in 1874. The work (including lengthening the hull) was done by Walker, Crouch & Lindwall.

Her new dimensions were: length bp 355ft 10in (she had previously been 332ft 10in), breadth 44ft. The compound engines had a nominal horsepower of 700 with cylinders of 62 and 112 inches diameter, with 5ft stroke. There were eight circular boilers with a heating surface of 10,290 sq.ft.

With the transplant completed, she returned to the West Indies run with an estimated speed increase of one knot, but with coal consumption reduced by 50%. How desirable that was may be gathered from the following table, produced in 1870, which compared the performances of *Shannon*, as a paddle steamer, with three screw ships. By far the most efficient was *Elbe*, Royal Mail's first compound engined ship:

Ship	Tons of coal per round voyage	Cost of coal per round voyage	Average speed (knots)
Shannon	3,604	£4,468	9.45
Elbe	1,411	£1,582	11.83
Nile	2,244	£2,698	10.62
Neva	2,163	£2,533	11.20

Seine and *Shannon* were indirectly concerned with John Elder's contract to build *Elbe*. There was a stormy Court meeting on 2 December 1868 when the managers reported on tenders for converting both *Seine* and *Shannon* to screw propulsion (six years before *Shannon* finally received her new engines). Elder & Co. was among the firms invited to tender. Generally the Court agreed that if better ships were needed for the West Indies transatlantic service, a newbuilding was preferable to a conversion. Admiral Whish (a future Chairman) moved that 'it is desirable for the more perfect working of the transatlantic service to add another steamer to the RMSP Company's fleet'.

This prompted another director, John Greenwood, to launch into a bitter tirade on the Company's management, in particular the finances in connection with the Panama, New Zealand and Australian Royal Mail Co. (looked at in the entry for *Ebro* [I], *Tiber* and *Liffey* [II]). The problems with that investment, particularly the cost of extending RMSP's services to Colon, came under fire; there were further expenses for temporary arrangements in the Caribbean, and 'considering also the present state of the finances and prospects of the Company', the placing of orders for new ships, he claimed, was sheer madness. Far better that RMSP revert to its old West Indies schedule and do away with the Colon extension.

No-one was inclined to second his motion, and Admiral Whish's original one was carried. Elder built the new ship (which became *Elbe*), with an option for RMSP to trade in *Atrato*, *Seine* and *Shannon* at a combined value of £20,000. The option was taken up only in the case of *Atrato*.

When the time *did* come for *Shannon* to be converted, the work nearly didn't happen again, for the directors were asked once more to choose between a conversion and a newbuilding. Late in October 1873 they decided to proceed with *Shannon* and invited tenders. Walker, Crouch & Lindwall bid £13,500 for altering the hull and fitting a new spar deck – this work included lengthening the hull and providing her with a clipper bow in place of the straight stem. They purchased the old engines for £6,250, while a separate agreement was reached for 'extra work'. Maudslay, Sons & Field beat Napier for the machinery contract at £51,500.

Shannon's loss, described in a moment, was reported to have come during her second voyage as a screw ship. If that was so, the conversion work must have taken an exceptionally long time, for it was already under way in April 1874, a year and four months before she was lost. At all events, on the outward passage to St Thomas she made the fastest crossing yet by an RMSP ship – 3,650 miles in eleven days. The homeward passage from Colon began early in September 1875. At about 5.15 a.m. on 8 September Capt. Leeds was on duty – the Jamaica pilot was on board but had not yet taken over. The ship headed at full speed towards Kingston and was about eighty miles SSW of Port Royal, her course shaped to pass ten miles to the east of Portland Rock so as to clear Pedro Bank, a nasty area of shoals and sandbanks. A powerful current here has always caused mariners to pay a great deal of attention when plotting a course. Capt. Leeds did so on this occasion, but the current running on 8 September was later described as 'heavier than ever previously known', and as a result *Shannon* ran firmly aground on a coral reef known as Pedro Keys. She travelled well over the reef and came to rest roughly amidships. Capt. Leeds ordered his engines full astern and set the crew to lightening ship by dumping cargo. She remained fast aground.

With about fifty passengers on board, it was a credit to the master and officers that there was no hint of panic. They were also, to a large degree, responsible for the splendid behaviour of the crew, who responded quickly to orders and made no attempt to plunder the liquor store or baggage. The purser, pilot and a few crew set off in a boat for Port Royal, an eighty-mile journey completed at 11.30 the next morning. They reported to the Port Commodore, who arranged for HMS *Dryad* to sail out to *Shannon*. Meanwhile the ship's 'delegation' moved on to Kingston. RMSP's Port Superintendent, Capt. Cooper, quickly recruited the services of the cable-laying steamer *Investigator*, and then HMS *Heron*.

Nothing more was heard until the following night, when *Dryad* returned to Port Royal with fifty-one passengers and their baggage, and 107 packages of specie. The passengers were given accommodation in Kingston. Shortly afterwards *Investigator* turned up with most of the crew.

Shannon, with 500 tons of cargo thrown overboard, was still dry inside. *Investigator* returned and anchored some way from her. Cables were attached but the attempt to pull her off failed. When *Dryad* returned the following Saturday, her crew saw that the reef had cut through the hull. She was slowly filling and water had risen to three feet above the orlop deck. When she swung slightly later that day, hopes of getting her off were raised, especially as water had not yet reached the engineroom. *Investigator* again got a line on board and *Shannon's* engines turned full astern once more. Almost at once there was a muffled sound from within the hull – a steampipe had burst. Water swirled into the engineroom, rose quickly and extinguished the fires.

Boisterous weather and a heavy swell now battered the hull and she was expected to break up shortly. Capt. Leeds, with several officers, engineers, the carpenter and boilermaker, five firemen, the chief steward and a barman remained on board to salvage what they could. Some ship's fittings and cargo were taken to Kingston. During the entire operation the work, initiative and leadership of Capt. Leeds drew everyone's admiration. When, in December, the Board of Trade held its enquiry at Greenwich Police Court, it was satisfying to all who had been involved that Capt. Leeds emerged with no stain on his character.

At Kingston, Capt. Cooper had quickly summoned *Nile* from Colon to take *Shannon's* voyage home, and her passengers therefore reached Britain only a few days late and none the worse for their excitements in the Caribbean.

Shannon did not die without a fight. Some time afterwards she was still reasonably intact and Royal Mail sent men and equipment from the Marine Salvage Co. to refloat her. In July 1876 came the news that they had failed. RMSP's local representatives complained about the terrible inefficiency of the salvage company, and when £500 was claimed under a 'no success' clause, Royal Mail referred it straight to the solicitors. They were doubtless bitter at having the chance of salvage thrown away. Instructions were given for the ship to be sold locally and without further advice to the Court; the tone made it clear that after smarting over the salvage fiasco they wanted to rid themselves of this embarrassment as quickly as possible. What an ignoble end for a ship which had broken the Company's speed record earlier on that final voyage. That part of Pedro Bank became known as Shannon Shoal, a name still used on navigational charts.

Neva

Royal Mail had little time to reflect on the horrors of the October 1867 hurricane at St Thomas – it urgently needed a replacement for *Rhone*. She had been such a pivotal unit in the Company's bid to regain popularity with the travelling public that her loss had the potential to be more serious than the immediate event. She and *Douro* were the finest and most prestigious vessels in the fleet.

The search for a new ship had that status as its governing factor, together with a need to enter service as quickly as possible in order to maintain the mail contract and the line's reputation. That narrowed the search to a first-class screw vessel of 2,500 to 3,000 tons, which was reasonably well advanced in construction but not so far forward that changes could not be made.

What they required lay at Caird's yard at Greenock, an iron screw steamer being built for Norddeutscher Lloyd. Her name had been selected – she was to be christened *Rhein*, the Germanic spelling for the River Rhine. What a coincidental name against that of the ship she was to replace – RMSP wasn't inclined to retain it. Less than a month after the directors had learned of *Rhone's* loss they had found *Rhein*, negotiated with NDL and, during December, offered £90,000 for her. An additional £10,000 was allocated for alterations to make her as close as possible to *Rhone*. When she entered the water on 10 February 1868, Mrs Bevis (wife of her master-designate) christened her *Neva*.

Her dimensions were: length 348ft, breadth 40ft, depth 33ft. Gross tonnage was 3,025. Her inverted cylinder engines developed 600 nominal horsepower. On trials in Stokes Bay during June she reached $14\frac{1}{4}$ knots.

Neva was given brig rig, with main, top and topgallant yards. More than 150 feet separated the two masts, between which was a particularly prominent raked funnel, nine feet in diameter. A spar deck, flush from stem to stern, was filled with a cluttered collection of accessories and fittings – steam winches and capstan, cook house, hen coops and pens for sheep, cattle and pigs. Ventilation pipes from the spar deck reached every part of the ship's four decks. The hull was divided into ten watertight compartments.

Accommodation was provided for 390 passengers – about 280 to 290 first class and the remainder evenly distributed between second and third. Her great saloon was probably among the largest of the day, a hundred feet long and the full width of the ship; it had seating for 160. The walls were lined with oak and walnut and the furniture was solid walnut. Pillars and cornices bore a mixture of white paint and gilt, while cushions on seats, sofas and lounges were green morocco leather. Electro-plating was used for items like glass racks and door handles. A similar standard of décor and fittings was found in the first class staterooms.

Neva, *hurriedly purchased by RMSP, while under construction for Norddeutscher Lloyd, to replace* Rhone. *She was a popular mail ship and was sold in 1890.*

Having been bought for the St Thomas and Colon service, it was not until the summer of 1871 that she was sent to South America. Her voyages up to that point had been largely uneventful. Once *Elbe* was ready for service, Capt. Bevis transferred to her, so in January 1870 Capt. Woolward took command of *Neva*, taking his eight-year-old son in a successful bid to cure the whooping cough he had suffered during two previous winters.

A few months later, in the summer months, *Neva* battled a hurricane 450 miles from St Thomas. As signs of the approaching storm became clear, Capt. Woolward ordered all sails lowered, and the boats and deck fittings secured. She hove to and waited. A newspaper dramatically reported: 'The wind came whirling, roaring, rolling, with as terrible a sea as ever a human eye beheld… After 24 hours of anxious waiting and terrible tossing, the ship was able to make headway slowly…' There was no significant damage to ship or person, which was more than could be said for a French steamer not far away, which ended up without boats, with seven feet of water inside her (which extinguished the fires), one crew member killed and a passenger who died of fright. In addition to handing Capt. Woolward a glowing written tribute, *Neva's* passengers collected over £25 and presented him with a silver barometer.

Once she had been placed on the Brazil and River Plate run in August 1871, *Neva* was employed there for the rest of her career. In May 1872 her crew earned a day's pay for each day that the ship had a disabled vessel under tow. During the following year there were legal proceedings after a collision between *Neva* and the barque *Fluellin* off Start Point. The barque was making about 6 knots on her way from Sunderland to Bombay with coal. Seeing *Neva* attempting to cross his course, Capt. Robert Livingstone put the helm hard over but could not avoid contact. *Neva's* bowsprit penetrated *Fluellin's* bulkhead and forecastle, her bowsprit, jibboom, cat- and knight-heads and rail being carried away. Parts of the forecastle and main deck were started.

A boat was launched from *Neva* and Capt. Livingstone was asked if help was needed; he answered in the negative and so the steamer, little damaged, continued her passage to Southampton. *Fluellin* put in to Portland harbour for repairs. RMSP later reached an agreement to pay *Fluellin's* owners more than £500 compensation.

In a general review of the fleet in February 1875 the directors decided to order new engines and boilers for *Neva*. They were provided the following year by Day, Summers & Co. Her new average speed was about 12 knots. After they had been fitted, her career was largely uneventful. Facilities added during her declining years included refrigeration (only for stores, though the Company emphasised how popular that was with passengers) and electric light, yet her link with the days of sail remained as she used canvas extensively until the end.

Between 1886 and 1890 a number of particularly fine ships joined the RMSP fleet. Older vessels like *Neva* became redundant. After a successful career of eighty-five voyages, more than seventy of them to South America, she was sold for breaking up in 1890.

Boyne

On 19 October 1870 RMSP's Chairman, Capt. Mangles, proposed that a new ship should be built for the South America mail service. Tenders were invited from Laird Bros of Birkenhead, Denny of Dumbarton and the Glasgow firms of Tod & Macgregor, Napier and Elder. As an afterthought, Day, Summers of Southampton was added, but Denny won the contract. The arrangement included taking *La Plata* as part payment for the new ship. Denny's engineering division built the 500 nominal horsepower compound machinery. The cylinders had diameters of 57in and 100in, with 51in stroke.

'Fittings and arrangements in every department are of the very best character,' one description claimed. 'The main saloon is a splendid apartment extending for the full width of the ship and is very tastefully decorated and furnished.' There is, however, a dearth of more detailed description. *Boyne's* gross tonnage was 3,318, length bp 360ft, breadth 40ft and depth 34ft.

She left Denny's yard a day under a year after they had received the contract – 16 November 1871. Under the command of Capt. W.W. Herbert she sailed to Southampton for trials in Stokes Bay. On the way she had an argument with a craft named *Waif*, but the collision was not serious and did not delay *Boyne*. She ran trials over the Stokes Bay measured mile. With her engines averaging $58\frac{1}{4}$ rpm, the four runs achieved 16, 11.215, 15.721 and 11.803 knots – a mean average of 13.685 knots. A Force 4 wind and strong tide were responsible for the wide difference between east and west runs. The trials (so crucial for a new ship but so rarely described) were watched by several RMSP directors, two Admiralty surveyors, a Board of Trade surveyor, the Southampton postmaster, William Denny and Capt. Jellicoe (the Company's Southampton Superintendent).

They were 'well pleased' and *Boyne* was cleared to take the December mails to Brazil and the River Plate. That clearance also required passing an Admiralty on-board survey; and if a ship was later scheduled to enter a different mail service she would have to be surveyed again. The rules were strict and uncompromising, and extended beyond the suitability of the ships themselves. Early in 1872, for instance, *Boyne* and *Neva* were involved in a row between the

Boyne, 3,318 tons, built by Denny Bros in 1871 for the South America mail route.

Admiralty and RMSP over the use of unapproved transport for carrying mails across the River Plate. This was a periodic squabble because the Company had to deliver the Argentine mails in time for correspondence to be answered before the ship left Buenos Aires. The only way it could do that was to transfer mails to a local vessel at Montevideo.

Boyne made fifteen voyages, all to South America. On one of them her passenger list included the Brazilian Emperor Dom Pedro II, who was returning to Rio de Janeiro after a visit to Europe – the ship was given an enthusiastic welcome at Rio. All of her voyages except the last were under the command of Capt. Frederic Reeks, who had joined RMSP in 1842 as a midshipman in *Tweed*. The circumstances in which Capt. Reeks left the ship in June 1875 reflected a bad summer all round for *Boyne* and the men in her. The captain's navigation was criticised, and then information reached the Company that he 'had been guilty of insobriety'.

He resigned and Capt. R.H. Macaulay was given command of a fine ship which was popular with passengers. She sailed from Southampton on 9 June, but never returned to the United Kingdom. The outward leg and much of the homeward run was completed without incident. At 2 p.m. on 11 August she left Lisbon, rolling as she crossed the turbulent Tagus bar. On board were 108 passengers, about 114 officers and crew, mails, cargo (principally coffee, tapioca and hides) and £20,682-worth of specie.

On the evening before arrival at Southampton, in patchy visibility, a barque passed two or three miles distant. Capt. Macaulay, on the quarterdeck, ordered the lead to be made ready for another sounding at 8 p.m. – they had first taken soundings three hours earlier. At 6.30 p.m. the masthead lights were run up; Frederick Clark, an Able Seaman, saw this task completed and commented on the thick weather before going on duty as forward lookout. At 7.40 p.m. he saw breakers ahead; then rocks.

He called out 'Rocks right ahead', but his warning wasn't acknowledged. Then he cried 'We're going right atop the rocks; you'd better put the helm hard a-port'. But the weather shredded his voice before it reached the bridge and it was not until his third call that he received an acknowledgement. 'We are ashore', he shouted. 'The rocks are right under the port bow'.

Second Officer Butler replied 'Alright, I can see them'. He ordered hard a-port and moved to the telegraph to stop engines, but his captain had beaten him to it. For a full minute and a half after stopping engines, *Boyne's* momentum carried her on and she grounded with a rending of metal. Visibility was scarcely 150 yards.

Water poured into the hull in torrents. The engineroom filled rapidly and two coal-trimmers, trapped below, were not seen again. *Boyne* quickly heeled over, but Capt. Macaulay managed to prevent panic. Within fifteen minutes all the passengers and most of the crew were in the boats, with the ailing Chief Officer (who had been ill since Pernambuco) as flotilla commander. A diving cutter working nearby offered assistance and piloted the lifeboats into Molenes Bay. *Boyne's* distress signals were answered by a passing barque.

When they reached shore, the survivors were taken into the homes of local people, and later moved to larger towns. So well were some looked after in St Malo that they presented a cash gift and a silver crucifix to the Catholic Sisters who took care of them. The captain and one or two crew members remained on board as the ship settled lower and at a steeper angle on the rocks. Divers reported that the hull had been bitten right through and there was no hope of refloating her. At 1 a.m., having salvaged the specie and mail, and much of the baggage, Capt. Macaulay left his ship.

After four years of service Boyne *was wrecked during a homeward passage from South America. This view of the wreck, near Brest, appeared in* Illustrated London News *in August 1875.*

Distorted accounts reached London at lunchtime on the day after she grounded. Her arrival at Southampton had been expected at any time; instead, telegrams were posted outside newspaper offices telling of the vessel's loss. Some passengers and crew reached Southampton on 19 August from St Malo, in the London & South Western Company's steamer *Guernsey*. Cheers echoed between *Guernsey* and RMSP's *Minho* when the ferry passed on her way into the docks; *Minho* was preparing for the next mail voyage to South America.

The Board of Trade Enquiry in October was, as always, thorough. Every witness praised Capt. Macaulay's seamanship and his competence on the bridge; his constant vigilance over the Fourth Officer was commended (the Fourth was taking watches because of the Mate's illness), as was his conscientious practice in routine matters of navigation. He had spent twenty-two years with Royal Mail.

A quartermaster alone expressed doubts about the frequency with which the lead was lowered. Macaulay insisted otherwise; he had got a sight at noon and considered that the ship would pass well clear of the rocks around Ushant. A particularly strong tide and in-draught was recorded as the reason for grounding, caused 'solely by neglect in not using the lead more frequently when approaching Ushant in thick weather'. The Court, held at Southampton Town Hall, said that had another sounding been taken at 7 p.m. Capt. Macaulay would probably have realised the error and saved his ship. He was subsequently charged with a number of offences under the Company's Regulations, relating to soundings and fog.

Boyne was sold for 2,000 francs to a local company, for breaking up.

Ebro (I); *Tiber* and *Liffey* (II)

The early story of these ships surrounded RMSP's apparently insatiable desire to be involved in the UK – Australia mail service. Despite having had its fingers badly burnt in a venture in the 1850s (see the entry for *Oneida* and *Tasmanian*), the Company was anxious for another try a little later. In 1866, new mail contracts were issued for the Australia service and, for the first time, one was granted for an operation travelling via the Panama isthmus. With the advent of the Panama Railroad this route had become viable, though long distances across the Pacific remained a major hurdle.

A new company – Panama, New Zealand & Australian Royal Mail Co. Ltd (PNZA) – was to operate the service, using its own ships for the Pacific crossing. They were *Rakaia*, *Kaikoura* and *Ruahine*. RMSP was, from the start, an integral part of the service, for it provided the Atlantic voyages from England to Colon.

From what little is known about the PNZA ships they appear to have been similar but not true sister ships. Their lengths varied from 273ft (*Rakaia*) to 288ft (*Ruahine*). Gross tonnages were 1,509 (*Rakaia*), 1,591 (*Kaikoura*) and 1,589 (*Ruahine*). They all came from different builders: *Rakaia* was built and engined by Randolph & Elder at Glasgow in 1866, *Kaikoura* by Lungley on the Thames also in 1866, and *Ruahine* by Dudgeon at Poplar, London in 1865. *Ruahine*, being the first built, had some time to wait before entering service, a fact which suited RMSP because *Danube* (under construction) was suffering inordinate delays and *Tamar* had to return to England for new paddle wheels. Thus *Ruahine* was chartered as a stopgap for Caribbean intercolonial services from August to December 1865.

The Australian service began in mid-1866, and before long RMSP found itself immersed in a case of déjà vu – just as the Australian operation in the 1850s had got into difficulties, with Royal Mail inheriting ships it didn't want because they were securities for RMSP investments, so now exactly the same began to develop with PNZA. A five-year saga began in April 1867. Various financial proposals were discussed, which appear to have culminated in RMSP advancing £40,000 at 6% interest to the troubled PNZA, with mortgages on the three Pacific ships as surety.

The service continued for a year or so until, in July 1868, RMSP agreed to inject more money – but not without opposition. Two directors, John Greenwood and James Mathieson, were against further involvement, and the gulf between the two sides grew wider as the months passed; by December the two of them were strenuously advocating that RMSP 'realise its securities' after a meeting of PNZA's creditors. A week later PNZA plunged further into trouble. Mathieson and Greenwood, in a fiery meeting, tried three times to veto further involvement, including a demand that RMSP's shareholders be asked their opinions on the matter. They were outvoted, and in March both resigned their directorships.

By January 1869 PNZA appeared to be insolvent, for *Ruahine* had been seized by the Panama authorities. In April *Ruahine* and *Kaikoura* were in Sydney and arrangements were in hand to send them back to England. So parlous were the finances that coal could not be afforded and they came under canvas alone.

While the three ships did not join RMSP's fleet until 1871, the period between their return to England (when they were laid up in Southampton Water) and their official entry into the fleet involved a complex situation. Since the ships had been mortgaged to RMSP, they automatically became the Company's property after the collapse of PNZA. However, numerous creditors, not least PNZA's debenture shareholders, were part of the equation. As Royal Mail was holding the major assets of the defunct company – its three steamers – there was now an onus on RMSP to satisfy the shareholders before the ships could be released officially into Royal Mail's hands. Some thousands of pounds were paid out by RMSP either late in 1870 or early 1871, and the ships then entered its fleet.

In general, though, the Company had considered that it controlled the ships since, possibly, late 1868. When PNZA was being investigated that August, one of RMSP's managers, Robert Marshall, was sent to Australia. When reports were released suggesting that PNZA could not be made profitable, RMSP moved quickly. The Company's half-yearly report for April 1869 stated: 'Mr Marshall had no alternative but to take steps for assuming possession of the ships mortgaged to this Company'. On 22 November that year *Rakaia* left Southampton on a voyage for RMSP, calling at Lisbon, St Vincent, Pernambuco, Bahia, Rio de Janeiro, St Thomas and New York, returning to Southampton on 20 March 1870.

Also in 1869 came initial efforts to sell the ships. In September an offer from Persian buyers to purchase *Kaikoura* for £28,000 was rejected. In January 1870 there started an extraordinary period, lasting the better part of two years, in which a Mr Sheat bombarded Royal Mail with offers to buy all three. What was behind those purchase attempts was not revealed, but someone who has an offer of £78,000 turned down wouldn't be expected to then offer £42,000. By the time that happened, in September 1871, the approach was more of a demand (including a threat of legal action), and was instantly referred to the solicitors. The conclusion must be that Mr Sheat was acting on behalf of PNZA's creditors.

At all events, it was decided that selling the ships was not the best option; in the longer term they were better off bringing the vessels up to the desired standard and using them for service expansion. The hulls were examined and declared adequate. In October 1871 *Kaikoura* and *Ruahine* were placed in the hands of Day, Summers & Co. at Southampton, where conversion work included new compound engines. *Rakaia's* movements at that time are uncertain but it appears that she was not re-engined.

By the late spring of 1872 the Company was considering how best to employ the ships. For some time there had been growing pressure to increase the frequency of South America sailings – the service had been operating for two decades with quite phenomenal regularity, but without any expansion beyond the extension to the River Plate. Now it was decided that the PNZA vessels would open a second monthly service, leaving Southampton on the 21st of the month (soon put back to the 24th). A significant development was the use of European ports of discharge on the northbound voyage, and then for loading outward as well. The initial port was Antwerp, but before long vessels were calling at a range of ports – Bremerhaven or Hamburg homeward, Spanish ports or Cherbourg outward.

Their new names were announced during June. *Rakaia* became *Ebro*, *Kaikoura* became *Tiber* and *Ruahine* became *Liffey*. Between them they made twenty-six voyages to South America, not counting *Rakaia's* voyage back in 1869. *Ebro* made seven before being switched to the West Indies station. On her first voyage she battled a storm which carried away her foretopmast; then a mooring line was tangled round the propeller during the third. Little else from her fairly short time with RMSP was recorded. Before Christmas 1879 she was placed on the sale market, but not until early 1881 was she sold to the Marques de Campo, Madrid. He kept her until about 1886, when she went to Compania Trasatlantica, who renamed her *Baldomero Iglesias*. They kept her until 1898, and after a brief time under the French flag she left the Register in 1901.

The career of *Tiber* was, if anything, less eventful even than *Ebro*. After eleven voyages to Brazil and the River Plate, she was sent to the West Indies in 1875. Four years later she figured in a somewhat bizarre incident which featured the Company's steamer *Belize*. That ship, on a West Indies voyage, had been put ashore off Savannah-la-Mar and her master was ordered home. A new captain was sent out to take over, and on his first voyage put *Belize* ashore off Savannah-la-Mar! He, too, was ordered home – a bit like a cricketer trudging off the field after a first-ball duck. *Tiber* was sent to assist the stranded ship on the second occasion. A week later *Tiber* was at St Thomas. Her second and fourth officers took one of the ship's boats outside the harbour for a bit of recreation, a not unusual pastime. On this occasion the weather suddenly deteriorated, the sea rose and the men were thrown from the boat and drowned.

In 1882 she was on her way into Porto Plata, San Domingo when she ran aground early on the evening of 10 February. Few details of the accident have survived. It seems there were no injuries and at least some of the cargo was salvaged, but the ship was a total loss.

Liffey made eight voyages. The comparatively small number of South America voyages made by them reflects that they were really too small for the service – the disadvantage of inherited vessels was the need to tailor services to pre-existing ships. Having said that, it will never be known how many South Atlantic voyages *Liffey* might have made, for she was lost while still on the service.

She left Southampton for her eighth voyage on 24 July 1874. On the morning of 22 August she was faced with a situation reminiscent of that in which *Boyne* was lost. She was near the mouth of the River Plate, about to round the northern headland, when a thick fog suddenly descended. Unknown to the ship's officers, an extra strong current had set *Liffey* too close to the coast. She went ashore on Cape José Ignacio, close to Maldonado, Uruguay, grounding at 9.53 a.m. – and almost at once visibility improved enough for the shore to be seen. Capt. J.H. Donne sent the passengers ashore in boats. Beyond the immediate aspects of a shipwreck one of the greatest hazards can be the behaviour of the crew – in this respect *Liffey* fared badly. While some were engaged in lowering and manning the boats, others raided the canteen and seized all the liquor. Soon becoming drunk, they rampaged around the ship 'like a troop of Indians', breaking open passengers' baggage, pillaging and stealing all the valuables they could find.

When they went ashore, the mob took with them the remaining rum and brandy. The ship's officers were powerless to stop them, concentrating instead on forming barriers, with the aid of carbines from the ship's arsenal, to protect the passengers. They did this so well that the passengers later collectively wrote to Capt. Donne expressing their gratitude. The shipwrecked people were cast ashore at a remote spot and three days passed before help reached them. The crew had long since drunk themselves into a stupor.

A month later a Naval Court of Enquiry was held at Montevideo, on board HMS *Cracker*, presided over by Cdr R.C. Buckle. Their verdict was thus:

We... find the courses steered to have been correct and such as would have, under all ordinary circumstances, taken the ship well clear of all danger had it not been for the unusually strong current running to the northward, which Capt. Donne was unaware of, and therefore could make no allowance for. We also consider that, good bearings having been taken at eight a.m., a cast of the lead would have been unnecessary, and therefore, under these circumstances, we are of opinion that no blame whatever is attached to Captain J.H. Donne.

In consequence of the fog being of so short a duration, the Court consider that no blame is attached to Mr J.H. Parkin, the Chief Officer, on account of not easing the engines, and that he did everything he could for the safety of the ship, both before and after she struck.

In conclusion, the Court, from the above-stated circumstances, returns to Captain J.H. Donne and Mr J.H. Parkin, chief officer of the Royal Mail steamer Liffey, *their certificates of competency, at the same time remarking it considers they both evinced great zeal and energy for the safety of the passengers, mails and cargo on the occasion of the loss of the Royal Mail steamer* Liffey; *and the two officers' certificates are hereby returned accordingly.*

However assiduously the captain and Mate may have acted, that was an unprecedentedly generous outcome. A further Enquiry, held at Southampton on 27 October, was not so lenient and led to both Capt. Donne and Mr Parkin being asked to resign.

So *Liffey* was gone. It is quite amazing to record, in an era when accidents were so common, that this was the first loss of an RMSP ship on South America services, after more than twenty years of operation.

Minho (I) and *Mondego*

During the 1870s, much of the tonnage with which RMSP augmented its fleet was second hand. Two vessels acquired in this way were *Minho* and *Mondego*, purchased in 1874. They were built two years earlier for John Ryde of London, with dimensions of about 350ft length, breadth 37ft, depth 27ft 6in. These iron screw steamers had compound inverted two-cylinder engines which developed 450nhp, the cylinder diameters being 50in and 86in, with 48in stroke. They were built on the Clyde, *Mondego* (2,564 gross tons) as *Santiago* by Tod & Macgregor and *Minho* (2,541 gross tons) as *Leopold II* by Barclay Curle. Each builder also supplied the engines.

The first of *Minho's* forty-three voyages to South America began on 25 May 1874. Her sister ship, entering the fleet in September after a review of services, made more South America voyages than *Minho*, but both were sold in 1888. They were engaged in the 'B' route itinerary.

The first to record an accident was *Minho*, which grounded off Brazil's Abrolhos Rocks on 11 September 1876. She was not badly damaged but it was the last straw for Capt. E. West, whose long history with Royal Mail contained a number of cautions for accidents. He resigned and was given half pay for six months – in comparison with Royal Mail's responses to other such matters, this was towards the low end of the disciplinary scale.

In November 1878 *Minho* began a period of complicated schedule changes triggered by the yellow fever 'season' in South America and the consequent threat of quarantine. On that voyage she called at Lisbon, St Vincent, Pernambuco, Maceio, Bahia, Rio de Janeiro and Santos, and returned via Rio to Southampton and Antwerp. Thereafter the schedules for both ships were changed regularly – occasionally European ports like Carril and Vigo were added.

They took over a third monthly sailing (departing on the 1st of the month) when it was re-instated in September 1881. It omitted the River Plate and made more extensive use of North European ports for discharging. A further change in the summer of 1885 saw *Minho* returning from Rio de Janeiro to Britain via Barbados, St Thomas and New York. Royal Mail had periodic flirtations with that route over the years.

Officers and crew in *Mondego* were praised in January 1879 after she had been in collision with the steamer *Glamis Castle*. Royal Mail pressed for a settlement of £20,000. A year later, a launch from HMS *Agincourt* got across *Minho's* bows off Portugal and was run down. Two men from the launch were drowned but Capt. Dickinson and his officers were not held to blame. One of the many unsolved sea mysteries involved *Mondego* at Christmas 1885. Steaming quietly through the English Channel in good weather, at the start of a voyage to South America, her master, Capt. A.C. Green, couldn't be found. The ship was searched from stem to stern but there was no sign of him, and no evidence was found to explain his disappearance. *Mondego* put in to Plymouth where a replacement captain was appointed.

Built for Ryde & Co. as Leopold II *in 1872, RMSP bought this vessel in 1874 for Brazil and River Plate services and renamed her* Minho *(I).*

By 1887 both ships, surplus to requirements, were laid up, probably in the Solent. That November an idea was aired to give *Minho* new boilers and triple expansion engines, and fit her as an emigrant carrier. There was probably potential for this trade, but it is arguable if such an expensive refit would have been cost-effective. At all events, they thought better of it and shortly afterwards decided to sell her for £7,500. During November the same year *Mondego* was sold for £9,500.

Both were sold to Archibald Ross of London, though in *Lloyd's Register* they didn't appear under his ownership at the same time. *Minho* was listed with Ross only in 1888/89, *Mondego* appears the following year and stayed with Ross until around 1892, when she left the Register. *Minho* was soon re-sold to a Turkish owner, Idarei Massousieh; she was renamed *Aslan* and registered at Constantinople (Istanbul). In this guise she operated past the turn of the century, until being wrecked in April 1901.

Guadiana

Guadiana made her first voyage for RMSP in June 1875. Her purchase for £55,000 that May resulted from a decision by the Court to 'purchase another *Minho*' following a review of South America services – clearly trade was buoyant. There is some mystery about her origins, beyond the fact that she was built by the London & Glasgow Co. on the Clyde in 1874. According to the directors' minutes, the vessel they were buying was the already-existing *State of Florida*; there was, indeed, a steamer of that name built in 1874 (for the State Line SS Co.), but she did not become *Guadiana*.

A three-masted iron screw steamer, her dimensions were length 332.1ft, breadth 36.3ft, depth 28.6ft. Her gross tonnage was 2,504 and two-cylinder inverted compound engines produced 400hp. Cylinder diameters were 46in and 82in, with 46in stroke.

Her career of thirty-eight and a bit voyages was entirely to South America. A year after entering service, on 28 August 1876, she became, during a homeward voyage from the River Plate under Capt. A. Gillies, the first Royal Mail ship to call at Vigo. The Company's agent was Don Estanislao Duran, whose family remained Royal Mail's agents at the port throughout the Company's operations. A small fire caused some damage to the ship in the spring of 1877. A year later, presumably through quarantine difficulties from Brazil, she was refused permission to enter Buenos Aires. That incident pursuaded the Company to begin separate services – one to Brazil and another to the River Plate – in order to escape the delays which quarantine entailed. *Tamar* and *Trent* were purchased that autumn to cope with that.

Guadiana's voyages then passed without incident until November 1884. She was by then engaged in the four-month voyages to South America, the Caribbean and New York. Shortly after midnight on 15 November she touched bottom on Nantucket Shoal – the injury to the ship was minimal. Two voyages later she was less lucky. She left Santos on 13 June 1885 for Barbados, St Thomas and New York. Her crew numbered sixty-nine and there were twenty-five passengers – not a large complement. Some 1,800 tons of Brazilian coffee filled her holds. After loading at Rio de Janeiro she left on 18 June. Sailing north, she passed Cabo Frio and set course to pass outside the Abrolhos Rocks, a menace which has trapped many a ship over the years. The navigation light on the rocks was not seen; her course was altered slightly but she struck the rocks just before 7 a.m. on 20 June. According to her master's report, a strong westward current was the cause – how many Royal Mail ships were lost or stranded because of 'unknown strong currents'?

Guadiana filled quickly but everybody safely reached shore at Caravellas. The mails were saved, too, but the ship was a total loss. With *Humber* having been lost at much the same time in the North Atlantic, this latest disaster was the final straw for the South America-West Indies-North America operation (especially as shipping was suffering one of its periodic depressed phases). The route was closed.

Elbe and *Tagus* (I)

With the invention of the compound engine, which came from Randolph & Elder on the Clyde in the mid-1850s, the efficiency of marine engines was improved enormously, reports varying from 30% to 50% reduction in coal consumption. Extra benefits flowed from that. For example, with less bunker space needed there was an equivalent increase in money-earning cargo spaces; and fresh water could be used in the boilers rather than corrosive seawater, thus lengthening the life of the boilers.

Earlier references have emphasised RMSP's cautious approach to new technology but, even allowing for that, it seems surprising that the Company took so long to adopt the clearly beneficial compound engine. It was the spring of 1870 before the first entered service, installed in *Elbe*. She was ordered from John Elder & Co. in December 1868 in preference to an engine conversion for *Shannon*. Around Christmas 1869, Elder was given a contract for two sister ships, which became *Tagus* and *Moselle*. *Elbe* and *Tagus* each made about seventy trips to South America in long careers of more than 100 voyages each. *Moselle* wasn't used on this route.

To avoid confusion about the builder of these ships, it should be explained that Charles Randolph and John Elder had joined forces as marine engineers in 1852, later building ships as well on the old Robert Napier site at Govan. The time at which these ships were ordered was a critical period for the firm; Randolph retired in 1868, and with Elder now as sole partner the company name was changed to John Elder & Co. His term in that capacity, however, was short, for Elder died in September 1869 at the age of forty-five. The company was continued under his name and in time became the Fairfield SB & Eng. Co.

The Post Office examined *Elbe* on her completion in March 1870, and pronounced themselves satisfied. They described her as 'a credit to the Company's overseers and the builders'. Elders took the old *Atrato* in part-payment – not so much old, really, at well under twenty years of age, but thoroughly outdated. *Elbe* had a gross tonnage of 3,063 and was a brigantine-rigged iron screw steamer. Her dimensions were: 350ft length, breadth 40.2ft, depth 33.3ft. The diameter of the two inverted cylinders were 62in and 112in, with a 48in stroke, which produced 600hp. *Tagus* was similar though slightly larger at 3,299 gross tons, length 358ft, breadth 41.1ft and depth 33.4ft.

By keeping her yards until the end of 1902, *Elbe* became the last square-rigged ship in the fleet; *Tagus's* yards were removed in 1894. Their best average speeds over an entire voyage were very close, but a little misleading. The figure for *Tagus* was 12.99 knots and for *Elbe* 13.28; however, *Elbe* achieved her 'personal best' later in life after her machinery had been exchanged for another major improvement, the triple expansion engine.

With the advent of the Panama, New Zealand & Australian RM Co. service, RMSP extended its West Indies mail service to Colon, and it was in support of that move that *Elbe* was built. Five years passed before she first visited South America. In her early days on Caribbean routes she was a bit like a bull in a china shop. Twice in her first eight months she ran aground off Jamaica. Then, after breaking down a day out of Southampton in June 1871, she caught fire at Colon during the next voyage.

The cause of the fire was, to put it mildly, extraordinary. Two casks of Jamaica rum were in the after orlop deck. At Colon the officer in charge of the hold was pursuaded by crew members to broach one of the casks. He bored a hole, and then another was made, at the top, to let in the air. At that point quantities of rum spurted all over the officer – and over the lantern which was providing light for the clandestine operation. The fierce fire which resulted was extinguished quite quickly (at that period *Elbe* had become the first RMSP ship to be fitted with a 'steam fire-annihilator'), but the officer was burned to death and several crew badly injured.

Capt. Woolward, who commanded both ships, regarded *Elbe*, in her earlier years, as too heavily rigged and not entirely safe in bad weather. After that had been remedied he decided she was 'a very nice ship… beautifully fitted up, and looks like a nobleman's yacht on a large scale'.

He experienced difficulties in both *Elbe* and *Tagus* with the high-pressure cylinder's slide valve. In *Elbe* it sometimes prevented the engine being started, and *Tagus*, it seemed, fared no better – however beneficial compound engines were, such design faults were a constant problem. A replacement valve fitted at Southampton would fail a few days into the voyage and was replaced by the old one, which had been re-faced – this merry-go-round continued for several voyages and was overcome only when the Chief Engineer was allowed to modify the machinery.

As a result of *Elbe's* many stops at sea, Capt. Woolward made some observations on the use of sails in steamships. While they were stopped, with the propeller in the water, the ships remained 'with wind abeam and no other way, sail or no sail. I had her under full sail on one occasion for 36 hours, with a fine, fair breeze, and tried everything I knew to keep her on course, but she would only lie with the wind abeam'. Consequently he advocated doing away not only with sails, but also masts ('an expensive and useless luxury'). Nevertheless, sails were a godsend at times – in 1881, for instance, *Severn* broke her propeller shaft in mid-Atlantic and Capt. Hicks took her 799 miles under square and fore-and-aft sails before falling in with a tug for a tow to the Azores. Her passage under canvas lasted twenty-nine days – an average of just 27.5 miles per day, but infinitely preferable to the options without canvas power.

An undated but quite early photo at Southampton of Elbe, *RMSP's first compound-engined ship. She was built in 1869 for the mail service to West Indies and Panama, but later made many South America voyages and survived beyond the turn of the century.*

In November 1874 *Tagus* was alleged to have run down a brig off the Lizard – her people were convinced that the ship didn't touch the brig, but she was found liable. At about this time the ship established something of a record by carrying 402 passengers in what must have been very cramped conditions. Many had been taken on from a disabled French liner.

August 1875 saw *Elbe* embark on her first voyage to South America, and she carried her run of incidents over to the new service. Less than a year after switching routes her master, Capt. Moir, was in trouble at Pernambuco for refusing to hand over a passenger wanted by the Brazilian authorities. The captain, it seems, was not one to have his fingers burned twice; fourteen years earlier he had commanded *Trent* when the seizure of two Americans brought Britain and America to the brink of war.

In October 1878, *Elbe* went aground during the passage from Le Havre to Southampton. Lifeboats were called out but she was not badly damaged. Her commander on that occasion was Capt. W.W. Herbert who, in his later years, was so enormously rotund that he had to sit in an outsize chair on the bridge. In January 1876, at Colon, *Tagus* was rammed and sunk at her berth by RMSP's *Severn*, which had been 'manoeuvring'. *Tagus* was raised and repaired at the considerable cost of about £30,000.

During a refit for *Tagus* in 1883 the opportunity was taken to install 'Hall's cold dry air machine', the first refrigerating machinery of any kind in a Royal Mail ship. For many years such installations were for provedore purposes and not cargo. Having said that, there is evidence that *Tagus*, on at least one occasion, *did* carry meat cargo. This is presumed to have been a small shipment carried in the stores refrigerating room when space permitted.

When *Tagus* went ashore near Bahia, Brazil, in 1886, salvaging her was again an expensive operation. Years later one of her passengers, Florence Magnussen, wrote an account which mirrored the human drama even with an accident which the record books dismissed in a brief paragraph. *Tagus* (Capt. J.D. Spooner) left Rio de Janeiro on 24 June 1886. Mrs Magnussen, then Florence Taylor, was coming home with her parents and sister, the girls bound for school in England. In the early hours of 27 June *Tagus*, unnoticed at first by those on board, ran aground.

Mr Taylor woke his children and told them to dress. Clutching lifebelts and blankets, and with all the other young passengers, they were brought 'to the prohibited smoking room and locked in, the eldest a girl of fifteen, the youngest a baby girl in her nurse's arms'. At daylight they were allowed on deck. While there was no immediate danger, the captain, after sending off a boat to Bahia, fifteen miles distant, decided to land his passengers on the nearest beach. This could be seen about four miles from the ship, with an intervening reef over which the surf was high. Mrs Magnussen remembered it thus:

About 11 a.m. the largest lifeboat was filled with all the women and children before leaving the davits, an officer at the stern and the rowers in their places. Once in the water it was terrifying as one minute we seemed to be going to crash into the side of the steamer until the officer warded the boat off. Captain Spooner had made my father captain of [his] boat and all had to obey his orders. Father was the first to come over the side in a cane chair and to see him swaying backwards and forwards was heartrending; any who fell into the sea hadn't a chance for the sharks were there in thousands.

All the fathers came first. Then there came a bit of excitement when a tremendously long and lanky Englishman came down. As he landed in the boat my father said 'You take an oar, Mr X', to which he replied 'What do you take me for, a blooming sailor?' Immediately a shout came from the sailors 'Haul him up again', followed by a remark to the captain, who was standing above, 'For the last boat, sir'. So up again he went! I wouldn't like to say what thoughts went with him; to call himself an Englishman!

Due to mist and drizzle, it was impossible for those in the boat to see the gap in the reef through which they had to steer. So the captain guided us by blowing the horn to right or to left. As we neared the land the natives came running with a sheet on the end of a long pole to show us how to avoid the surf, whereupon the girl of fifteen, suddenly seeing them, yelled 'Cannibals, Cannibals' at the top of her voice.

How far from the truth! The people of Itaparica, the settlement they had reached, gave up their thatched huts and helped provide a huge fire on the beach. The castaways did not get much dinner that night; one hen badly roasted on a stick and some tinned tongue and cheese, biscuits and tea. They remained on the island for three days during which time their baggage was carefully ferried ashore in the ship's boats, together with the mails and £170,000 in specie.

It was a strange cavalcade that eventually made its way to Catu from where a small steamer would take them to Bahia. The able-bodied walked barefoot. Some of the children were mounted on horseback and others on the broad shoulders of local men. One lady, unequal to the journey, was carried in a hammock slung from a pole. The mails and specie followed in bullock carts. At Bahia they were met by the Company's agent, who had arranged for English families to house the party for a few days. *Tagus* was soon refloated and arrived at Bahia to re-embark her passengers. Though patched up locally, she underwent permanent repairs on her return to Southampton. The passengers, who signed a testimonial to Capt. Spooner, were delighted to hear that an Admiralty Court at Bahia acquitted him and his officers of blame for the stranding.

While Itaparica was hosting passengers from *Tagus*, tenders were being considered in London for converting *Elbe* to triple expansion engines. When she was given the new machinery she was also fitted with a new square saloon, electric light, a refrigerating plant and pneumatic bells. Oswald Mordaunt of Southampton, who carried out the work, wanted to lengthen the ship as well but the suggestion was turned down. Her new engines were fitted and the Board of Trade surveyed her; she set out for trials on 19 September 1887. During one of the runs her main steam pipe burst, with the fearful toll of nine men killed and one seriously injured.

A feature used in both ships was Cunningham's 'patent reefing topsails'. A widely-used device, the sails were slit from the top to the middle, where there was a spar to which they could be rolled up. The bottom portion was furled in the usual way. Another feature provided for *Tagus* was a steam launch to replace one of her lifeboats. This was an uncommon feature in the 1870s and *Tagus* was the first RMSP ship to be given one.

Both ships continued to operate mostly on Brazil and River Plate routes. There was an unusual moment at Southampton on the afternoon of 3 November 1892, when *Elbe* and *Tagus* sailed in company down the Solent at the start of their 90th and 91st voyages respectively, both bound for South America. As the turn of the century approached, each passed her hundredth voyage. *Tagus* reached 103 before going to London breakers in 1897. *Moselle*, the sister-ship which had never seen South American waters, was wrecked on Voyage 96, near Panama in 1891 – in addition to the ship being lost, her captain was taken by sharks.

Elbe, first of the trio to be completed, was in service until 1902 and had 109 voyages to her credit. Useful to the last, she was chartered by Cunard, just before her final passage to a French shipbreaker's yard, for an emergency dash to a damaged liner where she took off her passengers and mails. That mission accomplished, this venerable ship ended her career.

La Plata (II)

Just as the loss of *Amazon* by fire had immediately seen a new ship purchased to replace her, with the name *La Plata*, so precisely the same thing happened after *Douro* foundered in 1882. Within a month of her loss, there was an agreement to buy the Wigram steamer *Norfolk*, and she, too, was given the name *La Plata*.

Wigram's steamers were regulars on the Australia run and they expanded the operation in 1881, the year when triple-expansion engines made such a difference to the economy of long voyages to Australia. A twin-funnelled iron spardeck steamer, *Norfolk* was initially barque-rigged, a vessel of 3,196 gross tons. Despite being part of a service which so benefitted from the triple expansion engine, she – having been built in 1879 – had compound machinery. She was built by R. & H. Green at London, and her engines came from Humphreys & Tennant, also of London. Her principal dimensions were: length 332.4ft, breadth 40.1ft and depth 32.9ft.

The people of Australia were impressed with her. As traditionalists they liked the old-fashioned painted ports (which disappeared in RMSP ownership), but they were also taken with her solidness, which included iron girders throughout and half-inch iron decks beneath the planking. She was the epitome of the developing middle-range passenger-cargo ship, with a long saloon (110ft long, but very narrow) and five smokerooms and lounges. For her time she represented a size and quality exceeded on the Australian routes only by the likes of P&O, Norddeutscher Lloyd and Orient-Pacific.

She brought 300 passengers on an Australian voyage late in 1881, and that was her last visit for she was quickly snapped up by RMSP. Some changes were made after her purchase, but not a great deal; her tonnage measured a slightly increased 3,240 in RMSP operation. She took the Brazil and River Plate mail voyage on 9 October 1882 under Capt. A.C. Green. Probably all of her RMSP voyages were to South America, though there are gaps amounting to a year or two – she made a minimum of thirty-two South Atlantic voyages, and probably closer to forty. Most were mainstream ninth of the month mail voyages, but on occasion she took the B schedule (24th) and at least once went to Brazil only.

They were singularly uneventful years – an ideal situation at any time, but especially so with the run of disasters which occurred during the 1880s. The first time she appeared in the directors' minutes was when her sale was proposed. That was raised on 2 March 1892.

La Plata (II), purchased from Wigrams in 1882 to replace the lost Douro *(I). Originally a popular ship on the Australia run, she was equally well received on RMSP's South America mail service.*

The Court was told that she 'stood on the books at £39,965' – which was a far cry from the price they could expect in that decade of recession. She began her last voyage on 21 April 1892, to Brazil only. During August she was put up for auction, with a reserve price of £12,000. The bids did not reach the reserve, and in September a private purchaser was expressing interest. That fell through, and during October she was laid up in Southampton Water. She was finally sold in May 1893.

The purchaser was Orienta Steam Yachting Association (A.H. Gaze) of London; she was renamed *Orienta* and became an early full-time cruise ship. In one form or another she remained a cruise ship for a good many years. After only a year she was renamed *Norse King*, with Norse King SS Co. of Newcastle, then went to Albion SS Co. Finally she emerged as *Argonaut*, owned by W.H. Lunn, who operated the Co-operative Cruising Co. out of St Paul's Churchyard in London, an arrangement which remained until she left the Register in 1909 (having reportedly sunk in a collision the previous year).

Orinoco (II); *Atrato* (II); *Magdalena* (II); *Thames* (II) *and Clyde* (II)

As milestones in Royal Mail's progress, the importance of these ships cannot be overstressed. *Orinoco*, 4,572 tons, was not so much the first of a group as a prototype from which significant developments followed in the other four.

When *Orinoco* was launched at Caird's yard on the Clyde in September 1886, the clipper bow, which had taken something of a back seat since the 1860s, returned with a vengeance. She spanned two eras in more significant ways too. By the 1880s RMSP's priorities were changing, with mail subsidies severely pruned and the Company therefore forced to increase passenger and freight revenue. It was, too, a transitional period for passenger facilities between the cramped conditions of the early years and the advent of spacious (and, in many cases, gracious) accommodation which revolutionised sea travel once superstructures provided upper decks. If anything highlighted the development from *Orinoco* to the later vessels in this group, it was that factor: the later ships had superstructure decks while *Orinoco* possessed only a moderate amount of deck housing.

The compound engine ended its domination early in the 1880s with the introduction of triple-expansion machinery; *Orinoco* was the first RMSP ship to receive the new engine. This was also the period when steel hulls were beginning to replace iron, and *Orinoco* was the Company's first steel ship. As a consequence of new propulsion technology and increasing ship sizes, the use of sail was being rapidly scaled down. As a sign of that, *Orinoco* was the last RMSP ship to be built with square-rig. Those were her more obvious advances and throwbacks, but other innovations were included. Messrs Siemens supplied electric light, for instance, and a refrigerated stores chamber was provided.

Shortly after her completion, Royal Mail placed an order with Robert Napier for two somewhat larger ships (*Atrato* and *Magdalena*); before they were completed, two more were ordered – *Thames* and *Clyde*, a touch larger again. These four were the Company's first ships to exceed 5,000 tons. *Atrato*, 5,347 tons, was launched on 22 September 1888. She had a loadline length of 400ft, breadth 50ft, depth from spar deck 33ft 4in, and loaded draught 22ft. Cargo capacity was 2,524 tons, coal capacity 1,109 tons and storeroom capacity (including refrigerated chambers) 6,000 cu.ft. On trials she reached 16 knots, well in excess of her designed service speed.

Constructed of steel to Lloyd's Class 100A1, she met Admiralty requirements for chartering or for use as an armed merchant cruiser. Despite that, in April 1888 (before she had even been launched) the Admiralty advised that both *Orinoco* and *Atrato* were 'not deemed of sufficient power and capacity to receive efficient armaments to entitle them to a subvention'. The clipper bow and counter stern of *Orinoco* were repeated in *Atrato* and the three which followed. *Atrato* had three decks, plus a hurricane or promenade deck, forecastle and short whale-back poop. The accommodation was heated by steam. The staterooms for 176 first class passengers were described as 'exceptionally large'. Berths had patent spring bottoms, while sofas were adaptable as a single berth and most were covered with Utrecht velvet. Baths, with hot and cold water and shower unit, were marble. Some of the panelling was painted enamel white and elsewhere it was wood-grained. Each stateroom had a 14in sidelight.

On the upper deck was the carpeted first class saloon (which served the traditional joint uses of dining saloon and lounge), a large, fine room filled with sofas, tables and heavy Victorian revolving chairs. With the saloon running the full width of the ship there were square ports along both sides, fitted with Japanese screens. The ceiling was 'tastefully panelled overhead, and finished in white and gold', and there were walls 'of polished hardwood, decorated with Italian wood'. Tables and chairs were mahogony, Utrecht velvet was again used for sofa coverings and there were silk and tapestry curtains.

A handsome double stairway, with wood rails, balusters and carved Newell posts, gave access to the main deck cabins and the promenade deck. A music room, with sofas, silk curtains over the ports and Brussels carpets, was dominated by a large dome. On the same deck was the ladies' boudoir. The smoking room was fitted in polished hardwood and had electro-plated and aluminium-bronze fittings. There was lino-covered floor and its seating comprised hardwood morocco leather-covered chairs. The square ports featured glass jalousie sashes and silk curtains or spring blinds.

In second class, forty-two passengers were catered for. The fittings were a little less ornate but still an advance on earlier ships. Sofa coverings, for instance, were black hair cloth; the dining saloon was panelled in pine, 'tastefully painted', and had mahogany pilasters.

Portable galvanised iron fittings for nearly 400 emigrants were to be fitted on the main deck abaft the engine and in the 'tweendecks . Whether they were, in fact, fitted in *Atrato* is uncertain. European migrants would be expected in considerable numbers to South America, but on West Indies routes most third class were inter-island passengers packing the decks for a comparatively short journey. While *Atrato* spent much of her career on Caribbean routes, her early voyages were to South America and she may therefore have received a migrant outfit.

Her rig was a three-masted schooner, with steel pole masts. There was talk in the early design stages of using four masts. No reason was given, but it was possibly that an extra mast of fore-and-aft rig would provide an added traditional safeguard – the Company would have been conscious of the reduced sail power compared with the square-rig of *Orinoco*. The sails were not used for a great many years anyway – apart from *Orinoco*, *Atrato* was the last of the group to discard them. That was about 1900, while *Orinoco*, after losing her yards in 1891, continued using fore-and-aft rig until 1902.

Of the ten watertight bulkheads, six were carried up to the spar deck. The after bulkhead was strengthened to support the stern tube. Each bulkhead was fitted at its base with sluice valves which were controlled from the upper side of the main deck. Iron watertight doors were manually operated. Two galleys were installed, one for first and second class passengers and the other for third class and crew. In the latter the builders were instructed to supply a bakery 'sufficient for 1,000 emigrants', a hint as to RMSP's expectations for the future of this traffic.

Deck timbers and rails were mostly teak. Elsewhere, American rock elm and pitch pine were used for constructional purposes. 20,000 gallons of fresh water were carried in plate iron tanks. Standing rigging was galvanised iron wire rope, while for the running rigging European and Manila hemp were used. Sails were long flax Gourock canvas. *Atrato* was given five 30ft lifeboats, one 28ft steam launch, two 28ft cutters, one 25ft gig and one 18ft dinghy. The lifeboats and steam launch were of mahogany and teak and the others were English elm.

Muir and Caldwell's steam steering gear was chosen; other equipment included a 'Chadburn's tell-tale rudder indicator between the rudder and the bridge', and a reply telegraph between bridge and engineroom. The rudder was fashioned from steel-plated hammered scrap iron, and was able to be shipped and unshipped at sea. It had 42° of turn each way. Refrigerated storerooms for meat, vegetables and wines used a Haslam dry-air refrigerator with a discharge rate of 10,000cu.ft of air per hour. Cabins, saloons, passageways, storerooms, engineroom, boiler rooms and so on were fitted with electric light.

Propulsion machinery was inverted direct-acting triple expansion engines. Eight boilers were arranged in two rooms, the stokehold running fore and aft along the centre of the ship. Working pressure was 150lbs per square inch.

In essence, *Magdalena*, *Thames* and *Clyde* were similar, though the latter two were some 250 tons larger. A short boat deck was built over the promenade deck, and an ordinary poop replaced the whaleback, on each ship after *Atrato*.

The contract price for *Thames*, including machinery, was £148,500; the others would have been similar.

The Ships in Service

Orinoco did not visit South America, but the maiden voyages of the other four, evenly spread over a year and a half, were all to Brazil and the River Plate. *Atrato* sailed in January 1889; *Magdalena* September 1889; *Thames* April 1890; *Clyde* July 1890. Without exception they gave long and excellent service, and apart from *Atrato* (sold for further trading in 1912) each was retained until broken up. One of the few mechanical problems they encountered was a fundamental weakness in the furnaces. Unable to withstand the heat without becoming 'depressed', they were lined with zinc in 1891.

A larger than usual variety of incidents and upsets sprinkled those long years of service. In February 1892, for example, a box of specie from Buenos Aires was stolen from *Clyde* and a dummy box put in its place. Then, in January 1894, *Clyde's* consignment of treasure from Rio de Janeiro was found to be short by £2,400. This kind of thing became all too common; at the turn of the century some gold vanished on its way to Peru, part of the journey being in *Orinoco*. The repercussions went on for years, with investigations and legal proceedings in Panama and Peru. To put it mildly, they were extraordinary. For example, one man who had spent more money on trips to America and France than he had earned in his life explained this by saying he had 'seen a vision in the night' which prompted him to dig at the base of a tree where gold was buried. That, apparently, wasn't sufficient for charges to be laid. The last heard of the matter was a woman known as Josefa Rivas de V blackmailing just about everyone who had been implicated. Running a shipping line was not all ships and schedules.

Within the space of a few weeks in 1894 *Magdalena* was 'fired at' as she was anchoring at Bahia and *Thames* sank a schooner while entering Ensenada; then *Clyde* collided with an Argentine man-of-war, *Almirante Brown*, again at Ensenada. Later the same year *Clyde* broke down near Vigo, an accident to her machinery resulting in two men being badly scalded. Some three years later *Atrato* collided with the steamer *Lowlands*, and later cut the bow off the Isle of Wight steamer *Princess Beatrice* and rammed the dock wall at Southampton.

In 1903 *Orinoco* and the sailing vessel *Hawthornbrook* collided; a further collision, on the last day of 1904 at Montevideo, involved *Magdalena* and the Norwegian barque *Ilos*. On 21 November 1906 *Orinoco*, entering Cherbourg harbour, was run into by the

German Blue Riband liner *Kaiser Wilhelm der Grosse*. That was the worst of the collisions involving these ships, several people being killed in the *Kaiser* (which was almost three times *Orinoco's* tonnage) and one in the Royal Mail ship.

Various improvements were carried out over the years. In 1899 Day, Summers were contracted to raise the boats on each ship except *Orinoco* 'to a boat deck clear of the promenade'; the cost exceeded £5,000. *Clyde*, *Magdalena* and *Atrato* were given bronze propellers in 1903 – that cost another £5,000. In December that year it was decided to improve their accommodation. *Thames*, *Clyde* and *Magdalena* had their Cabins-de-Luxe refurbished, and then it was decided to convert the ladies rooms in all five ships to more Cabins-de-Luxe.

Freight carriage was becoming more sophisticated. In 1900 the River Plate mail ships were given small amounts of refrigerated hold space for meat cargoes; then, during 1901, a Mr Lawton asked if he could, at his own expense, fit refrigerating machinery in *Atrato* for the carriage of fruit. Many years before, a similar suggestion had been vetoed but this time the Company agreed. However, it was not fitted in *Atrato*, for shortly afterwards Mr Lawton's plant was placed in *Para* and soon afterwards the machinery blew up, killing its inventor and several other people. Not until May 1905 did RMSP finally sanction cold storage for fruit in *Atrato* and *Orinoco*.

Individual Careers

Of the four units which traded to South America, the first to be completed was *Atrato*. She left Southampton for her maiden voyage on the afternoon of 17 January 1889, carrying the Brazil and River Plate mails, over 200 passengers, £12,000 in sovereigns, £400 in bar silver, £2,000-worth of jewellery and a full general cargo. Her outward ports were Carril, Vigo, Lisbon, Pernambuco, Maceio, Bahia, Rio de Janeiro, Santos, Montevideo and Buenos Aires. She made several more voyages to South America before transferring to the West Indies service.

She was sold in October 1912 to The Viking Cruising Co. of Regent Street, London, whose owner was Samuel J. Beckett. Renamed *The Viking* (the definite article being used to identify her from the Isle of Man ferry *Viking*), she was used for cruising in northern European waters. When war broke out in 1914 she became a unit of the 10th Cruiser Squadron and bore the name HMS *Viknor*. On 1 January 1915, fresh out from the Tyne after her conversion to an armed merchant cruiser, she joined 'B' Patrol off the north coast of Scotland. North of the Shetlands, she intercepted the Norwegian-America liner *Bergensfjord*, for which the cruisers had been directed to watch out. A passenger, who eventually admitted to being a German wanted by the British Government as a suspected spy, was taken on board, together with a number of other people.

Bergensfjord was escorted to Kirkwall and *Viknor*, with her prisoners, left for Liverpool. They did not reach the Mersey. *Viknor* was in the region of a recently-laid minefield and it was thought that she struck a mine and was lost with all hands, though the weather was exceptionally bad and could have been responsible. At all events, bodies and wreckage were later found along the northern Irish coast.

Thames and *Clyde* (the latter regarded as the fastest of the group) spent much of their careers in the South Atlantic. Apart from incidents already referred to, there was rarely anything to record from their routine schedule, a trade described by a captain in more recent times as 'a comfortable route on which the ships wandered down to Buenos Aires and back'. Though predominantly on this route, *Thames*, *Clyde* and *Magdalena* at times voyaged to the West Indies and also to New York, especially later in their careers when RMSP was fostering the Caribbean cruise market from North America. Always, though, they returned to South America, and *Thames* and *Clyde* were on the route when they were sold. By then each was well past her hundredth voyage.

The departure just before Christmas, 1899 was due to be taken by *Thames*. For unknown reasons she was withdrawn and replaced by *Nile*; then *Nile* was requisitioned at short notice for transport work for the Boer War and so the Buenos Aires sailing was finally taken by *Atrato* – thus she made one more passage to South America after spending much of her life in West Indies trades.

Neither *Clyde* nor *Thames* did a great deal to warrant references in the centenary history. They were, however, involved in Spithead Reviews. *Clyde* visited the Review in 1902 in honour of Edward VII's Coronation, and nine years later *Thames* was used at the equivalent event for George V's Coronation. *Thames* gained a certain notoriety when, in the West Indies, her chief officer hit on the idea of liberally daubing with pink boot-topping paint the heads of West Indian deck passengers who had been found to have not paid their fares. Fare-dodging and travelling beyond the booking destination was a perennial problem with both deck and steerage passengers.

Atrato (II), built in 1888, was Royal Mail's first ship to exceed 5,000 gross tons. A cruise ship after her sale, she was lost during the First World War when operating as an armed merchant cruiser.

A rare picture of Thames *(II) in the white-hulled livery which the mail ships were given in 1901 and 1902. She is seen with the tug* Neptune *at Southampton.* Neptune *had a long career and towed* Titanic *out of her berth on 10 April 1912.*

Clyde and *Thames* were sold for breaking up in Scotland, the former in June 1913 and the latter in August 1914. *Thames* then reportedly became a block ship at Scapa; her figurehead was rescued and erected at Lyness Naval Base on Orkney, with an inscription beginning: 'Part of the figurehead of SS *Thames*, sunk as a blockship in Holm Sound in 1915…'

Before *Magdalena* entered service she took the Lord Mayor and Corporation of London to a Royal Naval Review at Spithead, a spectacle laid on for Kaiser Wilhelm II by his grandmother, the ageing Queen Victoria. She then joined *Atrato* on the Brazil and River Plate service and quickly established a reputation for comfort and reliability.

Shortly after the turn of the century her colour scheme was changed, in common with the other mail ships, when they became the 'great steamers white and gold' immortalised by Kipling. The directors were told in June 1898 that officers in the West Indies were 'wearing white tunics contrary to regulations'. The matter was taken up by Capt. Hicks, the Company's Superintendent at Southampton, who supported the wearing of white uniforms in the tropics. RMSP, unexpectedly, not only agreed to the idea but extended the use of 'whites' to hot weather 'at home or abroad'. This may well have sowed the seed which resulted in the ships becoming white as well. The short period (except for cruising) in which white hulls were used ended, broadly, because of the general soot, grime and rust which stained the hulls. The decision to revert to black, however, was specifically taken because of the Company's parlous financial position. Cost-cutting measures were put in place during 1902, and it was revealed late that year that the cost of maintaining white hulls was about three times that of black.

Magdalena plied back and forth across the South Atlantic for voyage after voyage; and then, as newer vessels came into service, she was relegated at times to what was by then the less prestigious West Indies service. In the Caribbean in 1909 she tried unsuccessfully to tow *Trent* off a sandbank. *Trent* was later refloated with little damage; a year later *Magdalena* herself grounded on the same bank, remaining fast for four days.

By 1914, at twenty-four years of age, she had practically ended her useful life. She was still operating when the First World War broke out, however, and on 16 December 1915 the Director of Transports requisitioned her. Two guns and an Admiralty gun crew appeared on board. Her war service was so unaffected by hostilities that she did not feature in the Company's war history. Mostly she sailed with troops and stores between Suez and the Persian Gulf, sometimes as far east as Bombay. An extra consignment of equipment came on board at Gibraltar in January 1917 – forty-five boxes of smoke-producing canisters to provide a smoke-screen in the event of attack.

Her long spell in a hot, dry part of the world had squeezed every drop of moisture from the ship, leaving her as dry as tinder. Smoke canisters of the kind she had on board, known as 'E' type, were withdrawn by the Admiralty very late in the war because they were unstable and a potential fire hazard. That ruling came too late to prevent an incident on *Magdalena* which led to a bitter battle between RMSP and the Admiralty. On 29 May 1918 the ship was berthed at Suez after a voyage from Basra in the Persian Gulf. Shortly after 2 p.m. thick smoke billowed from the port side of the promenade deck. At first there were no flames, only thick, acrid fumes – which at least proved the effectiveness of the smoke-screen. Flames soon enveloped the port side, and only when fire floats came alongside was the blaze brought under control. Royal Mail claimed the repair costs – £12,475 9s 1d. After all, she was on Government service and faulty Admiralty supplies had caused the blaze. Surely there could be no doubt that the Admiralty was liable? Not until 1921 did RMSP reluctantly drop its action, after reading law reports on the loss of

The last-built of a fine group of ships, Clyde (II) *was completed in 1890 for the Brazil and River Plate mail service and was sold for breaking up shortly before the First World War.*

another company's freighter; the Government clearly was determined not to pay out a penny. Feelings were bitter but companies like Royal Mail were helpless.

Magdalena's Government service ended in 1920, and within a year Royal Mail had disposed of her. The last survivor of that splendid group of ships sailed to the breaker's yard at Birkenhead late in 1921. Her sale price was £1 8s 5d per ton.

Nile (II) and *Danube* (II)

These were the largest ships owned by RMSP before the first 'A' ship entered service in 1905; the last substantial mail steamers for the South America service in the 19th century. Slightly larger and improved versions of the *Atrato* class, they were the Company's front-runners to Brazil and the River Plate for more than a decade. They were ordered in the first half of 1892 from J. & G. Thomson at Clydebank, who won the contract against Denny of Dumbarton, and were the only ships built by J. & G. Thomson for Royal Mail (though others were purchased second-hand). Thomson's had operated for many years but was on the verge of a takeover by John Brown & Co. Ironically, this fine shipyard which would build so many great Cunarders then lost the name of the family who had nurtured it and instead took the name of a man who never had anything to do with it. John Brown had established the Atlas Steel Works at Sheffield, becoming the regional 'franchise' for Henry Bessemer's steel production process. By the time the company took over Thomson's shipyard in the 1890s, Brown had long since ended his involvement (and his shareholdings) after policy differences with the other directors.

Nile and *Danube* were possessed of a number of minor setbacks. One problem, though, faced during construction, was anything but minor – it was pointed out that there were insufficient lifeboats to accommodate a full complement of passengers and crew. That the matter was discussed at director level may have had something to do with the Merchant Shipping Act of 1894, which would have been at the draft stage. RMSP probably had an idea of its contents, which included new powers for the Board of Trade to control the level of lifesaving equipment on a ship. Mind you, the provision of a maximum fine of £100 for owners and £50 for masters was hardly an incentive to conform.

Nile was the first to enter the water, being christened on 21 March 1893 by the daughter of Spencer Curtis, a director of RMSP since 1879. *Danube* was launched by Lady Savory on 16 May. She was the wife of another director, Sir Joseph Savory, who (like Curtis) continued his role into the Owen Philipps era. Then came frustration, for completion of the ships was delayed by a dispute between carpenters and joiners. Work ceased at nearly every shipyard on the Clyde and Royal Mail had to postpone the start of a new fast Brazil and River Plate service, for these were the only ships with which the new schedule could be operated. *Danube*, in fact, did not undergo trials until nearly a year after launching.

Stokes Bay was the scene for *Nile*'s trials late in September. However confident a builder might be, the trials of a new ship must engender some uncertainty: will the ship maintain her contract speed? Just how critical this was for a firm like Royal Mail may be gauged from this contract. They were to maintain an average of 17 knots over the measured mile – no mean speed in the 1890s for any route bar the North Atlantic, and even on that route the Blue Riband record stood at about 20 knots at that time. If 17 knots was not maintained, RMSP was at liberty to not accept the ship. Alternatively it could accept her against a penalty on the following scale:

$\frac{1}{4}$ knot or less below 17 – £3,000

$\frac{1}{4}$ to $\frac{1}{2}$ knot – £5,000

$\frac{1}{2}$ to $\frac{3}{4}$ knot – £8,000

$\frac{3}{4}$ to 1 knot – £12,000.

Conversely, a trials speed between $17\frac{1}{4}$ and $17\frac{1}{2}$ knots would earn Thomsons a bonus of £500, and if in excess of $17\frac{1}{2}$ the bonus would be £1,000. The reason for such a strict agreement was simple. Once the ships were in service they would be operating a tight schedule under a Government mail contract, and any delays in voyage times would then see RMSP facing fines under penalty clauses.

Nile achieved her prescribed speed on trials, but her builders faced a different setback – there was a problem with her stability. Thomsons arranged for 150 tons of ballast to be placed in her bottom, following which RMSP was dissatisfied as her draft then exceeded the planned depth (always a critical matter in the River Plate). However, she was finally accepted and on 25 October the Company was able to approve the new fast schedule – which probably sounded more grandiose than it was, that it took one day off a River Plate round voyage.

Danube (II), built in 1893 for the Brazil and River Plate mail service. At 5,891 tons she was the largest ship in the RMSP fleet in the nineteenth century.

Each ship could accommodate 215 first class passengers, 36 second class and 350 emigrants. Add to that a crew in excess of 100 (there were over 50 in the Engine Department alone), and there might be 700 or more people on board – a high figure for a ship of less than 6,000 tons, which might explain the inadequate provision of lifeboats. They were built to Lloyd's highest class and conformed to all Board of Trade rules – this included ten watertight bulkheads. Thomsons built their triple-expansion engines.

There were favourable reports on the accommodation. First class staterooms were 'unusually large, and every modern contrivance for the convenience of passengers has been adopted'. On the upper deck the main dining saloon was upholstered in polished oak. Immediately above was the music room, panelled in satinwood and cedar; abaft this was the ladies' saloon. Promenade decks, broad and long, were lit by electricity, and at their after end was the smokeroom. As slightly larger and newer versions of *Clyde* and *Thames*, their accommodation and equipment did not vary significantly. Visually, the most obvious difference was a straight stem in place of the clipper bows of their predecessors.

Built for the South America service, they mostly operated on that route. The first to make news was *Danube*, when she was involved in a minor collision with *Cairngorm* while leaving dock only a month or two after entering service. A cryptic note in the directors' minutes stated: 'Settled for £17 and part of a hawser'. After two years there was a 'mutiny' on board *Nile* by third class passengers who demanded, and got, extra space allocated to them from the second class accommodation. In response to that, two second class passengers and their booking agents made claims against the Company and complained to the Board of Trade. It seems likely that more than the regulation number of third class had embarked, which was still quite possible in the confusion of several hundred migrants boarding, an equal number of visitors to see them off, some not booking until they were on board and others who managed to get away without paying at all.

Both ships ran down fishing boats in the late 1890s, but in neither case was the mail ship found liable. *Nile's* accident, in Vigo bay, was attributed to the fishing boat suddenly altering course. *Danube* sank her victim off the Portuguese coast and the line's Lisbon agents laconically reported that such things *did* happen sometimes because the fishing boats had no lights.

A happier event interrupted *Danube's* routine in June 1897. Royal Mail agreed to her use at a particularly important Royal Naval Review at Spithead, to mark the diamond jubilee of Queen Victoria. For this splendid occasion it was fitting that RMSP's largest ship should take the prestigious role of conveying members of the House of Lords in the long seaborne procession to celebrate sixty years on the throne for the Queen who had signed the Company's original Charter at the start of her reign. Royal Mail received £750 for the use of the ship, plus ten shillings a head for refreshments. Later the Company received notice of the 'satisfaction of the Peers with everything connected with the *Danube*'.

Oil masthead lights on both ships were replaced with electric ones in 1897. Both vessels were suffering a little trouble at this time. *Nile's* rudder deteriorated and had to be replaced – hardly what one would expect after a handful of years. Her sister-ship then missed a voyage because of flaws in the high and low pressure connecting rods. Early in 1898 an improvement was sanctioned, when the stores refrigeration was altered to the more efficient carbonic anhydride system. The first contract for the carriage of chilled beef from

South America was with the River Plate Fresh Meat Co. in mid-1900. *Nile* and *Danube* were among the ships fitted with a small amount of cargo refrigeration at that time.

During the summer of 1899, when a plague swept Spain and Portugal, calls at Peninsula ports were curtailed and *Danube*, which had landed passengers at Lisbon, was quarantined in the River Plate. For years the problem had been the other way round, with yellow fever in South America causing quarantine in Europe. Early in 1900, *Nile* was taken off the service – at an early stage of the struggle against the Boers in South Africa she was taken up for trooping duties, for which the Admiralty paid 27s 6d per gross ton per month. She was the first of five Company ships to help the war effort, leaving Southampton on 11 January 1900 for Capetown, with a battalion of Lancashire Militia on board. At Queenstown the King's Rifle Militia (North Cork) joined, so that more than 1,300 passengers made the voyage.

During March 1902 there began an ever-so-polite episode of one-upmanship between the Transport Department and RMSP. The Company was asked if it would offer a ship to take part in the Royal Naval Review to celebrate the accession of the new King (Edward VII). The Admiralty offered £1,000 a day for *Nile*, to which the Company replied that it would place the ship at their disposal free of charge to carry the King's guests. A courteous snub came by return of post: *Nile* would not be required to carry the King's guests, but what would the Company do 'as regards guests of the nation, named by His Majesty?' The snub was reciprocated: 'The Company declines to carry the nation's guests gratuitously'. When a fortnight had passed without reply, RMSP decided on its own account to send *Elbe* – now thirty-three years old – and to charge £21 per head. Within a week or two *Nile* was in trouble anyway, and a contract was given to Day, Summers & Co. at Southampton to renew her stern frame.

In January 1903 Owen Philipps joined RMSP. One of the first reports he was faced with was an optimistic one – Capt. Dickinson's account of *Danube*'s debut at the new Madero Dock in the River Plate. There had been plenty of rhetoric about new facilities which would provide much-needed improvements for loading in the Argentine; at last it was operational. To celebrate the occasion, a reception was held on board *Danube* at Buenos Aires in February 1903. In June that year *Nile* suffered a broken crankshaft at Rio de Janeiro and was stuck there for weeks until a new one was shipped out.

At that period the directors authorised construction of a cabin-de-luxe in each ship at a cost of £816. A week later the order was amended to two each. A month later, on 1 April, the Court was told that bands had been established on board *Nile*, *Clyde* and *Thames* – they were soon included on the other main line ships, too. All of that activity, hot on the heels of Philipps' arrival, smacks of his immediate impact.

The freight situation, boosted by the new Madero Dock, was not allowed to stagnate – and what a crucial matter this was, for in May 1905 a contract was signed with La Blanca Co. 'for the carriage of chilled beef from Buenos Aires at a rate of $\frac{9}{16}$d per lb and it was decided that the *Nile* and *Danube* should be at once fitted with extra refrigeration plant and insulation, estimated cost being £2,966 per ship'.

By 1907 the early 'A' ships were entrenched in the service, and when an order was given for increasing the third class capacity on the 'small South America mail steamers', it referred to *Nile*, *Danube*, *Thames*, *Clyde* and *Magdalena*. Their years as the line's largest and finest ships were over and there remained only relegation to supporting roles. In 1911 *Nile* was sold to the Pacific Mail Steamship Co. and later undertook trooping duties in the First World War. Further down the track she was transferred to the United States Navy and after abortive negotiations for her sale to China in 1922, remained under the American flag until broken up at San Francisco in 1925.

Danube remained on South America routes into the 20th century, but in the decade before the First World War was periodically transferred to the Caribbean. After Brazil and River Plate voyages in 1913, there is uncertainty about her movements. During the second half of 1916 she made three consecutive voyages (voyages 104 to 106) from London to Brazil – her only visits to South America after the outbreak of war. In 1917 she 'ran for a few months between New York, Jamaica and Colon', and was then requisitioned to bring a food cargo to Britain.

Her Government service then involved conversion to a troopship, a role she continued on repatriation duties after the Armistice; at the end of 1918 she carried the exiled Serbian Government for a portion of their triumphant return to Belgrade. During 1920 she was sold to London shipowner Claude Langdon, who renamed her *Mediterranean Star*. She was broken up at Genoa in 1922.

Aragon (I); *Amazon* (II); *Araguaya*; *Avon* (III); *Asturias* (I), *later Arcadian* (II); *Arlanza* (I); *Andes* (I), *later Atlantis*; *Alcantara* (I) and *Almanzora*

Shortly after Owen Philipps took over the chairmanship of RMSP in the spring of 1903, he raised the question of new tonnage for the Brazil and River Plate mail service. It was then constantly under review for more than a decade. The story behind the advent of the 'A' ships, though, started late in the nineteenth century. The directors were aware as early as 1897 or 1898 that service improvements were needed. The size of its mail ships, while not the only factor, reflected the lack of progress – the Company had owned a ship of almost 3,500 tons in 1853 but had not reached 6,000 tons half a century later.

On the South America service, a mixture of trade recession and apathy in the 1890s was compounded by a loss in revenue through increased competition and quarantine difficulties which caused inefficient scheduling. RMSP had used freight only to a moderate degree to boost its income with mail steamers, and even when technological developments allowed larger freight spaces, cargo tonnages didn't grow as much as they might have. That became more significant with the advent of refrigerated meat and fruit trades.

Emigrant traffic took a step forward in 1899, when a meeting of Conference lines in Paris adopted a common policy to make the migrant trade more organised and productive. As a result, in January 1900 Royal Mail finalised a migrant contract with the Brazilian authorities. Rather more substantial accommodation than had been offered in the past would be provided, though with many hundreds on board during peak periods it was still far from comfortable.

Thus there grew a need for diversification – to accommodate ambassadors and the wealthy; business people and migrants; refrigerated and general cargoes; and the need still to maintain tight schedules for the mail contract. It was the same combination (except for refrigerated cargoes) that had always existed, but now the balance was different, for comparatively little of the income came from the carriage of mails, so commercial earnings were more crucial.

By 1902 the directors must have realised that trading conditions were changing far faster than the Company was. With no substantial improvements being proposed, unrest in the Court of Directors became acute. The outcome was several resignations and the election of Owen Philipps as a director in January 1903. His appointment coincided with news that RMSP's main French competitor was about to send two 7,000-ton steamers to the River Plate.

The 'A' ships which resulted from all of that were pivotal to the Royal Mail story. By November 1903 (when he had been Chairman for some months) Philipps turned his attention to new mail ship tonnage for South America. He had talked with the Hon. Charles Parsons about the prospects for his promising new invention, the turbine engine, but judged that a year must pass before the turbine concept could be evaluated; Royal Mail could not wait so long. Two weeks later he proposed that for the time being one new mail ship be ordered from Harland & Wolff. The choice of Harland's was not surprising – an agreement between the companies was already in place, with Harland's rendering a monthly account of expenditure plus 5% for profit.

Before the first 'A' ship was launched, Norddeutscher Lloyd withdrew from the first class River Plate passenger trade. While that eased the competition a little, there was no room for complacency. However prestigious one large ship would be, it was nowhere near sufficient for the level of returns envisaged by Philipps. Thus while the first ship was still on the stocks, he began negotiations for two more. Both went to Belfast, one each to Harland & Wolff and Workman Clark. The latter was the last Royal Mail passenger liner built by any other firm than Harland & Wolff. They were to be a little larger than the vessel already taking shape as *Aragon*, which was launched on 23 February 1905 by Countess Fitzwilliam. The second Harland & Wolff ship was *Amazon* and the Workman Clark vessel *Araguaya*.

The question of their machinery was again an issue. Philipps was champing at the bit to use turbines – he could see the benefits of the system but was not prepared to use them until their success was proven. The first ocean-going turbine liner was Allan Line's *Victorian*, which Workman Clark was building while Harland & Wolff was building *Aragon*. A sister-ship to the *Victorian* – the *Virginian* – was built by Alexander Stephen. It would be some time before a verdict could be reached, and so Royal Mail's new ships were given twin-screw reciprocating machinery. The fact that turbines were not employed for the 'A' ships until the final block of four, starting with *Arlanza* in 1912, reflects that there *was* a problem. Coal consumption was excessively high, and so the system was not successful until new gearing allowed the turbines to run at high speed while the propellers ran at an economical low speed.

During September 1905 the Chairman again raised the need for more tonnage. The Court authorised him to negotiate for a fourth 'A' ship, 'if more advantageous terms might be arranged'. Those better terms were secured the following February, comprising a

99

payments extension from two to three years. Harland & Wolff received the contract for *Avon* in the same month that *Amazon* was launched by Mrs Mai Philipps, the Chairman's wife. Lady Aberdeen christened *Araguaya* in May 1906 and *Amazon* was approaching completion in early June. She made a short cruise for invited guests, and then the Press were invited for a luncheon – a show of public relations as new to the Company as were these splendid ships themselves. Meanwhile, Owen Philipps was negotiating for RMSP to increase its share of the emigrant traffic.

On 13 June 1906, he explained to the Court that the Managers 'were impressed with the necessity of procuring additional tonnage in order to protect and develop the Company's position in the various trades. Authority was therefore given for an order to be at once placed with Harland & Wolff for a mail steamer for the Australian service'. Earlier that year RMSP had purchased The Pacific Steam Navigation Co.'s interest in the Orient-Pacific Line, which had been operating to Australia since the 1870s. The arrangement included RMSP inheriting four ageing ships; this new 'A' ship was intended to improve the tonnage on the Australia route. The new ship (named *Asturias*) made two voyages to Australia before the Company severed its involvement in the service. Though conceived for that route, she followed the general style of the 'A' ships and spent most of her career on the River Plate run before her conversion to a cruising liner.

After completion of *Asturias* in January 1908 even Owen Philipps was content for a time. He now had five liners whose entire concept was, for Royal Mail, utterly new. Some public rooms were two decks high; décor was a feast of Edwardian artistry; all first class staterooms were on or above the main deck; for the first time many cabins had connecting doors to allow family units; suites-de-luxe (built by conversion in earlier ships) were sumptuous affairs; first class cabins contained beds instead of bunks. And if the first class accommodation was most noteworthy, there were also matters like the huge third class capacity and capacious holds with custom-designed refrigerated spaces.

The most overtly impressive feature, however, was their size. The first of them exceeded in tonnage the previous largest vessel by more than 60%, for *Aragon's* gross measurement was 9,441 (later increased to 9,588). Each later ship was a little larger than her predecessor: *Amazon* 10,037; *Araguaya* 10,537; *Avon* 11,073; *Asturias* 12,002.

Voyage results quickly proved the wisdom of ordering such ships. In her first full year of service (1906) *Aragon*, though the smallest of the five, made handsome profits on each of her four voyages – a total of £45,368, or an average of £11,342 per voyage. The most successful non-'A' ship that year, *Clyde*, returned profits on the same service of £19,539 on three voyages – an average of £6,513 per voyage.

Several factors led to the addition of four further units to the 'A' ship fleet. The River Plate service was now doing very well as the premier route, after so many years as second fiddle to the West Indies. Cruising was starting to play an important role, beginning with *Amazon* in 1908. Before long *Avon* was periodically withdrawn from the South America route to make annual cruises, both from England and New York. Philipps thus decided on further expansion. Each year from 1912 to 1915 a new liner entered service: *Arlanza*, 15,044 tons; *Andes*, 15,620; *Alcantara*, 15,831; *Almanzora*, 15,551, the largest being more than 6,400 tons greater than *Aragon*.

As the nine vessels were spread over a ten-year period, progressive improvements in machinery, construction and accommodation were evident. A notable difference was that the group of four which completed the series had triple screws (the others had twin screws). The outer propulsion units were reciprocating engines and the centre screw was driven by a low pressure turbine, a combination reported to provide virtually vibration-free steaming.

Each of those last four ships was designed for the South America service, but in the case of *Andes* there is a complication – did she belong to RMSP or to The Pacific Steam Navigation Co. (PSN)? There is strongly differing evidence. However, her maiden voyage deck log has survived (extracts are reprinted in Volume 1), from which we know that it was an RMSP voyage to Brazil and the River Plate, though under the command of a PSN captain. The next six were the same, but she is known to have made at least one voyage to the west coast of South America, for she was in Chilean ports in March 1915.

Lloyd's Register states that RMSP was her owner for the first year. She was then owned by PSN from 1914 to 1916 (when she was serving as an armed merchant cruiser), reverting to RMSP late in 1916 and remaining so until her late years under Government ownership.

Exploring *Aragon*

To individually describe each ship would demand more space than is available here. We can look initially at the first in the knowledge that while there were developments and improvements in later ships, and individual characters in terms of fixtures, fittings, décor and the like, *Aragon* provided the core concept from which the later vessels developed. Her outward appearance was graceful and balanced, with counter stern, two upper decks with open promenades and a tall, raked funnel. She introduced the 'split bridge' design which featured in quite a few Royal Mail ships from then on. Its purpose was to distribute the heavy loads of freight and machinery more evenly by placing a hold between the bridge and main passenger accommodation; the engines were below the main passenger spaces.

Aragon's machinery consisted of two sets of direct-acting quadruple expansion engines with cylinders of 25, 36, $52\frac{1}{2}$ and 75in diameter, by 54in stroke. She was, of course, built of steel. Wilson & Pirrie's 'latest steering gear' was fitted, used in conjunction with Brown's telemotor. Bunkers, built with stiffened steel plates, held 2,000 tons of coal, with holds three and four designed as reserve bunkers. The five holds were each served by two hydraulic cranes or derricks of $1\frac{1}{2}$ and 2 tons capacity.

Twelve lifeboats were on the boat deck, one on each side being of steel and the others of wood. There were also a gig and dinghy aft. Ventilation was an important consideration. Fan systems carried air to every part of the ship, with special provision 'to be coal-dust-tight where they pass through passenger spaces'.

Her first class accommodation comprised 124 staterooms and six suites, providing 294 berths. Of the dining saloon, an RMSP brochure claimed:

it bids fair to surpass the most handsome afloat. The tables (seating 200 passengers) are arranged on the latest restaurant system. The elegance of the whole structure, combined with the magnificent stairway and approach to the Main Deck, forms a rare example of marine architectural beauty. The style is renaissance – in oak, white and gold furnishings adorned with cupids and sea trophies. The Dome, modelled after that of the Genoese Palace, is most ornate and brilliantly lighted.

The following extracts are from Harland & Wolff's specification:

First Class
…Saloon to seat about 210 persons. Also library, lounge and smokeroom… All labels on doors of public rooms, notices etc to be enamel outside, endolithic inside, and in English and Spanish. Labels with numbers of rooms to be over the middle of the door… The sofas in the sitting rooms of the suites to be Chesterfield pattern, and each to have one end to turn down so that it can be used as a bed when necessary.

The stateroom bulkheads to be framed and panelled, and each ordinary room to be fitted with two of Hoskins' iron beds, No. 574, 2 feet 3 inches wide, with spring bottoms, and one sofa, except the 48 single berth rooms, each of which are to have one bed and seat. Sofas to be upholstered in velvet, spring-seat, and fitted with lee-rail. The larger rooms to have one double-folding lavatory with table, and the smaller ones, a single-folding lavatory with table. Each room to be provided with a wardrobe and drawers where possible. Hooks, door furniture, and other metal fittings to be in white metal. Beds to have painted lee-rails. Door hooks to be approved by the Company. Cabins 175-194 have no wardrobes.

Cabins to be painted white and finished in best white enamel. No cabin key to be common to two locks. Hooks for clothes to be of a pattern which opens out and forms several hooks. Hook-on table to be provided for 25% of beds. Hoskins' patent ladders for upper berths. Sponge baskets to be fitted in cabins. Drawers of lavatories to be larger than usual. Cane bottom folding seats to be fitted to every cabin if possible.

The saloon to be finished in white and gold of a neat and ornamental pattern, the ceiling being panelled. The floor laid with parquetry. Tables and revolving chairs as per plan. All small tables in first class saloon to have a portable leaf to separate the table into two parts, one with four seats and one with five. These leaves to be made to slide in and out. Dinner waggon to be fitted between each two small tables. Side tables to be placed between scuttles to avoid draught. Children's saloon forward of first class saloon, on port side, as per plan.

The first class library and main entrance to be in one, with lounge abaft same, to be neatly finished in polished hardwood, panelled ceiling. To be furnished with bookcase, writing tables, easy chairs, and other furniture, as usual…

The smoke room to be finished in polished hardwood and India-rubber topped tables, revolving chairs etc. Sofas and seats to be upholstered in morocco leather, and to have all usual necessary fittings. Floor to be laid with rubber tiles. Entrance hall on bridge deck to be furnished in polished hardwood, panelled ceiling, and floor to be laid with India-rubber tiles. The deck above smoke room to be extended at after end, forming a verandah or shelter, which is to be fitted with tables, seats etc.

Second Class
To consist of about 27 rooms, fitted with 74 berths including sofas. Saloon to seat 62 persons. Smoke room, ladies' room and entrance in deck house.

Aragon *(I), which entered service in 1905 as the pioneer of the first 'A' ship series.*

Araguaya, *10,537 tons, built by Workman Clark in 1906. She was the only one of the original nine 'A' ships not built by Harland & Wolff.*

The second class staterooms to be enclosed with V-sheeted bulkheads; the larger rooms to be provided with three of Hoskins' iron beds with spring bottoms (one to be used as a sofa when required), and the smaller ones with two beds. Each room to have a single-folding lavatory with supply tank and receiver, bronze fittings, and the whole similar to first class but of a plainer description. Where two berths come under a scuttle, the frame space carrying the scuttle to be unlined to give air to lower berth.

The second class saloon to be panelled in plain white; to have polished hardwood tables and revolving chairs, sideboard, and other usual fittings.

The second class smoke room and ladies' room to be neatly panelled in oak, or other polished hardwood, and provided with suitably upholstered seats, tables etc…

Lavatories – The first class lavatories to be placed as shown upon plan, the WCs to be of Doulton's make with push valves, urinals of fire-clay of cradle type, baths of solid nickel with hot and cold water supply. The floors of WCs and lavatories to be laid with black and white tiles. Second class lavatories to be similar to first class and with lift valves, but not so elaborately finished, and the baths to be of vitreous enamel. Soap granulators to be provided over each lavatory basin.

Third Class

Space to be provided for about 616 persons, but beds to be fitted only in Nos 1, 2 and 3 upper 'tweendecks, and rooms under forecastle for about 370 persons. Those in Nos 2 and 3 to be enclosed in rooms, remainder open. The beds to be of iron. Mess tables, seats and other usual and necessary fittings to be provided. Hatches above third class accommodation to be fitted with gratings for ventilation.

Third class beds to be of Hoskins' make, open berths being two in height. Entrance and lavatories in the deck house between Nos 1 and 2 hatches. Hospitals, stairways, entrances and fittings of every description to pass Board of Trade requirements. All third class closets to be of the trough description, and to be divided off into separate rooms and seats made to lift up.

Elsewhere in *Aragon* five cargo holds were fitted; Nos 1 and 2 lower holds and No. 5 were insulated for frozen cargoes. Nos 1 and 2 lower and orlop 'tweendecks and No. 5 upper 'tweendeck were for chilled meat and fruit. The remainder held general cargo. The insulating material was silicate of cotton and the refrigerating machinery Hall's Duplex Marine Type carbonic anhydride with compound surface condensing steam engine.

Tanks between the tunnels and ship's side at the after hold contained about 2,000 tons of fresh water, and further fresh water tanks were fitted in the double-bottom – 4ft 4in high at the centre – beneath the engines and boilers. Salt water tanks were placed on the Sun Deck and in the funnel casing.

The ship's lights (mast, side, riding and signal lights) were a mixture of electric and mineral sperm oil lamps. The compasses consisted of 'one Lord Kelvin's standard on top of the wheelhouse, one Lord Kelvin's steering compass in wheelhouse, and one liquid compass aft'. Chadburn's telegraphs were fitted; a double-dial model for the engineroom telegraph (for port and starboard engines) and a steering and docking telegraph linking the bridge and the poop.

Third class dining saloon in Andes *(I).*

Loudspeaker telephones connected the bridge and engineroom, and the wheelhouse and docking bridge aft. An emergency electric bell system was installed and all accommodation was heated by steam radiators (except for the six suites, which had electric radiators) and lit by electricity. The lighting generator plant consisted of three 800-light dynamos, each driven by a separate compound inverted engine at 300rpm.

Those, then, were the principal features of *Aragon*. The ships which followed embodied advances and improvements, and their accommodation spaces were given the individualism which always distinguishes a ship.

Apart from the change in propulsion for the later ships, there were some significant variations. In the final four the forecastle and poop were done away with, though a housing was retained aft, while the most noticeable change for passengers was in the layout of the first class dining saloon. From *Aragon*'s specifications it seems that there were some small tables, but much of the seating was at traditional long tables. By the final block of four, long tables were used less, replaced by small tables, mostly four-seaters. And the ugly, heavy swivel seats were replaced by elegant dining chairs. The change wrought by those simple measures altered the character of the rooms. Important developments during the evolution of the series involved the superstructure decks – that is looked at shortly.

Araguaya

The only 'A' ship not built by Harland & Wolff, *Araguaya*, was regarded as a particularly fine ship. There is no doubt that Workman Clark and their sub-contractors put their heart and soul into her. Shortly after she entered service, RMSP produced a booklet which described her:

> *The portions of the steamer assigned to passengers are arranged in five decks lettered A to E. The floor plan of the dining saloon is arranged on Deck B, but the beautiful saloon dome rising above the centre pierces Deck C, Deck D, and is finally crowned on Deck E by its culminating cupola. The façade of this saloon superstructure presents an exceedingly fine effect, and the portion which is found on Deck C is adorned with beautiful frescoes depicting Brazilian scenery…*
>
> *Deck D, besides the portion occupied by a certain number of single-berth rooms, and the sweep of the decks assigned to promenade and amusements, contains the Smoking Room at the after end, and the Social Hall in the front. The former, which is especially well designed in oak, is surmounted by a card-room on Deck E. These two handsome apartments with their frescoes of old-world ships and Jacobean lanterns and furniture, form unusually attractive specimens of their class.*
>
> *The Social Hall contains a handsome grand piano, set at the forward end against the dome which rises from the Dining Saloon. The Library, which finds a place in this elegant apartment, contains a supply of books of reference and standard works, together with a number renewed each voyage from one of the shore libraries.*
>
> *In between the Smoking Room and the Social Hall stands the Dark Room devoted to the use of photographers. Nowadays pictorial art enters so fully into social life that passengers on the up-to-date vessels of the RMSP appreciate in a very practical manner these conveniences for changing and development…*
>
> *Like all the RMSP Mail steamers, the* Araguaya *has been fitted with boat accommodation capable of carrying every person on board even when the vessel contains her full complement. These craft are arranged for the most part on E Deck, the open space of which forms an excellent playing-ground for children.*
>
> *On the South American voyage, deck games play a large part. The facilities afforded on board the* Araguaya *for this form of exercise, so desirable in the case of passengers whose existence otherwise becomes too sedentary, rank high even among her sister ships. Deck cricket, which demands more space than most of the other cognate amusements, can be played without interfering with the comfort of those to whom 'deck-chair' lounging constitutes the most attractive feature of shipboard life.*

The Ships in Service

Aragon's years on the mail run were largely routine after the accolades from her maiden voyage. Probably because later ships were both larger and, perhaps, a little finer, she was kept as a steady workhorse on the mail run and was not used for cruising. Apart from running aground off the Isle of Wight in January 1908, little out of the ordinary happened to her before the war. Except, perhaps, for the rather taciturn statement in a 1913 voyage report: 'Called at Coruña in error'.

Amazon also enjoyed a trouble-free pre-war career. Her maiden voyage began in June 1906. During the summer of 1908 she was chosen to make a cruise (or 'yachting holiday', as it was termed) to Norwegian waters. It lasted seventeen days and visited eleven 'places of interest' in Norway. The longest stopover was twenty-four hours at Odda on the Sorfjord where passengers could leave the ship for an overland trip and rejoin *Amazon* at Stavanger. The lowest fare from Southampton was £16. This, then, pioneered RMSP's 'one-ship cruise', a business which became increasingly important for the remainder of Royal Mail's years as a passenger ship operator.

Araguaya was next to enter service. Her variations – as the only non-Harland & Wolff 'A' ship – showed how much leeway builders were given in a ship's design. She had a somewhat fatter funnel than her contemporaries, for example, and ten of her twelve deck cranes faced aft, the opposite direction to the other ships. There were no derricks attached to masts, and the foremast was placed further aft than in the Harland & Wolff ships – it passed through the middle of No. 2 hold (being stepped on the lower deck), and hatchways were arranged on either side of it. Due to its rake, the foremast passed barely ten feet in front of the wheelhouse.

Araguaya was launched in July 1906 and four months later sailed for the River Plate on her maiden voyage. Opinion generally held that she was more handsome, inside and out, than her two predecessors. She was received rapturously at all ports, and at Buenos Aires the Argentine President was entertained to luncheon. Considerable advances in interior layout and décor had already been made since *Aragon*. Her domed Social Hall (lounge) attracted much praise and there were people who insisted that her accommodation and rooms were finer even than those of the ships which followed over the next few years.

At the River Plate in July 1908, the first of her few mishaps involved a collision in fog. Both ships sustained superficial damage. Among her most profitable voyages was the sailing on 23 July 1909, when she had on board specie valued at £1,383,292 – that exceeded by some £30,000 the value carried by *Amazon* two years earlier.

It is astonishing how high a percentage of South America mail voyages, in more than a century, were completed with barely a ripple of incident or drama. Perhaps the epitome of that involved *Araguaya* and *Asturias*, which in October 1910 sailed through a revolution without batting an eyelid. RMSP's Lisbon agents, James Rawes & Co., advised:

> We are glad to be able to report that Araguaya *sailed from Lisbon quite a full ship. She likewise had her cool chamber space filled.*
>
> *We regret we cannot send you details of passage earnings or agent's report, as we cannot get to our office. A revolution broke out here last night… At the present moment the Royal Palace is being bombarded by the men of war which have gone over to the Revolutionaries. Our own house is close to the Palace and we can see everything that is going on. The Royal Standard has just been shot away.*

On 6 October:

> *…After desperate fighting for nearly 36 hours, the Government troops surrendered yesterday morning and a republic was declared in the town and on the river by a 21-gun salute…*

And the next day:

> *We beg to confirm the telegram sent to you yesterday by Marconigram from on board* Asturias, *advising arrival and departure and giving you cargo and passenger particulars. As the Telegraph office was closed we had to avail ourselves of the* Asturias' *wireless, and owing to our not being able to get to the office in consequence of the fighting, we were obliged to send you the message in plain language…*
>
> Asturias *got away at about 6 p.m., taking from Lisbon sixty first class passengers… only about ten of the seventy passengers originally booked embarked, the balance of our passenger list being made up of people who were fleeing the city…*

So two 'A' ships calmly witnessed the momentous events which saw Portugal stagger in bloody revolution from a monarchy to a republic. Only one other non-routine matter affected *Araguaya* before the war – in June 1912 she was chartered by the Thames Yacht Club to attend a major regatta at Kiel, an event which attracted the presence of the Kaiser.

Araguaya was followed into service by *Avon* (which had been christened by Lady Pirrie, wife of Harland & Wolff's chairman). Not long afterwards she became the Company's first ship to be fitted with 'Mr Marconi's wireless apparatus'. During November 1908 Guglielmo Marconi proposed to RMSP that his equipment should be installed in the five 'A' liners. He would pay installation charges, provide and pay

Guglielmo Marconi and his 'black box', photographed in the late 1890s. His work would quickly revolutionise communication at sea and Marconi radio was installed in the 'A' ships from 1909.

operators, look after maintenance and repairs, supply forms and other paperwork and take care of the accountancy side. RMSP would provide accommodation and keep for the operators and supply the equipment to raise and support the aerial wires. A standard charge of £200 per year for each ship was suggested. Alternatively the equipment could be sold direct to the Company for £525 per ship.

The Company chose to hire the equipment. *Avon* received her wireless five months later and the others soon followed – this was little more than a decade after Marconi first came to England armed with a letter of introduction to the Engineer-in-Chief of the Post Office, and a 'mysterious black box' which was very much at an experimental stage. RMSP, then, so often cautious in adopting new technology, ranked among the pioneers of marine radio.

At the beginning of 1910 *Avon* was chosen to operate cruises from New York to the West Indies for four months. It had been decided to paint the ships 'cruising white' for those voyages and it seems that *Avon* retained the white hull for her first voyage back on the River Plate run for celebrations to mark the centenary of Argentina's independence.

Last of the initial group of five liners was *Asturias*, which was launched without ceremony in 1907. Her career began in the early days of 1908 when she sailed round to the Thames and became the first 'A' ship to visit London's river, and reputedly the largest vessel to have done so. Editors and reporters from leading papers were invited on board at Tilbury and a luncheon was held for Australian shippers and shipping clerks – it will be remembered that she had been built to augment RMSP's joint service with Orient Line to Australia, which explains her presence at Tilbury for her maiden voyage.

If success can be judged by public enthusiasm, then *Asturias's* maiden voyage was a triumph. She sailed to Australia via Suez and was greeted by large crowds at every port. At Sydney the quayside was crammed with people. Australia was a good place to 'road test' a new liner for public reaction, for these people – so far from the hub of commercial life – had always been immensely dependent on shipping and had gained a great knowledge of and empathy for ships and seamen.

Australians were used to the best that firms like P&O, Orient Line, Norddeutscher Lloyd and Messageries Maritimes could offer, which made their impressions of *Asturias* particularly pertinent. When she reached South Australia on her maiden voyage early in March 1908, the Adelaide *Advertiser* noted that:

> ...curiosity was intensified by the widely circulated report that Australians might look for something quite out of the ordinary in marine architecture – a colossus in comfort and general convenience for passengers. Passengers say that the reports were justified and the expectations more than fulfilled. The Asturias is a truly magnificent specimen of the marine architect's skill, a triumph in the matter of comfort, and a credit to her builders, the well-known Belfast firm of Harland & Wolff...
>
> A point deserving notice is that the staterooms are on deck, an improvement that will appeal strongly to the travelling public. There are handsome two-bedded staterooms (no upper berths), beautifully decorated, and with bathrooms attached; and the majority of these are arranged on the tandem principle with sidelights for each room. Single berth staterooms are a special feature, and the entire accommodation in the lower promenade deckhouse is arranged in this manner.

Aragon *(I) introduced in 1905 a new standard in shipboard travel – this was the first class lounge.*

There are several suites de luxe (so well known in the company's steamers), and these are magnificently furnished in white and gold with silk panellings. An electric passenger elevator is provided to serve four decks, and to land passengers either in the saloon, or the social hall, or lounge. The first class dining saloon bids fair to surpass the most handsome afloat. The tables (seating 300 passengers) are arranged on the latest restaurant principle. The elegance of the whole structure, combined with the magnificent stairway and approach to the main deck, forms a rare example of architectural beauty. The style is in renaissance, in oak, white and gold furnishings adorned with Cupids and sea trophies. The dome, modelled after that of a Genoese palace, is ornate and brilliantly lighted, and the saloon is specially ventilated by a complete arrangement of electric fans.

The decorations of the social hall and lounge, situated on the promenade deck, are in Austrian oak, the structure being surmounted by two handsome domes of stained glass. The smoke rooms, upper and lower, are on the upper promenade and boat decks aft, and are exceptionally well ventilated. They are decorated with Dutch tiles, giving views of different places of interest in the ports and countries to which the vessels of the company trade. The woodwork is carried out in oak panelling, handsomely carved. The arrangement of the rooms is attractive and comfortable. A staircase leads from one to the other, and the popular 'well' formation gives a balcony to the upper room. The rooms are mechanically ventilated with 13 electric fans. A nursery adjoins the first saloon on the main deck, and electric fans are provided throughout the first and second class accommodation…

In spite of the ship's personal popularity, the Australia service was not going well and RMSP's involvement ceased the following year. *Asturias* made one further voyage to Australia (voyage six), but otherwise was engaged on the Brazil and River Plate service. Between her two Antipodean voyages a collision occurred with New Zealand Shipping Co.'s *Rakaia*.

There was little difficulty adapting *Asturias* for permanent service to South America for she was generally little different from the others. The principal variation was the construction of an extra deck, a feature which continued with the final four ships of the series. With her immediate predecessor, *Avon*, Royal Mail had extended the promenade deck to the bridge structure, thus separating the bridge from the accommodation by only the upper promenade deck. In *Asturias* and later ships the extension of two decks to the bridge, which was pioneered in *Avon*, was retained, but because an extra deck had been added there was, visually, an apparent return to the older design as both promenade and upper promenade decks ended at No.3 hold.

The pre-war years to South America were busy and fruitful. The Company's centenary history mentions *Asturias* in particular (though it applied to all the 'A' ships) enjoying a boom time with passengers; large numbers of migrants were carried, and first and second classes were frequently full. With South America becoming immensely cosmopolitan, passenger lists took on an equally varied look. On one voyage *Asturias* carried passengers of thirty-six nationalities, which created many a headache for the purser's and chief steward's staffs.

There was a gap of four years before the last four vessels began to emerge. First of them was *Arlanza*, whose maiden voyage began on 21 June 1912. She had scarcely time to settle in before her schedules were disrupted by war. On a short cruise on 27 June 1914, Sir Owen Philipps (recently the recipient of a Knighthood) demonstrated a keenness to employ the influence of those who possessed it to support his agenda of cementing RMSP's position as a leading company. This was essentially a floating party in which one can sense Philipps publicly re-inforcing his position as a business leader and flagging RMSP as a force to be reckoned with in a way that it hadn't achieved for many years.

Most of the South American ambassadors (or ministers, as they were called then) were on board, as were members of the influential West India Committee. Other guests included Lord Aberconway, the Earl of Coventry, Admirals H.E. Purey-Cust and Campbell, the Marquis of Douglas and Clydesdale, the Earl of Dundonald, Sir Edward Elgar, Major-General Sir Douglas Hadden and Luh Tsang Chang, a former Prime Minister of China. If Sir Owen hoped that such a gathering would help influence his future, he had to place such thoughts on hold. Two months later Britain was at war. For a short time *Arlanza* continued her scheduled voyages, but early in 1915 the Admiralty requisitioned her for military duties.

Alcantara and *Andes* had even less time – under a year – to settle into the routine of the South Atlantic. The final ship, *Almanzora*, was under construction when the conflict began and was requisitioned before completion. Because of those which were lost in the war, at no time were all nine in commercial service together.

The First World War

England and Germany were officially at war from 4 August 1914. On that day *Aragon* was at Buenos Aires. Next to her was the German liner *Cap Trafalgar*, one of the European ships which had created powerful competition for RMSP. It was felt that she was anxious to mount an attack on *Aragon* (an event described in Volume 1). German liners had, for some months, been carrying guns and ammunition in their holds, and, as this was known to Britain, a number of its ships (including *Aragon*, *Amazon*, *Andes*, *Alcantara* and *Asturias*) were already armed with 4.7in guns.

On 16 August *Arlanza* – which was not armed – steamed towards the Canary Islands on a northbound voyage, scarcely aware that she might face danger before reaching England. The German liner *Kaiser Wilhelm der Grosse* was the source of danger. What a foe for *Arlanza* – a former Blue Riband holder with an average speed of 22 knots and a cluster of 4in guns pointing at *Arlanza* ensured that the British ship acceded to the German's order 'stop or I will open fire'. Under instructions her radio aerials were dismantled and thrown overboard. Then the *Kaiser* asked how many women and children were on board. The answer went back: '335 women, 97 children'. All told there were over 1,000 people on board. She was told to proceed. Capt. Down rang 'full ahead' – thankfully at this early stage of the war there was more consideration shown than would be the case later.

Almanzora had such a varied First World War career that in 1919 a booklet was published telling its story. This sketch from the booklet, of the first class social hall, shows it converted to a boxing ring.

So within a fortnight of the outbreak of war, two *A*' ships had brushed with the enemy, and it is a touch ironic that of the four vessels involved, the one which came closest to disaster – *Arlanza* – was the only one to survive the war. Late in August she managed to secure a berth at Southampton in spite of its closure to commercial traffic on 6 August – some dispensation was granted until the end of the month, after which the Divisional Naval Transport Officer advised the Company 'that no further facilities can be given to your ships other than those under Government contract'.

The loss of Southampton's facilities was a big blow and caused consultation with the solicitors. One problem was how to deal with alien passengers en route from South America to Europe – Royal Mail had sold through tickets to their destinations via Southampton, and the question arose as to RMSP's liability for honouring them via another English port or, if they were refused access to Britain, via Spain or Portugal.

Britain possessed, in the *A*' ships, a group of large, modern liners suited to many roles. Five were commissioned as armed merchant cruisers, all but *Avon* in the 10th Cruiser Squadron. Those which joined the Squadron were *Alcantara*, *Andes*, *Arlanza* and *Almanzora*. With the exception of *Almanzora* (which had not then been completed) they were commissioned in April 1915. *Almanzora* joined them five months later.

The objective of the 10th Cruiser Squadron was to form a northern blockade of Germany, one of the most difficult tasks of the war. Its ships had to patrol an area of about 200,000 square miles of inhospitable waters – the North Sea, Norwegian Sea and Arctic areas where winter gales were relentless or the seas were blanketed in fog. The threat from ice was often very real. When the hazards of war were augmented by a new menace – submarines – the Squadron's difficulties increased. Even routine matters were hard work, for suspicious vessels had to be stopped, boarded and searched, often in rigorous weather conditions. During the winter of 1914/15 the Squadron was supplemented with armed merchant ships and it became a policy, which merchant ship crews and owners remember with pride, for the merchant navy to play a majority role in the German blockade.

Thus was the scene set, in the spring of 1915, when some of the *A*' ships began their arduous duty. First to suffer from the weather was *Alcantara*, during her second patrol when she was detailed to search in the region of Jan Meyen Island for signs of German radio stations and submarine bases. Submarine attacks on vessels using the Archangel route indicated that a base must exist in Arctic regions. All that was found were the seventy-year-old remains of an Austrian-American exploration party and three fox cubs (which were kept on board as pets for a short time). In retreating from the area she became briefly trapped by ice but emerged relatively unscathed.

Late in 1915 *Arlanza* had a more substantial taste of ice. She was detached from routine duties for a voyage to Archangel in the White Sea, a region habitually icebound in winter. Her task was to bring a group of Russian officials to England for a conference with Britain and France. For good measure the ship also had on board over half a million pounds-worth of platinum. She left Archangel on 21 October 1915 and the next day, with minesweeping trawlers ahead of her and a convoy of merchant ships astern, she made her way across the Arctic Circle towards the Barents Sea. When it was thought that the mined danger zone had been passed, the trawlers departed and the merchantmen proceeded independently. An hour later *Arlanza* was mined near the forward hold.

A First World War photo on board an RMSP ship as an armed merchant cruiser in atrocious winter conditions. It is believed to be Almanzora *in Baltic regions.*

She jarred and shuddered and quickly dropped 'ten or twelve feet by the head'. Engines were stopped and watertight doors quickly closed – too rapidly for a couple of crewmembers who were caught beneath the descending partitions. The operation of those doors was not, however, as powerful as more modern ones and though badly shaken and bruised, the two men survived.

The Russian delegation was taken off the ship. Some, together with several seamen, fell in the icy water when the after-fall of their lifeboat was released before the forward one – all were safely recovered. One of the minesweeping trawlers, which was still in the vicinity, returned to help, but in rounding *Arlanza*'s stern had to take evasive action to avoid the lifeboats which were being lowered. As a result, she steamed into the liner's propellers, which were clear of the water as she was down by the head. The trawler was holed and quickly sank.

When it became clear that *Arlanza* was not going to sink, everyone returned on board. Arrangements were made for most to transfer to another vessel – *Arlanza* would winter in the White Sea, with nine officers and a hundred crew spending the time patching up the ship for the voyage back to Britain. A party set off across snow-covered tundra in search of a village from which to secure supplies. They travelled by reindeer sledge, and some ten miles across the Finnmark Plateau reached the Lapp village of Yukanski. The next event was the arrival of *Orotava* (one of the former Australia service ships which RMSP had inherited in 1906), which reached *Arlanza* after steaming into the White Sea in a furious blizzard. She took all those who were not in the wintering party and departed for England, leaving the rest to a long Arctic winter.

Two other 'A' ships were having an eventful time. On 29 February 1916 *Alcantara* was off the Norwegian coast. It was the last day of her patrol – after fifty days on G Patrol she was scheduled to return to port on 1 March for a refit. Her duty was being taken over by *Andes*, which was steaming towards her rendezvous. The armed merchant cruiser *Alcantara* intercepted a vessel purporting to be the Norwegian freighter *Rena*, which stopped when ordered to do so and the AMC closed her to make a routine boarding and search. At about one mile range the freighter revealed her identity as the German raider *Greif*, and opened fire. *Alcantara* replied and there followed a gunnery slogging match, at one stage across just 750 yards. Each inflicted terrible damage on the other. After thirty or forty minutes *Alcantara's* steering gear was disabled, and only when the after machinery was connected could she turn away and increase the range. She succeeded in putting *Greif* out of action – the raider was blazing from stem to stern and was abandoned by her surviving men. In her turn, *Alcantara*, badly holed, slowly heeled over, capsized and sank.

Meanwhile, *Andes* and two other ships, HMS *Comus* and *Munster*, had reached the battle area, and while *Munster* picked up survivors the other two pumped shells into *Greif* until she blew up and sank.

Did *Alcantara* know the raider's identity from the start? Leslie's *Royal Mail War Book* claims that *Andes* warned *Alcantara* of the vessel's identity; that, step by step, *Alcantara* carried out a charade of normality while approaching the enemy, and was fully prepared for the engagement. The Company's centenary history largely endorses this, saying that after being warned by *Andes*, the master of *Alcantara* had to make quite sure of *Greif's* identity before opening fire on the 'merchantman'.

Two other reports contradict that. Archibald Hurd, in his *Official History of the Great War*, Volume 2, stated that when *Alcantara* came up with *Rena* her people were ignorant of her true identity, and that a Norwegian freighter of that name was on her list of ships to be boarded. *The Times* said much the same thing, but on another point those two sources were at odds. According to *The Times*, *Greif* was steering a course which would carry her out into the Atlantic, while Hurd's history puts her course as north-east and her reply to *Alcantara's* challenge that she was the *Rena* from South America with a cargo of coffee.

Whatever the true story, *Alcantara* had already put *Greif* out of action and might well have disposed of her completely before *Andes* arrived had it not been for large quantities of cork in the holds which made *Greif* close to unsinkable. She succumbed finally after a mighty explosion. That could have been simply the raging fire reaching a store of torpedoes or shells; even a hold full of mines, as claimed by one historian. The ship was blown apart and sank beneath a pall of smoke. About 230 of her complement were lost, while from *Alcantara* the toll was sixty-eight.

By this time *Almanzora* was ready and had joined the Squadron. Her introduction to war service was bleak and forbidding, her decks covered in snow and every exposed fitting coated thickly with ice and frost. She patrolled the Denmark Strait in constant blizzards and heavy gales, and with temperatures so low that even the accommodation heating system was not sufficient to allow her crew to take off their overcoats and mufflers.

Almanzora was to serve in, and survive, both world wars – a great service commemorated for decades in the Company's head office with her ship's bell forming the centrepiece of Royal Mail's war memorial. Neither bell nor building are still there. The Royal Mail war memorials – together with *Almanzora's* bell – are now at St George's Centre, Chatham Dockyard. Her voyages in the First World War totalled over 190,000 miles. She was one of the lucky ships to emerge from the war almost untouched. Her worst injury was a damaged propeller and her nearest approach to action was to take part (with *Arlanza*) in an unsuccessful Atlantic search for the raider *Möewe*.

First World War gunnery practice on the Armed Merchant Cruiser Arlanza (I) *– a 6-inch gun being fired from the starboard after well-deck.*

During 1917, after the United States had entered the war and eased the task of the German blockade, the 10th Cruiser Squadron was disbanded and its ships given new jobs. *Almanzora* was allocated to convoy duty, which took her mostly to Canada and West Africa. Two voyages in 1918 found her in Brazilian ports, offering South Americans their first glimpse of her in the grim dress of war before they saw her in trading livery.

The fifth 'A' ship used as an armed merchant cruiser was *Avon*. For much of the war she was renamed HMS *Avoca* and could be found far away in the Pacific, patrolling off the west coasts of North and South America. Her sole moment of drama owed little to the war being waged thousands of miles away. An SOS from British Government offices at Salina Cruz in Mexico sent her at top speed to retrieve British property which had been seized by a rebel army and taken away in railway wagons.

The formidable auxiliary cruiser sailed into Salina Cruz and a deputation interviewed the Governor. He was most happy to see a British man-of-war in his harbour because, of course, his whole aim in life was to please the British. What – British property confiscated? Yes, well, some of his subordinates *were* a little impetuous, but he would see what he could do. The men from *Avoca* urged him to do just that. In fact, if everything had not been restored by nine the next morning, they would regretfully have to turn their guns towards the Governor's fine city. All of the property was promptly restored. Before the ship left, her delegation thanked the Governor and assured him that should any further problems arise he could easily call upon *Avoca* for assistance – she would not be far away!

Two 'A' ships unable to enjoy such a relaxed war were *Aragon* and *Asturias*. Both took part in the Dardanelles campaign. *Aragon* first went there in March 1915 with 5th Hampshire and RAMC units. Between off-loading the troops and embarking wounded soldiers she was caught up in HMS *Queen Elizabeth's* bombardment of the fort at Sed-el-Bahr, but suffered no damage and sailed to Alexandria and Malta with nearly 1,500 military wounded.

She returned to the Dardanelles and remained until the evacuation was completed. Gen. Sir Charles Monro and his staff used her as their base, and Lord Kitchener was seen on board more than once. When the campaign was over, *Aragon* remained mostly in the Mediterranean as a troop transport. In December 1917 she embarked many troops and 150 nurses. Altogether there were about 2,700 people on board, bound for Alexandria with the destroyer *Attack* for escort in the later stages.

Approaching the Egyptian port, HMS *Attack* signalled that she would search for mines. She vanished ahead of her own spray, zig-zagging at high speed up the channel. At length HM Trawler *Points Castle* appeared, flying the international signal 'follow me'. *Aragon* did so, and headed into a few minutes of total confusion. Suddenly *Attack* came into view, countermanding the trawler's orders, signalling to *Aragon* 'You have no right to take orders from a trawler'. She intercepted the fishing boat, then signalled to *Aragon*: 'I am senior naval officer; follow my instructions'. She ordered the liner to turn and head out to sea once more, while the destroyer sped about like a mad thing at 30 knots. On board *Aragon* there must have been total bewilderment, but the officers faithfully carried out their instructions. As soon as they were in the open sea again a torpedo hit the liner near No.4 hold.

She began to sink. With calmness and perfect discipline, everyone was at emergency stations in a matter of minutes. First to leave were the nurses; then the ship dipped lower in the water and the order 'every man for himself' was given. Over 600 people died, though not all as a direct result of the ship's loss. Some were picked up during a courageous rescue by *Attack*, which was still searching for survivors when she, too, was hit by a torpedo, breaking in two instantly and sinking quickly with a heavy loss of life.

The whole episode, recalled later by *Aragon's* senior surviving officer, was inexplicable:

> The only explanation that the writer can put forward is that the commander of the *Attack* had a warning of mines in the channel, causing him to order *Aragon* to disregard the *Points Castle's* 'Follow me'. Evidently the enemy laid mines at the appropriate time in the knowledge that the ship would be kept out and thus present a target for torpedo attack...

Regarding the fine discipline on board he had this to say:

> It is a proud tribute to be able to pay to the soldiers and ship's company to say that not one of the nurses even got wet. All were landed safely and intact save one who, seeing a ship's boy hauled aboard her boat clad only in a short vest, promptly divested herself of her own nether garment (bless her!) in order to cover his embarrassment.

Those recollections prompted a response from Alex M. Hamilton, who was on board *Aragon* as an officer in the Royal Engineers. He wrote:

Who among the survivors took this picture is not known but it records the last moments of Aragon *(I), torpedoed off Alexandria in 1917.*

When the torpedo struck I reported to my boat station and assisted in filling the boat with nurses. Sliding down the ship's side, I was holding onto the outside of a porthole when I heard the second explosion. I have a hazy recollection of being crushed by wreckage and some six hours later was picked up unconscious, by a trawler, and landed at Alexandria where I spent six and a half months in Ras-el-Tin Military Officers Hospital... I recovered and am today [November 1962] supervising the business which I commenced after being invalided out in the year 1919.

That business was Alex M. Hamilton & Co., The Pacific Steam Navigation Co.'s agents at Belfast.

Asturias also served at the Dardanelles. The announcement that she was to be turned into a hospital ship came some days before war was declared. The first class smokeroom became an operating theatre; pipes for hot and cold water were fitted through the various decks to this room, and its rubber-tiled floor was taken up. Powerful lights had to be fitted and special rooms erected for processing x-rays and for a disinfecting plant. The dining room became a ward with eighty-five swinging cots, and the children's dining room was turned into bathrooms and toilets. Other wards were made by removing cabin partitions. Those were just some of the necessary tasks for her new role.

On 5 August 1914, when England had been at war for just one day, she left Southampton under sealed orders. They directed her to Scapa Flow, where the Home Fleet lay at anchor around the flagship *Iron Duke*. On board that impressive warship was Admiral Jellicoe, son of the Royal Mail director who had sailed in his first RMSP ship towards the end of 1841. *Asturias* was quickly put to work. At Le Havre she berthed beside a coaling works and her sparkling white paintwork, the broad green hull band and red crosses all vanished beneath a black layer. The first hospital train to reach her with its wounded soldiers was a line of cattle trucks painted with red crosses. Le Havre gave *Asturias* a telling taste of her future in the war.

Her sphere of operation was mostly the Mediterranean, from St Nazaire in the west to Gallipoli in the east. In the spring of 1916 the King visited her and lunched on board. They were frugal times and he asked for nothing more exotic than an egg – even that request had the Chief Steward searching through his ageing supplies for one that would 'behave in a decent manner'.

When a German torpedo was fired at *Asturias* in February 1915 it was made clear that allied vessels flying the red cross could no longer consider themselves safe. That particular torpedo missed its target, but there was a different story two years later. Germany had by then announced that it had moved the goalposts – hospital ships in the English Channel and the southern part of the North Sea could expect to be attacked. On the night of 20/21 March 1917 *Asturias* was torpedoed without warning. Germany's excuse was that 'there was evidence' that hospital ships were taking advantage of their privileged status to carry troops and munitions – they were certainly carrying troops, but they weren't exactly in a condition to pose a threat.

Fortunately, *Asturias* had disembarked her wounded passengers at Avonmouth and only the crew and fifty nurses were on board when the vessel, her Red Cross lights shining brightly, was attacked. Her situation quickly became critical. The captain ordered the engines to be shut down while the crew and nurses took to the boats, but the water had risen so quickly that the engineroom controls could not be reached. Some people were drowned when a boat was lowered while the ship still moved sluggishly.

Asturias *(I) in her role as hospital ship during the First World War.*

The lighthouse at Start Point was in view and the captain urged his slowly-sinking ship towards land. After forty-five minutes she was listing badly to port and was down by the stern. But at length, after painfully slow progress (her boilers, one by one, being doused by seawater), she beached gently at Bolt Head. The remaining boats were quickly lowered and made their way into Salcombe. After a month ashore she was refloated and towed to Plymouth. When she was drydocked the full extent of the damage was seen. It was too much to cope with then, so she lay off Plymouth until the war ended and repairs could be carried out.

The surviving 'A' ships from the disbanded 10th Cruiser Squadron turned to troop carrying. Thus we have looked at the principal wartime events of all the ships except two – *Amazon* and *Araguaya*. They maintained the mail service to South America after *Avon's* transfer to a military role at the end of 1915. For much of the war *Amazon* carried out her voyages relatively unhindered. With so few steamers available for commercial service, those which maintained the Brazil and River Plate run had their holds well filled, and in spite of delays through waiting for convoys, zig-zagging on occasions and other difficulties, their voyages were often highly profitable.

It was a great relief to Royal Mail that those two 'A' ships sailed the South Atlantic safely for much of the war. In January 1917 *Amazon* was close to the great bay of Vigo when her master, Capt. A.P. Dix, spotted a torpedo speeding towards his ship. *Amazon's* helm was turned hard-a-port and she managed to turn sufficiently for the torpedo to pass close astern.

The U-boat which had fired it quickly surfaced, her commander presumably confident that the liner had been hit. Capt. Dix must have rubbed his hands with glee – *Amazon* carried only a token armament, but the gun was rapidly put to use. The first two shots were near misses and the next two hit the submarine, making her roll until the keel plates showed. Spectators lining *Amazon's* decks watched this retaliation with delight, for many were survivors of torpedo attacks. None doubted that the submarine was mortally wounded, but since no concrete evidence came to light, *Amazon* was credited with nothing more than a hit. It was, however, something of which those on board were understandably proud.

There was pride, too, among a group of passengers who travelled in *Amazon* at the start of the war. A group of twenty-six Britons domiciled in Brazil answered the call to arms by embarking in *Amazon* at Rio de Janeiro on 16 September 1914, heading for England and enlistment. Two were killed in action and eight were not traced after the war; the remainder, except one who remained in England, returned to Rio and formed the Amazon Club. Each year from 1921, on 16 September, they held a reunion dinner.

By 1947, when most had returned to England, the venue was switched to London. Naturally, as the years passed there were fewer and fewer survivors. The handful who remained in 1959 decided they were becoming too old to continue the tradition, and so the 45th anniversary reunion would be the last. All this time a silver cup bearing the names of the twenty-six volunteers had made its appearance at each dinner, and the members drew lots to decide who would hold it for the ensuing year. After the 1959 dinner it was handed over to Royal Mail for safe-keeping. A new *Amazon* was on the verge of entering service, and the cup was placed on board. There was one more highlight for the Amazon Club. On its 50th anniversary – 16 September 1964 – the four surviving members were invited to lunch on board the new *Amazon* and were presented with silver tankards. When *Amazon* was transferred to Shaw Savill Line a few years later, the cup was presented to the British community at Rio de Janeiro.

To return to the earlier *Amazon*. After her triumphant encounter with the submarine, she was not troubled again for more than a year. The war was drawing towards its conclusion, with both sides so battered and bruised by four years of conflict, and so short of seapower, that losses by enemy action fell away sharply. During 1918 two RMSP ships were lost – *Amazon* and a small cargo steamer. On the morning of 15 March, with two destroyers scurrying about her in a fury of activity, *Amazon* was torpedoed at her coal-filled No.4 hold. Everyone left the sinking liner safely, and from their boats they watched her stern go awash and saw her slide perpendicularly beneath the waves.

In spite of the trauma of the situation (or perhaps because of it) there was a moment of humour before the destroyers took them on board. The U-boat which had sunk *Amazon* unexpectedly popped up right beside one of the bobbing boats. The astonished survivors looked at each other and someone said 'Shouldn't we do something?' A voice from the stern answered: 'Well, we haven't got any guns. We'll have to ram her'.

While they considered that suggestion the submarine vanished, and one of the destroyers hove into view. While the rescue operation was in progress the submarine again popped up, and this time there were guns at the ready. In fact, HMS *Moresby*, while picking up survivors, had also been pumping out depth charges and one found its mark. When the damaged German sub surfaced, *Moresby*'s guns completed the job. Everybody from *Amazon* was saved – she was the last 'A' ship to be sunk and the only one to go without loss of life.

The bulk of the wartime South America service fell on the intermediate 'D' class steamers, but *Amazon* had some support from two other 'A' ships for a time. *Avon* remained in commercial service for over a year and *Araguaya* until the end of 1916. Just before her requisitioning *Araguaya* was chased by a submarine and escaped through superior speed and good seamanship. She was then converted into a hospital ship and, as such, saw out the rest of the war without incident. For a couple of voyages she served the Ministry of Transport, but from then until November 1919 she was employed by the Canadian Government. Her nineteen voyages as a hospital ship between the UK and Canada carried 15,000 patients back to North America.

After the Armistice

Following the Armistice the Company took stock of the 'A' ships. Three had been lost and *Asturias* lay disabled at Plymouth. The other five needed major overhauls and conversions to turn them back into passenger ships fit for ambassadors. They were not all released at once – *Almanzora*, for example, did not commence her first commercial voyage until 14 January 1920. But, unit by unit, the ships returned to the South America service to enjoy what remained of the years of 'false prosperity' when the movement of freight and passengers built up quickly and there were too few ships to cater for the trade.

That lasted until 1920, after which a slowing down led to less successful times. This trend continued, with slight reversals, through the 1920s and into the Great Depression. Thus the 'A' ships were operating in abnormal conditions of one kind or another from 1914 until the 1930s. By 1926-1927 their places as the front-runners in the fleet had been taken by the new *Asturias* and *Alcantara*.

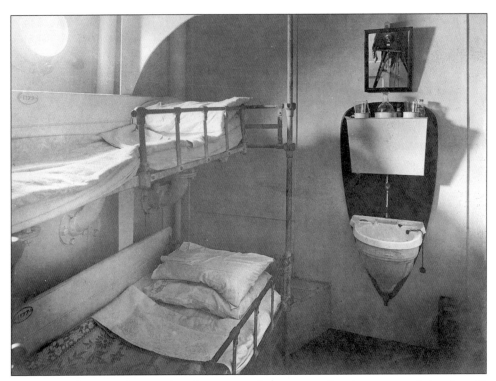

Third class cabin in Andes *(I). A stark contrast to the sumptuous first class accommodation, but still an improvement on the cramped 'tweendecks of earlier ships.*

While the South America service continued as RMSP's dominant trade route, the role of cruise liner was becoming increasingly important. The first sign of renewed interest involved *Asturias*. She had been compensated for by the Government as a constructive total loss, but as Royal Mail badly needed ships it re-bought her. She was towed, much the worse for wear, to Belfast. Building and repair yards were at a premium, and *Asturias* lay by the Ulster yard until 1922 before work began. The task was gigantic and took a year to complete. It included conversion to oil-burning engines and she emerged as a two-class cruise liner with a new name, *Arcadian*, recalling her pre-war namesake which had been lost during the conflict.

With the exception of *Arlanza*, all of the surviving 'A' ships left the River Plate run on occasion for cruising duties. By 1929 *Arcadian* and *Araguaya* (which by then was also a cruise ship) were rather outdated and the conversion of another ship was needed. So *Andes* went to Belfast; cargo spaces were cut out and new public rooms and more spacious accommodation were built. Oil-burning machinery was installed as well. All told, the changes were more radical than those made to *Arcadian*, caused by a mixture of experience and confidence in the future of cruising.

The withdrawal of *Andes* from South America services was made possible by the recent appearance of two new liners on the service, *Alcantara* and *Asturias*, but the changes spelt the end of the road for *Arcadian*. She had been transferred to the New York-Bermuda service, but when the newly-converted *Andes* began her cruising career, Furness, Withy brought out two large liners for the New York-Bermuda run, *Queen of Bermuda* and *Monarch of Bermuda*, and it was considered uneconomic to offer a part-time rival service with a much older ship. In October 1930, therefore, *Arcadian* was laid up and remained out of commission for more than two years. Then, in convoy with White Star's *Baltic* and *Megantic*, she sailed to Japan to be broken up.

Andes emerged with a gleaming white hull and a new name – *Atlantis*. The name *Atlantis* was an inspired choice, for it retained the traditional Royal Mail 'A' prefix but with something of a mystical flavour. She operated so successfully that Royal Mail kept her profitably employed throughout the sometimes difficult 1930s. Her popularity became almost as legendary as the source of her name. A barrage of publicity literature helped to sell her berths and keep her name constantly before the public. Three colourful brochures a year was an average output. Not the least interesting of the material was a large range of coloured postcards. I have thirty-two different cards of her, produced between 1931 and 1938, and probably that is not the complete set. During the same period similar material was produced for the newer liners *Asturias* and *Alcantara*, both for their South America service and cruising, and for the other surviving original 'A' ships.

Araguaya's first class social hall, photographed in the 1920s, probably after her conversion to full-time cruise ship. A plaque above the stairway gives details of her First World War service.

123

The fact that Royal Mail was demonstrating its commitment to this kind of large-scale promotional technique reflects that the new Company, in the wake of the collapsed RMSP, possessed the same kind of marketing vision which formerly had been the domain of Lord Kylsant. It was a vision which formed part of the enormous popularity of *Atlantis*.

From the first voyage under her new name until the outbreak of the Second World War she made 126 cruises. Earlier (as *Andes* still), after her return to commercial service in November 1919 until August 1929, she helped maintain the South America service with only occasional breaks for cruising. One of her masters was Capt. Walter H. Parker – *Andes* was the last RMSP ship he commanded. He recalled that she was 'a beautiful ship, and most comfortable'. His last voyage in her was so unexpected that when he left Southampton he had no idea it *would* be the last. Before sailing he had, in an off-the-cuff comment, mentioned that he preferred North Atlantic routes to South Atlantic. The year was 1927, when that crucial event – the purchase of White Star Line – took place.

Four days out from Southampton, Parker received a telegram at Lisbon. The Company, noting his preference for the North Atlantic, proposed transferring him at the end of the voyage to *Ohio*, which was to enter the White Star fleet as *Albertic*. Parker had to instantly decide whether to entirely change his career path – a cable was expected before he left Lisbon. His reply was 'yes'; and so he continued his final Royal Mail voyage. His table was graced by Rudyard and Mrs Kipling. It is unclear whether this was a voyage arranged by the Kiplings or whether they were at last taking up the offer of a free passage made many years before by Owen Philipps, just after publication of the poem in which he lamented having 'never reached Brazil' by 'rolling down to Rio' in a Royal Mail ship. He may not have reached Rio in the *Don* or *Magdalena*, but his wish was fulfilled.

The outward passage, then, was filled with happy memories, but the northbound one was less pleasing. Parker received a radio call from St Vincent, Cape Verde Islands, where an influenza epidemic was sweeping the island and medical supplies had run out. *Andes* could supply what was needed and headed for Porto Grande. Here, having made up a special raft, they stopped half a mile offshore after dark, 'fired a detonator which brought off a small tug, lowered the raft and proceeded on our voyage inside of ten minutes'. On the following day there was an emergency appendicitis operation on board – so urgent that there was no time to move the patient to the hospital and the operation was performed in the cabin.

In her later years as *Atlantis*, though her voyages were generally incident-free, she reached the newspaper columns from time to time. In January 1935 she responded to an SOS from the freighter *Hindustan* – a seaman, badly injured by a fall, had severed a primary vein and the ship had no doctor. When *Atlantis* reached the scene, her doctor patched up the seaman, who was brought onto the cruise liner for further treatment. In March 1939 Princess Marie Louise was on board for a cruise to the Seychelles, where she inspected a Guard of Honour of the local police force.

Atlantis was the premier cruise liner of her day. She was seen in the Pacific, South East Asia and the Far East, the United States, South America, all round Africa, the Mediterranean and West Indies, and in the ever-popular northern waters of Norway and the Baltic. By 1938 her fares for the traditional long winter cruise (about two months) ranged upwards from 120 guineas. In that year there was some uncertainty about her

A cabin-de-luxe in Araguaya.

future. During January, RML felt that she still had two or three years left, but later in the year Lord Essendon, the chairman, said that she might be withdrawn after her winter cruise from January to March 1939. By then the new *Andes* would be close to completion, and either *Asturias* or *Alcantara* could then be withdrawn to become the new full-time cruise liner.

Those plans, of course, came to nothing because of the Second World War. Luckily *Atlantis* had not, in the event, been sold and in August 1939 she was converted hurriedly into a hospital carrier; five months later more comprehensive alterations turned her into a hospital ship. She served the Red Cross until 1945, and her voyages were almost as widespread as her cruise schedules had been – they took her to Norway, South Africa, the Middle East, North Africa, Egypt and elsewhere in the Mediterranean, New York, Sweden and more.

It seemed that where there was action, there, too, was *Atlantis*. For two years she carried wounded soldiers from the campaigns of the Western Desert. Immediately after the capture of Diego Suarez, Madagascar, she steamed in to pick up casualties. Survivors from the battle of El Alamein were brought to England at the end of 1942, and then she carried American casualties from North Africa to New York. During 1943 she took part in a prisoner of war exchange between Britain and Germany, at the Swedish port of Gothenburg. Men from the British Liberation Army fighting close to the German borders were then her passengers for fifteen months. Altogether she carried over 35,000 sick and wounded, and steamed 280,134 nautical miles.

First class lounge in Arlanza *(I).*

That brief summary conveys none of the human story which pervades a vessel on such wartime duties. One of her officers at the time, later Capt. Douglas Brookfield, wrote in the Royal Mail Association's newsletter in 1993 about the prisoner of war exchange at Gothenburg. *Atlantis*, with German PoWs on board, was approaching the port:

> *About 12 o'clock the captain said to break out the largest Red Ensign we could find, as we were the first British merchant ship to sail into Sweden since the beginning of war. The Second Officer, 'Ginger' Phillips, looked in his store and found a large red duster, I think nine yards, which would only fly at the gaff but looked splendid.*
>
> *As we rounded the last bend the dockyard came into view, and the quays were crowded with British war wounded who set up terrific cheering at such a volume that I think old Hitler must have heard it in Berlin. We docked ahead of the German hospital ship and Queen Louise of Sweden came on board to thank the Captain and OC troops for bringing the ship safely into Swedish waters. We made the exchange and next morning sailed for Liverpool.*
>
> *Two days later we passed New Brighton about 11 a.m. on 26 October 1943, another sunny day. The Wallasey promenade was crowded with thousands of school children, cheering home the heroes of Dunkirk and other theatres of war, to arrive at Princes Landing Stage to another tumultuous welcome which brought a lump to the throat.*

For most of the war the neutral status of *Atlantis* as a hospital ship was observed, but she was twice the target of German bombs while at anchor off North Norway in May 1940. There were reports that at 7,000ft, hospital ship markings could not be identified, so *Atlantis* subsequently bore a gigantic red cross on the boat deck, 54ft across.

Her Government service did not end in 1945. Still fitted as a hospital ship, in the following year she carried 450 war brides and 135 children to their husbands in Australia. It was a festive voyage which left Southampton to the strains of *Waltzing Matilda* over the loudspeakers and ended at Melbourne with the ship dressed overall, a band playing on the quayside and hundreds of husbands, almost lost beneath vast bouquets of flowers, besieging the ship. Later in the year she was at it again, this time bringing Italian-born wives of Polish soldiers from Naples to England. At least one baby was born every day. On the last day two babies were delivered and the ship's cat had kittens – an optimistic note on which *Atlantis* could end her second successful term of service through a world war.

Royal Mail had no further need for her, so the Ministry of Transport bought her in 1946 and she was refitted as an emigrant ship, initially for service to Australia, where migration boomed in the post-war years, but for much of her time she operated on charter to the New Zealand Government. Her former cruising passenger load of about 600 was raised by 50%. *Atlantis* maintained this service until 1951 before being replaced by the more modern *Empire Pride*. Her career, after nearly thirty-nine years of extraordinarily varied service, ended with her sale to the British Iron & Steel Corporation. She reached Metal Industries' yard at Faslane on 27 March 1952.

Almanzora undertook only limited cruises in the 1930s, being reserved primarily for the South Atlantic. Like *Atlantis*, she was earmarked for disposal in 1939 but the war intervened. In spite of the looming crisis, RML scheduled her final voyage to end in September 1939. Accordingly, farewell parties were held at South American ports for officials, local companies and the like. Having thus signalled the end of her career, she

Atlantis *as a hospital ship. She is seen at Newport, Mon., in December 1942.*

faced the unusual situation of immediately making a further voyage, for she took the sailing which was to have been the maiden voyage of *Andes*.

After spending a year or so at Scapa Flow as a Depot Ship she was requisitioned as a troopship, seen often in Middle East waters and, later, India and South East Asia. At Suez in 1941 a stick of bombs straddled her but caused only superficial damage. Two years later, during an air attack in the Mediterranean, one enemy plane was brought down but crashed into *Almanzora's* hull, its fuel tanks exploding on impact. Dramatic though those moments were, with plane wreckage strewn over the ship, *Almanzora* emerged relatively unscathed. In a thankfully quiet war campaign, that was her most exciting day, though there was satisfaction in July 1944, after responding to an SOS from a stranded ship, to safely bring aboard her people. That was doubly satisfying when they discovered that the ship was *Orbita*, which had been an RMSP ship in earlier years.

During March 1945 she repatriated much of the Czech Government (who were landed at the Romanian port of Constanza) and Russian troops at Odessa. September 1945 saw her at Madras, receiving a visit from Gen. Sir William Slim. She then went to Singapore for the re-occupation of Malaya. Over 1,600 people, wearied and weakened from more than three years under the Japanese, boarded her for the voyage home. Early in 1946 *Almanzora* repatriated many Dutch nationals in a short but uncomfortable journey to Amsterdam – the weather was bitterly cold and there was an outbreak of measles. If her passengers were miserable from that, they were cheered on arrival when Princess Juliana came on board to welcome them.

Some misconceptions about the last year or so of *Almanzora's* life were put straight in *Royal Mail News* in 1993 by her then 4th officer, Michael Mortimer. After being released from Government service she was chartered to Elder Dempster as a fill-in ship on the West Africa run while new liners were being built. Like the ageing ship she was, *Almanzora* needed a breather at regular intervals: 'To keep the old lady going, 10 days were needed in Southampton between voyages'.

When the frequency of voyages was reduced, *Almanzora* was able to repatriate members of the Jamaican Air Force to the Caribbean. She had to contend with an astonishing number of stowaways – it appeared the total tally was ninety-nine. Only after all that, and one further passage to West Africa, did *Almanzora* take up station, early in 1948, for lay-up near Cowes, Isle of Wight, where the little paddle steamers *Medina* and *Solent* had been built for the Company a century earlier. Later that year she was surveyed and it was decided that the expense of refitting such an old ship was not justified. Thus she, too, was sold to BISCO, reaching shipbreakers at Blyth in September.

Avon had earlier been a popular cruise ship and from the end of the First World War until 1930 much of her time was spent cruising, for which she was given a white hull. Apart from losses in the War, she was the first 'A' ship to leave the fleet. Her sale to Thos. Ward & Co. in 1930 took her to Briton Ferry for demolition.

As for *Araguaya*, after being handed back to RMSP by the Canadian Government in 1920, she was reconditioned before resuming her place in the River Plate trade that October. For four years she remained on that route apart from occasional cruises. Her only blemish was a collision with the French steamer *Haut-Brion* off Boulogne in July 1923. By the following year she 'no longer matched up' to the competition on the

1. Possibly the first postcard issued by RMSP. A generic card for South America services, it depicts Rio de Janeiro. The ship is either Danube (II) or Nile (II) and the card was issued around 1903. The artist was Charles Dixon.

2. Postcard of Clyde (II) from Raphael Tuck's Oilette series, probably issued in the first decade of the twentieth century. The artist was Neville Cumming.

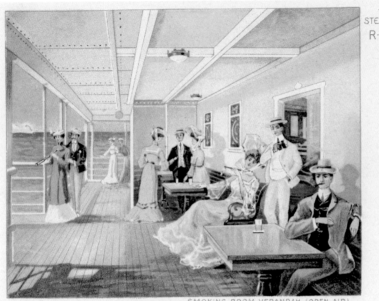

THE ROYAL MAIL
STEAM PACKET COMPANY
R·M·S·P·"ARAGON"

SMOKING ROOM VERANDAH (OPEN AIR)

3. *Prior to 1910, RMSP issued a series of postcards depicting scenes on board the early 'A' ships. They were generic scenes overprinted with the names of the ships on which they were issued. This one, for* Aragon *(I), shows the smoking room verandah.*

THE ROYAL MAIL STEAM PACKET COMPANY
Twin Screw R·M·S·P·"ARAGUAYA"
10537 TONS.

4. *Postcard of* Araguaya, *most likely issued shortly after she entered service in 1906.*

5. *Postcard by an unknown artist of* Aragon *(I), issued about the time the ship entered service in 1905.*

THE ROYAL MAIL
STEAM PACKET COMPANY
R·M·S·P· "ARAGUAYA"

SMOKING ROOM & STAIRCASE TO CARD ROOM

6. *Another of the generic 'A' ship postcards issued during the first decade of the twentieth century. This one, issued on* Araguaya, *depicts the first class smokeroom, featuring the spectacular entrance staircase.*

7. *Postcard of Darro (I), when the ship was new in 1912. The same painting, by Edward Wright, was also used for cards of her four sister-ships.*

8. *A Kenneth Shoesmith-designed brochure from December 1925 which introduced third class passengers to the brand-new Asturias (II). RMSP pointedly printed on the cover 'Maiden voyage of the World's Largest Motor Liner'.*

9. *(Left): In the 1920s and 1930s third class brochures were issued in many European languages, emphasising the breadth of the migrant trade to South America. This issue was for Yugoslavia in 1937, with artwork by Kenneth Shoesmith.*

R.M.S.P. "ALMANZORA." Vigo.

10. *Postcard of* Almanzora *at Vigo. It was issued between 1923 and 1926 and is among the earliest surviving RMSP products from Kenneth Shoesmith. He lightened the ship's black hull to lavender in order to make the ship stand out against an exceptionally strong foreground.*

LISBON:
M.V.
"ALCANTARA."

11. *Postcard of* Alcantara (II) *as a motorship. The painting by Kenneth Shoesmith depicts her at Lisbon and was issued about 1933, shortly before she was given steam turbines.*

12. *A memorial booklet to* Alcantara *(I) produced about 1919. This unusual concept comprised photographs of the ship, a written story and a description of her battle with the German raider* Greif.

13. *The Georgian-style first class Social Hall in* Asturias *(II), modelled on Ely House in London and Godmersham Hall, Kent – from the booklet issued when the ship was new in 1926.*

14. *Third class poster issued in October 1924 for use by travel agents. This immensely detailed document listed departures by both 'A' and 'D' ships, routes and transshipment ports, baggage allowance etc. Passage rates were quoted from every European nation from Albania to the Ukraine, while destination ports extended to Manaus, far up the River Amazon. The need for such a complex and regularly-updated publication reflected the large amount of migrant travel at that period.*

R. M. S. "ALCANTARA" 22,000 TONS GROSS.

15. Alcantara *(II)* postcard issued in the late 1930s. *The artist was Kenneth Shoesmith.*

16. *Shoesmith booklet from October 1934 when* Asturias *(II) and* Alcantara *(II) received steam turbines.*

ROYAL MAIL CRUISING STEAMER 'ATLANTIS' AT LISBON

17. (Above): The cruise liner Atlantis *at Lisbon in a postcard from the 1930s. She had been a familiar sight at Lisbon for twenty years, mostly in her original identity as* Andes *(I). Painting by Kenneth Shoesmith.*

18. (Right): A brochure issued for first class travel in the early 1930s, specifically targeted at South Americans travelling to Britain and Europe. Using artworks by an unnamed artist, its style was unique for Royal Mail – an immensely bold, almost brash, design purely in black and shocking pink.

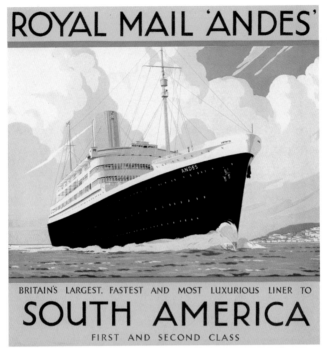

ROYAL MAIL 'ANDES'

BRITAIN'S LARGEST, FASTEST AND MOST LUXURIOUS LINER TO

SOUTH AMERICA

FIRST AND SECOND CLASS

19. *A large fold-out leaflet produced during 1939 to introduce* Andes *(II) to the travelling public before her anticipated maiden voyage in September. This would be one of the rarest RML artifacts now, for if the brochure was released (which is uncertain) it would have been withdrawn no later than August 1939 when work began on transforming her into a troopship. The artist is not known.*

ROYAL MAIL LINE ■ BRAZYLJA, URUGWAJ, ARGENTYNA, PARAGWAJ.

20. *A generic* Highland *ship postcard from the 1930s, produced especially for the considerable numbers of Polish migrants who occupied their steerage accommodation. This was one of comparatively few Kenneth Shoesmith paintings to depict a ship at sea rather than at a port of call.*

R . M . S
"A N D E S"

ROYAL MAIL LINES
TO SOUTH AMERICA

21. Andes *(II)* brochure from the 1950s, an expensive full-colour publication. It was produced shortly after stabilisers were fitted and opened with a special introduction headed 'A new era in sea travel - the stabilised ship'.

R.M.S. "ANDES" 26,000 TONS GROSS. Equipped with Stabilisers for maximum comfort.
Royal Mail Lines Sunshine Cruises to the Mediterranean, Northern Capitals, West Indies, etc.

22. *Postcard of* Andes *(II) issued in the 1950s. The painting, possibly the finest example of marine art used by Royal Mail, first graced a postcard in 1939, produced before the ship was completed and therefore possibly not released. The painting was by Frank H. Mason.*

23. *The first class Grand Hall in* Andes *(II). The picture was taken in the early 1950s, while she was still wholly engaged in the South America mail service.*

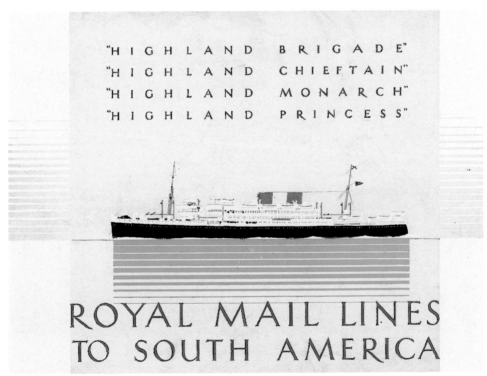

"HIGHLAND BRIGADE"
"HIGHLAND CHIEFTAIN"
"HIGHLAND MONARCH"
"HIGHLAND PRINCESS"

ROYAL MAIL LINES
TO SOUTH AMERICA

24. *Clearly a companion brochure to the one on* Andes *(II) from the 1950s, this publication was the last significant promotional material produced for the* Highland *ships.*

R.M.S. "MAGDALENA"   17,500 TONS GROSS

25. Postcard of Magdalena *(III)* from 1949. The painting was by Howard Jarvis.

26. Aragon *(II)* at sea. This photograph was used during the last years of the mail service for a generic postcard for all three 'A' ships.

ROYAL MAIL LINES

AMAZON
ARAGON
ARLANZA

TO SOUTH AMERICA

27. Brochure issued in 1959 for Amazon *(III),* Aragon *(II) and* Arlanza *(II) before the ships entered service. It therefore used artist's impressions of the ships and their public rooms and cabins, a rare opportunity for Howard Jarvis to extend his work beyond ship exteriors.*

28. A photo which encapsulates the relaxing appeal of sea travel. It was taken on the first class verandah during a benign Bay of Biscay crossing in Aragon *(II) in the 1960s. (Author's photograph)*

29. *First class dining saloon in an 'A' ship, 1960s. These ships carried smaller numbers of first class passengers than vessels like* Andes *(II) and* Alcantara *(II), resulting in more intimate public rooms.*

"AMAZON" 20,000 TONS GROSS.
Royal Mail Lines passenger service between United Kingdom, France, Spain, Portugal, Canary Islands, Brazil, Uruguay and Argentina.

30. Amazon *(III) postcard from 1959/60, a particularly fine painting from Howard Jarvis.*

R.M.S. " DARRO " 9,732 TONS GROSS
Royal Mail Lines' Cargo/Passenger Service between United Kingdom and Brazil and River Plate.

31. Postcard of Darro *(II), one of four large meat freighters built during the Second World War. The artist was Howard Jarvis.*

32. Sunset during a crossing of the Bay of Biscay during a Force 11 storm in Arlanza *(II), February 1967. (Author's photograph)*

A rare photograph of an 'A' ship in trouble – Almanzora *aground off the Portuguese coast near Lisbon on 7 September 1921.*

South America run. Since she was, broadly speaking, contemporary with some of her running-mates, it was probably a mixture of a downturn in trade and the fact that she was, if only by a small amount, the smallest and oldest of the surviving 'A' ships which caused her withdrawal.

Cruising, though, had continued to develop and *Araguaya* was sent to Belfast for conversion for full-time cruising. Her passenger spaces, particularly the cabins, were now extremely spacious, for she was to carry only 365 first class passengers. In her new role she was, like her consorts, very successful, and but for the Depression would doubtless have sailed through much of the 1930s. But in 1930 RMSP's financial troubles, which were on the verge of coming to a head, forced the Company to sell both *Avon* and *Araguaya*.

Jugoslavenski Lloyd bought *Araguaya*, intending to open a route to South America. The service did not materialise and she was used principally in the Mediterranean. Little changed except her name, which was now *Kraljica Marija* ('*Queen Mary*'). As the years passed her activities became increasingly desultory; there were occasional lay-ups and in the late 1930s she was reportedly sold to the Hellenic Cruising Co. At all events she had a further change of ownership and name in 1940, at a critical time for France between the outbreak of war and collapse of the French Resistance. Purchased by the French State and registered at Marseilles, she was renamed *Savoie* and was placed under the management of French Line.

Little more was heard of her. A wartime account talked of 'reports from Vichy France concerning a ship called the *Savoie* at Marseilles'. No-one at that time knew what she was doing, but later research suggests that she sailed once more to South America. Her new career, however, was short, for she was reportedly sunk by a torpedo in 1942.

We are left with the final years of one *'A' ship – Arlanza*. She has been left to last because she, alone of the *'A'* ships, continued in service to South America (apart from the First World War) from her maiden voyage until her sale in 1938. There is hardly a bad word that can be said about her during a quarter of a century of service. If she became slower in later years one could not expect less, and she was old-fashioned by the 1930s. But, like all great liners, she quietly created an atmosphere for herself and a popularity which held its own despite the mounting years.

There were landmarks to look back on. One of the finest rescue operations ever undertaken by a Royal Mail ship occurred in the Bay of Biscay during dreadful weather in December 1929. The 5,205-ton Italian freighter *Casmona*, which had been built at Sunderland back in 1901, was sinking. *Arlanza* was quite close, steaming at only four knots because of exceptionally high seas. Her officers and crew managed to rescue nearly all *Casmona's* men (a German vessel took off three) and brought them safely on board the liner. The gallantry and exceptional seamanship displayed by *Arlanza*'s men produced a flood of medals and presentations, from Royal Mail, Lloyd's and the Italian Government.

In the following year she carried King Alphonso of Spain from Southampton to Santander after he had visited Britain. A year later the Prince of Wales and Prince George embarked at Rio de Janeiro for the homeward voyage after opening the British Empire Exhibition in the Argentine capital of Buenos Aires. As the 1930s progressed she became less able to pay her way and it was decided to withdraw her in 1938. That August, cheering crowds on the quayside at Buenos Aires waved away another of the original *'A'* ships for the last time.

At Montevideo, HMS *Exeter's* Royal Marines Band played her out of port and the occasion was broadcast throughout Uruguay. Brazil did her proud as well, for it was apparent that, after this, there would only remain one (*Almanzora*) of the original group of liners whose appearance, in the shape of *Aragon* in 1905, had marked a triumphant advance for RMSP.

Arlanza reached Southampton on 6 September 1938 with a paying-off pennant 170ft long at her mainmast. She was contracted to an Italian shipbreaker for £36,000 but the deal fell through. A new sale for £30,000 was arranged and before the end of the year she was being demolished at Rosyth.

Asturias (II) and *Alcantara* (II)

Lord Kylsant firmly believed that the trade cycle would trend upwards as the 1920s progressed – an ideal time to introduce two large and expensive liners. Powerful competition was emerging from Continental lines, and from Vestey's Blue Star Line.

Manoeuvring platform in the engine room of Alcantara *(II).*

Kylsant's response was to make use of the Trade Facilities Act which, by 1924 (the year these ships were ordered), had been offering for some time low interest loans and Government guarantees for repayment. That facility was unlikely to continue much longer.

While that was a major factor in the timing of these ships, a further reason was that shipyards had been in peak demand in the post-war years and prices had been high; by 1924 some of that leverage on price had evaporated as order books diminished somewhat. Large, high class passenger ships were now a better proposition.

Once the order had been placed, Harland & Wolff's chairman, Lord Pirrie, voyaged to South America in 1924 to examine port facilities so that he could judge features to be built into the new ships. The result was a pair of liners each a little over 22,000 tons gross – for a brief period the world's largest diesel-powered ships. *Asturias* was the first to enter the water, christened by the Duchess of Abercorn (wife of the Governor of Northern Ireland) in July 1925. In September the following year *Alcantara* was launched – curiously, for such a fine liner, without a sponsor. *Asturias* left Southampton for her maiden voyage on 26 February 1926; *Alcantara* followed on 4 March 1927.

Each had a length of 630ft bp and 656ft overall, and a beam of 78ft. There were seven decks (with an orlop deck in the forward holds). Six holds were served by electric cranes. Three of the hatches were forward and three aft of the accommodation housing. Two cranes could lift five tons and the others one and a half. The double bottom would hold fresh water or water ballast.

Propelling machinery was Burmeister & Wain-type eight cylinder four-stroke double-acting diesel engines with air blast injection. At 115rpm, each engine (driving one of the twin screws) had an ihp of 10,000 and bhp of 7,500. The engines were built by Harland & Wolff.

In a lavish booklet commemorating the introduction of *Asturias*, every advantage of diesel machinery was dealt with, but no speed was quoted. Though the engine spaces were smaller than with steamers, and there were other advantages, one would expect a greater speed than in previous vessels, especially if those earlier ships had been built ten or twenty years before. Their advertised speed was, in fact, 17 knots, but as a rule they operated at least half a knot less. Royal Mail was certainly not happy with that. At one of the first board meetings of the newly-formed Royal Mail Lines in 1932 the directors discussed ways of increasing their speed. One sentence from the minutes was revealing: 'First of all the Board might satisfy themselves if it is not possible by some adaptation, or re-arrangement, to adapt the present machinery to give the 18 to 19 knots speed for which the vessels were supposed to be originally designed'.

Clearly the diesels did not meet expectations, either because of a miscalculated power output or because at the designed speed there was too much vibration. It is equally clear that the Company was peeved at the prospect of an expensive operation to make the ships as fast as the original contract had stipulated.

They, of course, were a new group of decision-makers. At the time the ships were built, not only was the use of diesels in such large ships something of an unknown quantity, but Lord Kylsant was in an embarrassing position. Lord Pirrie had died during his overseas trip in 1924 when he was assessing design concepts for *Asturias* and *Alcantara*, and following his death the chairmanship of Harland's was taken on by Kylsant. Thus when the ships were built, the same man was at the helm of both owners and builders.

They were the first Royal Mail passenger ships with cruiser sterns. Their two squat funnels were raked but had horizontal tops, a feature which quickly identified early Harland & Wolff motorships but which was aesthetically appreciated by few people (especially as the forward funnel, a dummy, was just abaft the bridge, scarcely a third of the way aft from the bow). Each had about thirty lifeboats, most double-banked along the main superstructure; a reduction of two on each side was made in later years when passenger numbers were reduced.

Their first class passenger spaces were not only the finest feature, but arguably among the finest on any ship; superlatives were unnecessary in vessels where ornate artistry permeated every room. The main room of *Asturias* was a Georgian-style social hall and ballroom. It drew inspiration from several fine houses in England, notably the high window bays of Ely House in London's Dover Street and a marble fireplace at Godmersham Hall in Kent. The white walls, two decks high, and the ceiling were richly decorated with cornices, gilded scroll-work and entablature. There were Ionic pillars and 18th century-style paintings, red velvet upholstered period sofas, carved wood balustrades by the entrance stairway, elaborate moulded wall designs and exotic light fittings. This was among the finest shipboard rooms of all time.

Another favourite in *Asturias* was the first class dining saloon, more ornate even than the social hall and decorated mostly in the style of the French empire period. It owed not a little to the Palace of Versailles. The walls (again two decks high) were graced by gilded

First class lounge in Asturias *(II), a sumptuous room which personified the grandeur of these two ships. The lounge was designed in the style of Houghton House in Norfolk.*

and inlay work, and an enormous painted panel covered about half the ceiling. There were verandahs, split by arches formed with violet-striated marbled pillars and matched by the purple morocco upholstery of dark mahogany chairs. Following a tradition which Royal Mail maintained for its first class passengers, all were accommodated at one sitting, for its capacity was about 408. Tables accommodated between two and twelve people.

The most striking feature of the first class lounge was an enormous bay window. A fine ornamental fireplace was overhung with a painting in the Dutch style, reminiscent of Jan van Huysum. The style of the lounge – early Georgian – was adapted from Houghton House in Norfolk. A bold feature from a period usually influenced by pastel or dark shades was a large area of peacock green walling with gilt mouldings.

For the reading and writing room the designers returned to large areas of white; tall Venetian windows, slender pillars and an elegant coffered ceiling, coupled with grey carpet, produced a cool and restful room based on designs by the Adams brothers who, over a century earlier, had created the furniture and decorations in Harewood House, Yorkshire. Two more fine mansions – Ham House in Surrey and Belton House in Lincolnshire – were the models for the first class smokeroom. Panelled in cedar and with carvings after Grinling Gibbons, it had the warmth and cosiness adapted so successfully later in the *Andes* of 1939. A fireplace provided the focal point, and above it hung another painting in the Dutch style. Other features – electric lights in cut glass bowls, powder-blue hide chair coverings, a novel sun-ray clock and so on – pandered to the tastes of appreciative passengers. There was plenty more to please them, too. For example, a spacious winter garden modelled on the Cordova Mosque in Spain and an indoor swimming pool whose design was inspired by Pompeii.

The suites comprised sitting room, bathroom, bedroom (with 'two luxurious bedsteads') and a wardrobe room. Bathrooms were also included with many of the single and double cabins, and every first class cabin had at least hot and cold water laid on – a facility not found in every liner of that era. Among the services and conveniences were a Kosher kitchen, hairdressing shops and a photographic darkroom.

The splendours of *Asturias* revolved around the first class, but in their own way the second and third class areas were similarly improved from what had gone before. The second class dining saloon, seating about 200, extended right across A deck; on D deck was the social hall and one deck higher the main smokeroom. There were two verandah smokerooms on F deck whose design was airy and comfortable for the tropics. The second class accommodation, in two and four berth cabins, was in the after part of the vessel, in a housing which surrounded the mainmast.

Over half of her passenger complement comprised third class. About fifty percent of them were in two, four and six berth cabins and the remainder in dormitory accommodation. They had an adequate quota of public rooms – lounge, smokeroom and bar, and two dining saloons. Their accommodation complied with the steadily-growing requirements of the Board of Trade and of the European and South American governments. Royal Mail's third class passengers are generally thought of as being European, and most were, but British passengers travelled third class as well – in the 1930s they could buy a return ticket in the 'A' ships for £24 to Brazil or £26 10s to the River Plate.

An unusual photograph of Asturias *(II) – she is pictured during engine trials late in 1934 after having her diesel engines replaced by steam turbines. However, her squat motorship funnels had not yet been heightened.*

Approximate passenger numbers for *Asturias* and *Alcantara* were 420 first, 230 second and 770 third class. The total complement of passengers and crew amounted to 1,780.

When *Alcantara* appeared a year after *Asturias* she showed that her sister-ship could be matched in decorative splendour. The same philosophy of drawing inspiration from the finest examples on land was adopted, and anyone viewing photographs of her first class public rooms could be forgiven for thinking they were looking at some of England's stately homes. The workmanship was breathtaking, and the effect of the original rooms was, in many cases, enhanced by her post-war refit when new furniture, light-fittings and carpeting replaced the old stock which had been stored and destroyed during air raids at Southampton and Malta. Her social hall, splendidly carved and dominated by wood panelling, was quite different from the equivalent room in *Asturias*. Its profusion of exquisite detail was bewildering in its intensity.

Some perceptive copy-writing went into a brochure advertising cruises to Madeira, Morocco and the Mediterranean when the vessels were quite new. The introductory text had this to say:

> *When Royal Mail built the* Asturias *in 1926 it was observed that a new era had begun in the history of passenger-carrying transport. When the* Alcantara *followed her sister-ship into the ocean ways of an already wondering world, there was sensation.*
>
> *That two sumptuous and superbly-constructed motor-driven liners – each 22,500 tons – should thus be launched into the world's marine, and take their place, almost as if nothing had happened, on the service to South America: this seemed incredible. But it was no more than the*

logical development of a tradition: of the Royal Mail tradition, eighty-eight years old, of progressive service to the public.

In ships, however, space matters. Thanks to the supplanting of enormous boilers by diesel motors, the accommodation in Asturias *and* Alcantara *is everywhere more generous than is possible in a steam-driven ship. Thanks to this, likewise, there is no wisp of funnel-smoke to incommode, no grain of dust or aftermath of coaling; instead, an airiness, a cleanliness and an immaculateness – which are the envy, since it must be so, of the best-run steamers in the world. And these things matter, too. Add to this their 660 feet of length, their 80 feet of breadth, their unequalled steadiness and stability in all weathers, and the distinguishing characteristics of the two largest motor-driven vessels that Britain owns are in essence complete.*

But the Royal Mail tradition went further. Elegance in interior design, grace and harmony in the appointments throughout, the beauty and the magnificence of the 'period' decorations in all the principal saloons; these in their aspirations towards the perfect have invested Asturias *and* Alcantara *with an unique splendour.*

The remark on the quietness with which such momentous ships entered service was astute: there was, indeed, little fuss except for localised celebrations during their maiden voyages. You can read into those words the degree to which Lord Kylsant could sense the marketing potential of the world's largest motorships. There would have been persuasive arguments from Lord Pirrie in favour of diesels, and if Kylsant assessed the potential as appropriate, the promotional aspects (so elegantly handled in the brochure) would have sealed the matter. So strongly was Harland & Wolff involved with early motor engines that it is reasonable to suggest that if RMSP had been allied with any of Britain's other great shipbuilding firms, *Asturias* and *Alcantara* might well have been steam-driven from the start.

Delving further into the same brochure we find these words:

Since the two cruises do not quite take the same itinerary it is not possible to tell the story in sequence. No matter; the beginning of the holiday is the same, the total sum of pleasure and entertainment the same, and the conclusion – that it was good enough to do again as soon as may be – also the same. The beginning, of course, is the ship; you will spend absorbed hours getting to know this splendid country mansion which turns out every now and then to be a ship!

During their early years, when they were owned by RMSP Meat Transports Ltd (a wholly-owned subsidiary of RMSP, established over a decade earlier), the economic climate steadily worsened. In the middle of a world-wide depression the Royal Mail empire collapsed. *Asturias* and *Alcantara* were not performing as well as had been hoped, yet they sailed through the long storm without lay-up, without sustaining such crippling losses that their disposal was contemplated. A number of cruises were the only pre-1932 occasions when they were not engaged in the River Plate mail service. They were years of steady operation when, despite a lower speed than competitive vessels, a loyal following was established.

During most of *Alcantara*'s first two years her master was Capt. Charles Adam, who developed a mid-Atlantic treat for his passengers. The two liners used to pass in the tropics and Capt. Adam would steer his ship as close as he felt was safe towards the on-coming

The breathtaking first class dining saloon in Alcantara *(II). There can be little doubt that the design, decor and sheer artistry in this ship and* Asturias *(II) were among the finest afloat.*

Second class dining saloon in Alcantara *(II). It was a step up from earlier ships and quite adequate for its day – but when compared with the picture of her first class equivalent it is evident that a gulf existed.*

Asturias. 'It was an exhilarating sight, passing as close as this,' wrote Captain E.N. Giller in later years (he had then been second officer in *Asturias*) 'with sirens blowing, flags flying and passengers cheering and waving'. When they were abeam, Capt. Adam put his helm hard-a-port to sweep across the wake streaming behind *Asturias* – a manoeuvre not always appreciated by his opposite number.

Though their cruises at that stage were not great in number, some were significant affairs. Only a few months after entering service, *Asturias* left Southampton, early in 1927, for a mammoth 101-day cruise under Capt. H.A. Le Brecht, the longest and most ambitious cruise ever undertaken by the Company (it is looked at in more detail in Volume 1).

In 1931 Lord Kylsant was summonsed to face charges at the Old Bailey. After a year had gone by, Royal Mail Lines, Ltd was formed and *Asturias* and *Alcantara* were transferred to the new company. The circumstances of their careers to that date could be labelled 'abnormal', both because of their slow speed and because of the worsening economic climate. The new regime had to set about stabilising matters, and the mail service was high on its list of priorities.

Urgent Need for Improvement

On 9 August 1932 Royal Mail Lines' Chairman (Lord Essendon) led an exhaustive study of the River Plate service. The minutes recorded the matter thus:

> *The Chairman reported that he had advised the interests concerned that in his opinion unless the Royal Mail have new and up-to-date tonnage in the South America trade, by the time the moratorium expires its goodwill in that service would have practically ceased to exist. The information he had obtained, as the result of enquiries he had conducted during the course of the last few weeks, showed that the food and the service were second to none, but that the great disability was the quicker passages, amounting to about five days, given by the German and French vessels.*
>
> *The popularity of the Royal Mail company was such that a difference of a few hours would probably be put up with, but when it came to a question of days, competition was so serious that it was bound permanently adversely to affect the Company's business unless some announcement were made as to the policy of new tonnage. Whilst it would be an exceedingly difficult matter, the Chairman was in hopes that it might be possible to make the necessary financial arrangements and obtain the necessary consents, but first of all, in his capacity of Chairman, he had to satisfy himself that such a policy would be justified by results.*
>
> *The German and French vessels at present engaged in the trade were capable of steaming at 22 knots per hour. If the Royal Mail company built a vessel of 23 knots it would mean a considerable addition in cost, and the Chairman doubted very much whether, under most favourable conditions, the expenditure would be justified, because from all accounts the German and French vessels were losing very large sums of money.*
>
> *The builders have been asked to provide tenders showing the different prices for a vessel steaming 19, 20, 21 and 22 knots per hour respectively under the geared turbine system, and alternatively under the quadruple turbo-electric system. When these figures were obtained he*

would ask the Management to provide an estimate of the trading results under reasonably normal conditions which might be hoped to prevail against the time the new vessel could be ready.

The Chairman further stated that he could not help thinking it might be advisable to have a conference with the German and French lines and indicate to them the intention of the Company to build speedier tonnage than that they were now operating, but inviting them to reduce their speed to 19 knots in consideration of the Royal Mail company limiting their speed to 19 knots.

If such a consideration could be come to, it might then be worth while considering, in case of need, taking out the engines of the Asturias and Alcantara and making them 18-19 knot vessels, which it is estimated would cost £500,000, the effect of which would be to give the Royal Mail company a service with three boats in the same length of time that it is now being taken by four boats. This would provide a uniform service and would also overcome the possible disadvantage of any success of the new vessel being at the expense of the older boats. But first of all the Board might satisfy themselves if it is not possible by some adaptation, or re-arrangement, to adapt the present machinery to give the 18-19 knots for which the vessels were supposed to be originally designed...

With *Cap Polonio* and *Cap Arcona*, Germany led the opposition, closely followed by Italy and France. The fierce rivalry which led to faster and faster ships on many routes was a luxury too expensive to make economic sense. With the South Atlantic rapidly becoming as hotly contested as the North Atlantic, it was a brave move for Lord Essendon to suggest a speed limitation between rival lines – especially at a time when the world was trying to clamber out from the morass of the Depression.

He got his agreement nearly a year later. With the circumstances in which the new Royal Mail company found itself, the prospect of new passenger tonnage so soon was remote, and it was not surprising that plans for a new ship were shelved. The Board determined instead to convert one of the existing ships to turbine propulsion, leaving the other with her diesel machinery to replace *Atlantis* as the cruise ship. In May 1933 it was decided to give both vessels turbines, build new bow sections of increased length and improve the accommodation. The contract was dependent on the re-engining raising the service speed to 18 knots. On 31 May, Harland & Wolff were asked to give assurances and guarantees that their proposed changes would be satisfactory. There was an exhaustive question and answer session, almost as though the directors were unwilling to believe that the work could meet with their approval – the performance of the ships so far must have instilled deep-seated distrust and frustration.

At length Harland's convinced the Board, their arguments supported by evidence of similar conversions to three Canadian Pacific ships and Holland-America Line's *Statendam*. The order was then placed. In order hopefully to eradicate excessive vibration from some of the auxiliary machinery (which was not going to be replaced) Harland's proposed to alter the crankshafts. Any potential difficulty with stability would be overcome by placing the new engines lower in the hull and storing much of the increased fuel stocks in the double bottom.

Royal Mail's speed limitation agreement must have been a tremendous relief. Though the conversions were expected to cost half a million pounds, they at least now didn't face the cripplingly high cost of a new ship. Not only would the finance for that have been difficult to obtain, trading conditions were against it. 'The prospects of a revival to any appreciable extent in the near future in passenger and freight traffic between the UK and South America are poor,' stated a Company report in March 1934. 'In fact, from all information that can be gleaned, any improvement is going to be very slow… It will be necessary for the *Asturias* and *Alcantara* to carry the burden of the first class mail service…' That assessment was borne out by voyage results for January and February that year when the River Plate mail service showed a loss of £5,000; in good times it was expected that each voyage would show a *profit* of at least double that figure.

The 'New' *Asturias* and *Alcantara*

While they were at Belfast for re-engining, their accommodation was given a facelift costing around £20,000 per ship. Of prime importance was an unsatisfactory layout of C deck cabins – RML went so far as to say that it was inferior to the equivalent areas in the ageing *Arlanza* and *Almanzora*. Large cabins replaced groups of smaller ones and extra private bathrooms were built, so that out of sixty-one cabins on C deck, forty-seven would have private facilities. All but two first class rooms would now have portholes or windows. Apart from laying a new floor in one of the first class lounges, little was changed in the public rooms – they hardly needed improving.

The task of producing a speed increase of about two knots was not left solely to the new machinery. Harland & Wolff designed new three-bladed manganese-bronze streamlined propellers, 17 feet in diameter and with aerofoil section, after numerous model tests at the National Physical Laboratory tank. The rudder was streamlined, too. But the largest job apart from re-engining was lengthening the bow section by ten feet. All of those alterations were aimed at marginally increasing the speed, so in the absence of any specific explanation for rebuilding the bow sections, it is assumed it was to improve the block-coefficient. In the process it played its part in improving their appearance as well.

Installing turbine engines in place of diesels posed a space problem, for the boiler room alone would take up considerable space. In a most successful arrangement, however, Harland & Wolff needed only three boilers which were fitted abreast of each other. They were Johnson watertube boilers, with integral superheaters, used in conjunction with Parsons' triple-expansion single-reduction geared turbines.

The new power output raised an intriguing issue. Royal Mail did not at the time publish performance figures. One newspaper highlighted the secrecy of *Asturias'* trials: 'The results are known only to a few experts of Harland & Wolff and of the owners'. It was known that she had exceeded the contract speed of 18.75 knots, but not by how much (though *Syren and Shipping* talked of 18.9 knots maintained over the measured mile). Very few sources since then – not even the centenary history – have quoted output figures. Harland & Wolff's carefully worked out specification actually provided an output of 24,000shp.

RML's anxiety to guarantee a successful outcome was reflected in the penalties clause: for each 0.1 knot below the agreed 18.75 the builders would forfeit £2,000; and if it fell below 18.5 knots the machinery would not be accepted. A further clause stated that 18.75 knots on the Skelmorlie measured mile must be achieved with a maximum output of 22,500shp. Thus Harland's 24,000 included a safety factor to exceed the required speed in service.

Third class washing facilities in Alcantara *(II).*

Third class bakery in Alcantara *(II).*

The interest in this matter is because the calculations which can be made to deduce an absolute maximum speed appear to equate to a little under 21 knots, and yet it is recorded that in 1940, as an armed merchant cruiser, *Alcantara* chased the German raider *Thor* for over four hours at 21.5 knots. The deduction, then, is that *Alcantara* and *Asturias* were given considerably more powerful engines than was generally realised, and this was achieved within the existing machinery spaces, which saved a lot of time, money and problems compared with the need to take down bulkheads and re-plan the lower decks.

Each conversion lasted five months. *Asturias* received hers between May and October 1934, which then permitted an outward voyage as far as Rio de Janeiro to gauge initial results before *Alcantara* went to Belfast in mid-November. The price for the work on both ships was lower than had been estimated – £366,790. In every respect the operation was a huge success. The need for an 18-knot service speed, the reduction of vibration and improvements in cabin layout were all competently achieved.

Alcantara, under Commodore Bertram Shillitoe, left Southampton on 4 May 1935 for her first voyage as a steamer. Two months later both ships (as well as *Atlantis*) were at Spithead for King George V's Silver Jubilee Royal Naval Review. The combined tonnage of those three ships was the highest ever to fly the Royal Mail flag at one of those occasions, and their passenger complement of over 1,500 was also a record.

After the waterborne procession had passed and the fireworks display was over, the trio sailed up-Channel in close convoy. At Dover *Atlantis* broke away and continued her passage to Tilbury, while the sister-ships turned back and anchored for the night close to Brighton. Holiday crowds saw two liners with splendidly improved profiles; with extra hull length, and 15ft in height added to the funnels (whose tops were now, thankfully, at right angles to the axis), they were handsome ships.

During October 1936 *Asturias* inaugurated a call at Le Havre, which temporarily replaced Cherbourg to see if there was any advantage in changing the French port. Apparently there wasn't for the change was soon abandoned and Cherbourg again became the port for the Southampton steamers and Boulogne for the *Highland* ships.

The few years left before the Second World War were, on the whole, good ones for the liners. Each, though, suffered one major inconvenience during 1936. One of the main power cables in the accommodation of *Asturias* fused and started a fire which claimed a firm hold in a C deck alleyway before it was discovered. Then, during April, it was reported that as *Alcantara* left Vigo the port intermediate turbine blading stripped. The voyage was made at reduced speed and on her return to England the turbine was dismantled – the blades were badly stripped and the rotor bent.

Early in 1938 Lord Essendon travelled to South America in *Asturias*. It was thought to be the right moment to disclose Royal Mail's plans for the future of the service; when *Andes* was completed in the autumn of 1939, he said, she, *Asturias* and *Alcantara* would maintain the route from Southampton. *Arlanza* and *Almanzora*, well over twenty years old, would be sold.

Things, of course, didn't go quite according to plan. At the start of the Second World War *Alcantara* and *Asturias* were requisitioned as armed merchant cruisers. In fact, *Asturias* was taken over before war was declared, for she left Southampton only hours after ending a Mediterranean cruise and was at Belfast before the end of August 1939, where the heart

A powerful photo of Alcantara *(II) during proving trials in 1935 after being fitted with steam turbines. Unlike the equivalent picture of* Asturias *(II), her new funnels had already been fitted.*

of her luxurious accommodation was torn down. Oxy-acetylene burners sliced away the dummy forward funnel. The hull and deck were strengthened to take eight 6in guns and several smaller ones. Commissioned as HMS *Asturias*, she sailed for Scapa Flow within a month of reaching Belfast.

Pressure of work in British yards forced *Alcantara*, after some of the more valuable items from her décor had been removed, to sail to Malta for her conversion. She was given one 4in gun for the voyage – what that was expected to achieve during the five U-boat attacks which plagued the convoy before it even cleared the Channel is unclear. She was badly damaged during the voyage, but not by the enemy. Capt. F.H. Fisher, RML's Assistant Marine Superintendent, on board to supervise the conversion, was 'taking exercise in the gymnasium, and was actually on the electric horse, when there was a thundering blow, and I imagined the ship had been torpedoed but it was not so'. During zig-zag manoeuvres *Alcantara* and *Franconia* had collided. The Cunarder ran into the Royal Mail ship, and then they came together heavily along the length of their hulls. The first impact holed *Alcantara* on her port side and pumps were needed at full pressure to keep incoming water at bay. Her conversion was delayed while she steamed to Alexandria for repairs.

When work began at Malta, her luxury fittings and fixtures were at first lovingly extracted screw by screw. Among the revelations to emerge was that the magnificent columns in the social hall were hollow, built around two-inch steel bars. The careful nature of this work was simply not practical, and before long Maltese workmen were ruthlessly tearing down panels and mouldings. The fine paintings were taken ashore, and

Alcantara (II) in her guise as a Second World War armed merchant cruiser. The photograph was taken in December 1942.

along with items of furniture and the like were placed in store. The operation was to no avail, though, for store and contents were destroyed during bombing raids.

Like her sister-ship, *Alcantara* lost her forward funnel and was the more handsome for it. In its place went First World War Hotchkiss guns; elsewhere there were 6in guns, some of which had first been fired in the Boer War forty years earlier. Thus prepared for all eventualities she left Malta around Christmas.

Her early war service was wide both in variety and region. On 28 July 1940 she was patrolling off the South American coast, almost due east of Rio de Janeiro. On that day she had her encounter with *Thor* mentioned earlier. The ships sighted each other during the morning. *Thor*'s master thought his adversary was P&O's *Canton* because she had only one funnel. *Alcantara*'s people had no idea what ship was firing at them and remained ignorant for some time afterwards.

Deciding that discretion was the better part of valour, *Thor* took off; there followed a chase, with Alcantara's engines at emergency full power, which eventually brought the range down sufficiently for her ancient armoury to be brought into use. The gun crews made effective use of it, too. Several hits set *Thor* on fire. Unfortunately the AMC not only had First World War guns but also ammunition of similar vintage. A shell clearly dated 1917 found the German's most vulnerable spot – it penetrated the magazine, but failed to explode.

How fate can dictate the outcome of a battle like this – a shell from *Thor* which hit *Alcantara* also failed to explode, but its impact tore a hole on the waterline – about three feet by one. The sea, funnelled in by her speed, surged into the engineroom and quickly flooded a number of vital pump motors. The engines had to be slowed and *Thor* escaped behind a smoke-screen. Fuel was transferred to *Alcantara's* side tanks to create a list and raise the hole clear of the water. Then it was plugged with rolled hammocks and she was able to head for Rio de Janeiro for repairs.

That November, at Southampton, a concentrated air attack bombarded the city with incendiaries. A few fires were started on board *Alcantara* but caused little damage. The Company's store, though, was destroyed; as at Malta, fine furniture and fittings from both ships were lost. On 30 June 1943, with more naval ships becoming available, *Alcantara* ended her role as an auxiliary cruiser. After some months lying at Bidston Dock, Birkenhead, she was converted to a troopship and started her first trooping voyage in March 1944. Until the war ended – and for some time afterwards – she sailed without incident to the Mediterranean (she was among the first ships to reach Piraeus after the liberation of Greece), Singapore, Indonesia, India, Ceylon and Canada.

Asturias, after her commissioning at the start of hostilities, seemed destined to just miss the kind of activity in which her sister-ship was involved. On several occasions actions were fought by vessels which had just replaced her; and she replaced *Alcantara* on the South Atlantic patrol after the *Thor* battle.

A telling picture of the shell damage inflicted on Alcantara *(II) during her gunnery battle with the German raider* Thor.

In 1941, when her mainmast was removed, more modern armaments were placed on board. The second class housing, abaft the main structure, was taken off and in its place an aircraft hanger was constructed. Aircraft catapult equipment was fitted. The work was carried out at Newport News, Virginia, and when she was ready she returned to the South Atlantic station where, for a time, she was the area flagship. On one occasion a floating dock she was towing to West Africa became so badly damaged it had to be sunk.

In July 1943 she was given charge of a second dock, for a voyage from Brazil to Freetown. The long tow was approaching its destination – they were about 400 miles from Freetown – when a torpedo exploded on the port side of *Asturias*, against the boiler room. Four people died in the blast, which ripped the hull open. Water quickly flooded the engineroom and all power was lost.

Despite an estimated 10,000 tons of water inside her, *Asturias* was towed to Freetown. She lay there with only a skeleton maintenance crew until the war was nearly over, when it was considered safe enough to tow her out to sea again. After temporary repairs at Gibraltar (by which time the war had ended) she was taken to Belfast for the monumental task of turning her into a passenger liner again. Her damage and general condition were so bad (for a year and a half Atlantic waters had washed through her midship section) that the Ministry of Transport compensated the Company on the basis of a constructive total loss. From then on she was owned by the MoT, but managed by Royal Mail.

When her resurrection was completed – it can have been little less – she was placed in the emigrant trade to Australia. Those were boom years for migrant traffic; so much so that on 26 July 1949 *Asturias* left Southampton with a record passenger load for Australian ports – 1,340. It was a record week all round, for in the space of four days four ships left England with 3,646 migrants, all bound for the land of the kangaroo. How many tales, how many futures, figured in those long passenger lists? One man on that July 1949 voyage was a young priest named Howell Witt. 'The good ship *Asturias*,' he wrote, 'steamed into Port Phillip Bay in August 1949, crammed to the gunwales with migrants'. The young priest was about to gain a baptism of fire in his new homeland with an appointment as Anglican chaplain at Woomera, the new rocket range deep in Australia's searingly hot desert country. When you mull over the endless stories emanating from such voyages, migrant ships surely hold a most evocative niche in maritime history.

At that period *Asturias* was still painted all-over grey. The forward funnel had not been replaced and neither had the mainmast. On the basis that grey was not really appropriate for her duties taking families to a new life across the world, at the end of 1949 her upperworks were painted white and the funnel buff. The grey hull was retained until the following May, when it became black with pink boot-topping. Thus the Government-owned ship was once more in Royal Mail livery.

When more specialised migrant ship conversions and newbuildings supplemented the fleet sailing to Australia, vessels like *Asturias* were no longer needed. In the early spring of 1954 she appeared in another new colour scheme – white hull and blue band, white superstructure and yellow funnel, signifying a full-time troopship. Her last years were employed in this role, much of the time in Far Eastern waters.

She had previously been used several times to transport soldiers. One occasion was in September 1953, when she brought to Gibraltar the last British military contingent to leave Korea after the armistice there. It was a voyage of celebration as happy soldiers, many with wives and families on board, crossed Asian waters and made ceremonial visits to Hong Kong and Singapore. Among the festivities and general euphoria, one incident was less welcome. Early one morning the boatswain's mate was patrolling the accommodation when he spotted a lethal-looking snake. He had the presence of mind to capture and kill it and then took it to the bridge for inspection. A rumour began to spread that a soldier was responsible.

The Chief Officer (later Capt. C.N. Wightman) went in search of more reptiles. In cabin E148 he found a canvas bag (which moved when gingerly nudged with a well-booted foot) and a wicker basket whose contents Capt. Wightman described as 'a large number of small venomous reptiles'. He ordered the collection to be taken to the bridge, a move which didn't go down at all well with Capt. Mason, who ordered them to be thrown overboard. Capt. Wightman later recalled:

The corporal was very distressed, and asked if he could be allowed to keep the canvas bag and basket. I granted this request without thinking of the difficulties involved. These slimy things had to be transferred to another container for ceremonial dumping. A sack was produced. The ship's officers were placed at the ready. I was armed with a chipping hammer, the second officer with a broom handle, and the fourth officer with a marline spike he had produced at short notice from somewhere. The corporal transferred his prizes into our sack and I'm perfectly certain that he was near to emotional collapse as he consigned his sack of specimens to the deep.

The captain now returned from the starboard wing of the bridge, where he had stationed himself during the dumping procedure on the port side.

Asturias continued trooping, usually with less excitement, until 1957. At a little over thirty years of age she was allocated to Shipbreaking Industries Ltd and reached Faslane on 14 September.

Alcantara continued trooping until August 1947. She then spent a year and a month at Southampton being reconditioned by Harland & Wolff. Much of her finery was new, since the bulk of the original material had been destroyed. Her dummy forward funnel was not replaced but, unlike *Asturias*, the mainmast was. When she left Southampton under Capt. Bernard K. Berry on 8 October 1948 at the start of her first post-war commercial voyage she became the last Company ship to rejoin the trade routes. There was a permanent passenger on *Alcantara* during Capt. Berry's time in command – his cat Spiv, which sailed 110,000 miles with him after being born in the bottom drawer of Berry's wardrobe in *Almanzora*. It was a saga which began at Belfast in 1946 when Spiv's mother, Twerp, wandered on board *Asturias*. After Spiv had been born, Twerp took unauthorised shore leave at Lagos and didn't return.

As for *Alcantara*, for a time the Brazil and River Plate mail service occupied her fully, but during the 1950s she made cruises during the summer months. She did not give a lot of trouble, but by the time her turbine machinery neared twenty years of age there were occasional blemishes. During a northbound voyage in 1954 the starboard engine broke down and she completed the passage (some of it through heavy seas) on the port engine alone and a counteracting helm. She averaged a creditable 14.3 knots.

Asturias *(II) during the 1950s. The occasion was not recorded, but she was carrying military personnel before her time as an official troopship. It was therefore probably in 1953, bringing home troops from the Korean War.*

Alcantara *(II) pictured in the 1950s with the finest of her profiles. Her forward dummy funnel, taken off during Second World War, was not replaced, but (unlike* Asturias) *her mainmast was.*

Her last commercial voyage was during April and May 1958; generator trouble delayed her last arrival at Southampton by several days. When she was handed over at Southampton to Japanese shipbreakers (her sale price was about £250,000) she became the first British ship to be sold to Japan for some twenty years. She was renamed *Kaisho Maru* for the voyage to Osaka, where her furniture and other fine decorative items were put on sale after being exhibited at the Takashimaya department store.

Highland Brigade; *Highland Chieftain*; *Highland Monarch*; *Highland Patriot* and *Highland Princess*

In 1932, under the Scheme of Arrangement which determined the futures of companies affected by the RMSP crash, ships of the Nelson Steam Navigation Co. were taken over by the newly-formed Royal Mail Lines. They included the ships discussed here, all of which were completed between 1928 and 1930 except for *Highland Patriot* (laid down at Belfast during 1931 as a replacement for *Highland Hope*, which had been wrecked).

Nelson Line had been shipowners since the late 19th century, when James Nelson & Son, cattle salesmen, moved into Argentina and set up a meat factory at Zárate, close to where the Paraná and Uruguay rivers merge to form the Rio de la Plata. In 1890, with refrigerated ships starting to appear, Nelson decided to buy a ship to carry its own meat to a chain of 1,500 retail butchers' shops in England.

Despite vigorous competition from home and abroad (not least, of course, RMSP), Nelson developed from the little *Spindrift* (which they renamed *Highland Scot*) to a position of such strength late in the 1920s that it could order five passenger-cargo liners of 14,130 gross tons. It was no longer an independent company, though, for its share capital, and that of the managing company H. & W. Nelson, was bought by RMSP in 1913. Sir Owen Philipps became Chairman and there were changes in the directorship, but outwardly Nelson continued to operate independently.

Prior to the five ships dealt with here, Nelson was not remembered as a passenger carrier to the extent that RMSP was, even though some ships *did* carry several hundred and built a faithful following. Perhaps the reason for their lower profile was a greater concentration on freight and third class migrant traffic, but that didn't prevent the first class accommodation being popular. These new ships, though, were typically ambitious for a Kylsant company, nearly twice the size of any previous tonnage. In principle, if not in timing, it was an astute move, not just for Nelson but also for RMSP. With plenty of competition on this service, there were now two major options both for freight and passengers from which the profits would benefit RMSP.

In the past Nelson had built mostly at the Cammell Laird and Russell yards, but as part of RMSP it ordered its new ships from Harland & Wolff. Each could carry about

4,500 tons of meat. Compared with *Alcantara's* 204,230cu.ft, the 521,060cu.ft of meat and fruit spaces in each *Highland* ship played a much more significant role.

On the passenger side the ships, as built, could each carry 133 first class, 66 intermediate and about 300 third class, an arrangement radically altered later. Notwithstanding the disappointments of diesel machinery in *Asturias* and *Alcantara*, the *Highland* series received double-acting four-cycle diesel engines driving twin screws. Not only were they smaller vessels, a speed requirement of about 16 knots also played a part in the greater success they enjoyed with diesels, along with lessons Harland's would have learned from the *A*' ships.

Their design was intriguing. It took the split-bridge concept to the ultimate, for where Royal Mail's earlier ships had at least one accommodation deck linking the bridge and passenger housings, in the *Highland* family there was a complete severence down to the shelter deck – this was a design concept later adopted by RML with the last *A*' ships of 1959/60. With the *Highland* group this was especially noticeable on some where the bridge structure was built onto the after end of an extended forecastle deck. At the forward end of the passenger accommodation the forecastle deck re-appeared but was known as the bridge deck.

An island housing, aft of the main passenger spaces, held the intermediate passengers, and below them and further astern, in the upper part of the hull, were many of the third class. Other third class were offered dormitory accommodation in the shelter 'tweendeck around Nos 4 and 5 hatches, an area which, as far as I can make out, could also be used for general cargo – the only space in the ship for uninsulated cargoes. In later years the

Highland Monarch *on the stocks at Belfast, prior to launching in 1928.*

third class facilities were, under pressure from European Governments, somewhat improved. The intermediate class was plain but perfectly acceptable, the predominating feature being wood.

In fact, wood was the dominant feature throughout the ships – so much so that I once tapped the hull of a *Highland* ship and was relieved to hear a metallic ring! The use of wood was overwhelming – virtually the entire bridge housing was of wood, and the first class passenger rooms – particularly the saloon and lounge – resembled fine Tudor pubs, dominated by oak beams and panelling, and feature windows with leaded glass. In today's age of fire-consciousness, safety officers would have apoplexy at the sight of so much timber, but I suspect that most other people would merely sink into one of the deep armchairs and absorb the quiet splendour and restful dignity.

The first class accommodation succeeded splendidly in creating an atmosphere of relaxed intimacy. The ships were small enough to achieve this. By making the public rooms in each ship somewhat similar, Nelson Line prevented the creation of much individual character for each ship; but the successful formula ensured a devoted following from many travellers who preferred their slightly less formal service to the Royal Mail express run from Southampton.

A feature of note was the layout of the promenade deck. A covered promenade ran the width of the ship at the forward end of the accommodation, and was continued aft for a fair distance. Set within this were the recreation room (used for dances and the like) and lounge, separated only by a double stairway. A short passageway aft from there led to the writing room and then into the smokeroom; open promenade decks flanked both rooms. This, interestingly, seemed to inspire the layout which would be used a decade later for the new *Andes*.

The route undertaken by the *Highland* ships was London to Brazil and the River Plate. For the few years they were under Nelson Line ownership their pale grey hulls (with a slight mauvy tinge) and red, white and black funnels made a striking picture. Of the diesel liners built by Harland & Wolff in the 1920s and 1930s, the *Highland* liners were possibly the only ones which were aesthetically pleasing. For some reason (perhaps their extreme shortness) even that strange phenomenon the flat-topped raked funnel looked good.

In August 1932 all Nelson Line ships were transferred to Royal Mail Lines. While they fitted in well visually, in their new livery, there was disappointment that the distinctive Nelson colours were no longer seen. The last voyage under the old colours was made by *Highland Monarch*, leaving Tilbury on 20 August 1932. Confusingly, it was also the first under Royal Mail ownership.

Their early years with Royal Mail contained a number of incidents which were locally troublesome but little worse. They began with *Highland Brigade* on 19 August 1932, when she grounded on the silt bed at La Plata and suffered rudder damage – within a few days of its formation, Royal Mail Lines was faced with its first repair bill for a *Highland*. During the last days of 1932 there was a fire in No.1 hold in *Highland Patriot*. It was thought that a match or cigarette was the cause. While fighting the fire the boatswain was overcome by fumes, became unconscious and fell down the hatchway. Capt. Robert H. Robinson was affected by fumes as well. *Highland Monarch* collided with the 1,700-ton Lloyd Brasiliero steamer *Manaos* at Pernambuco, Brazil, in August 1935. There was some damage to *Highland Monarch's* port quarter, and the bows of *Manaos* were stove in – she had to return to port for emergency repairs.

Superb Tudor-style first class dining saloon in Highland Chieftain.

Highland Monarch *during her short period in the Nelson Line fleet, approximately 1930. She is pictured at Tilbury with the tug* Sun VIII.

One Sunday in the following summer, as dusk fell over the low Essex marshes, 200 passengers in *Highland Chieftain* watched as they slowly passed landmarks they had left astern thirty hours before. After sailing from Tilbury the ship had called at Boulogne, and then the starboard compressor broke. Details were sent by radio to London, triggering a plan to minimise the delay. By the time a flurry of messages had passed between ship and head office, *Highland Chieftain* was limping back up the Channel. *Highland Princess* was in dock at London, so her compressor was quickly removed and taken to Tilbury. When *Highland Chieftain* was taken in tow, the compressor was brought out to her, winched on board and work started on a twenty-four hour non-stop replacement programme. It was a slick operation which ensured that her passengers were on their way again in the shortest possible time.

On 29 July 1938 *Highland Princess* was in trouble, colliding with the German vessel *Mecklenburg* in the River Plate and, as a result, running aground. Damage was slight and *Mecklenburg* was held to blame.

Thus, within six years of transferring to RML, each of the *Highland* ships had suffered in one way or another. Thankfully that kind of situation didn't continue and they operated with few incidents in later years. During that early period there was one rather different event, though the story was a little vague. *Highland Brigade*, off Cap Gris Nez, picked up faint distress calls and after a search picked up a twenty-six-year old Londoner who was reportedly 'sailing to Australia in a 15ft craft but had become lost in a fog off the French coast'. Boat and occupant were taken on board and landed at Boulogne.

Highland Patriot, *photographed during the 1930s.*

Royal Mail was soon faced with a need to alter some of the accommodation. In September 1933 Spanish emigration authorities advised that the third class facilities in the *Highland* series did not comply with their regulations, and warned that they 'would not continue to tolerate this state of affairs indefinitely'. At about the same time the Polish Government, whose citizens were among numerous nationalities to make up third class passenger lists, refused to book passengers in the *Highland* ships 'so long as they are without cabins, general rooms etc'. With the long-standing arrangements Royal Mail had fostered, the *Highland* vessels must have been something of an embarrassment in that respect, especially as the changes were neither complex nor expensive. The work was carried out by the Company's own Tidal Basin Works at London.

The directors considered in 1932 whether or not to rename them. None of the discussion was recorded – simply the decision to leave the names as they were. Perhaps if they had been allocated to new routes it would have made sense to give them traditional Royal Mail names, but the Nelson heritage and goodwill, particularly in the River Plate, was clearly seen as advantageous for ships already so well known there.

War Service

For the first year or more of the Second World War, the *Highland* ships were left to pursue their normal trade – their capacious refrigerated holds were important for bringing food supplies to Britain. By November 1939, though, their schedules had been turned on their heads, for *Highland Chieftain* (Commodore T.J.C. Purcell-Buret DSC) left England on 13 November 1939, *Highland Princess* (Capt. F.R. Miles RD RNR) on 18 November and *Highland Brigade* (Capt. A. Watts) on 5 December, all bound for the River Plate. They were doubtless held back until the Company knew if they were to be requisitioned.

The three ships roughly maintained their time differences throughout the round voyage, closing the gap a little so that all reached England within two weeks or so. And all had their holds filled to capacity, so there was around a million and a half cubic feet of much-needed cargo suddenly on Britain's doorstep. Their outward passenger numbers were described as 'fair to good'. Northbound, one carried eight, another four and the last six.

By the time all five ships had completed at least one wartime voyage, and moved further into the restrictive conditions caused by the war, there were frustrating little hurdles to overcome. *Highland Monarch* departed early in January 1940 and had to make the outward voyage in ballast. With only thirty-seven passengers (though twenty-three were first class), there wasn't a profit to be made; a full cargo for the return helped to balance that. *Highland Patriot*, built to replace the lost *Highland Hope*, was inward bound from the River Plate in May 1940 when she stranded near the Knock John Buoy in the Thames while hugging the coast for safety. Early attempts to free her failed; not until a quantity of fuel oil had been off-loaded into lighters, and a large deck cargo of tomatoes discharged, were tugs able to pull her free after two days. RAF fighters kept a vigil overhead to protect the helpless liner from German bombers.

Capt. Robinson was found not to be at fault as the Company attached blame to the pilot. There were very few occasions when Royal Mail had cause to grumble at the fine service given by the Thames river and dock pilots, in conjunction with tug skippers and crews. Many times I watched them guide the *Highland* vessels and, later, the even larger *'A'* ships of 1959/60 through the Royal Docks, around tight corners and through the narrow Connaught Road cutting with seemingly only the proverbial thickness of a piece of paper to spare. Hundreds of times over the years those great liners safely negotiated the twists and bends of the river channel and the concrete-edged obstacle course through the Royals.

During the early days of the war Capt. Robinson was zig-zagging for hours on end to escape a German U-boat, finally out-manoeuvring it and escaping through superior speed. Then in January 1940 a submarine attacked *Highland Patriot* in the South Atlantic – five torpedoes were fired and all missed; the *Patriot* opened fire with her inadequate armament, reportedly hitting the U-boat and driving it off.

Capt. Robinson's eventful time in the ship ended in the autumn of 1940. She was in the Atlantic, homeward bound from South America with a larger than usual number of passengers for the time (about forty), some of them volunteers on their way to England to enlist. In the early hours of 1 October a torpedo hit her. An engineer and three crew members were killed instantly and several others were injured. As soon as the torpedo struck, all lights went out; in fact all power in the ship was lost. The fire which followed the explosion – fuelled by the ship's plethora of wood – spread rapidly and created sufficient light for everyone to abandon ship, which was achieved in just seven minutes. Twenty minutes after the torpedo struck, a second was despatched, narrowly missing some of the boats on its way to *Highland Patriot*.

She blazed fiercely for several hours before sinking. HMS *Wellington*, seeing heavy smoke on the horizon, set course for her and picked up the 169 survivors from a line of boats moving in strict convoy away from the liner. The senior second enginer, J.B. Twist, had rescued two men from the engineroom, for which he was awarded the OBE. *Highland Patriot* was the only one of her class to be sunk during the war, and was the largest Royal Mail ship to be lost (though *Asturias* was recorded as a Constructive Total Loss). During

Highland Patriot *on fire after being torpedoed in 1940.*

the same year came the evacuation of Dunkirk. As *Highland Princess* was in London at the time, two of her lifeboats joined the awesome flotilla which sailed relentlessly to and fro across the Channel.

Among wartime actions later immortalised on the big screen was the Battle of the River Plate, when British warships cornered the pocket battleship *Graf Spee* at Montevideo. Rather than relinquish his ship to the British, Capt. Langsdorff took her to the river mouth and blew her up. Her crew and many of the prisoners she held were picked up and taken to Buenos Aires, where they were landed at a berth adjacent to *Highland Chieftain*, in which many of the captains and officers from captured ships made the voyage home.

Highland Monarch, it was learned later, may unwittingly have helped in the destruction of *Graf Spee*. One of the captured skippers told of a copy of the *Buenos Aires Herald* found in the engineers quarters of *Graf Spee*. Langsdorff reputedly read it, saw the schedule of shipping departures from Buenos Aires and among the names spotted *Highland Monarch*. His ambition to sink the liner was supposed to have influenced his decision to head for the River Plate, where the British South Atlantic Force laid its successful trap. For some years the upperworks of the scuttled *Graf Spee* jutted from the waters, an imposing reminder of the encounter for passing shipping. Ironically, in later years *Highland Chieftain* occupied a similar position, but more of that later.

While the Battle of Britain raged, the *Highland* ships were still trading but switched their terminal port to Liverpool. If the Mersey was regarded as safer, it didn't provide immunity from attack. September 1940 found *Highland Princess* in Canada Dock with a hole in her side from debris blasted from the wharf after a bomb exploded. A month later *Highland Chieftain* was more seriously damaged when a bomb made a direct hit. *Eight Bells* carried a telling description of the bomb's progress through the ship: 'It struck her on the starboard side, for'rd of the boat deck, penetrated through the lounge, went clean through a bed in a stateroom, through the service room adjoining the saloon, and exploded in the wine and spirit room on the lower deck'. Casualties were light but the ship suffered a major fire which took several hours to extinguish. Repairs required a lengthy period in drydock.

During that autumn and winter the *Highland* ships were taken in hand by the Admiralty for conversion to troop transports. There was a pressing need for passenger ships to carry troops, but so was there a need to bring foodstuffs to Britain. Presumably the priorities changed at this point, and their withdrawal may have had a bearing on Royal Mail's ability to have four large meat carriers built during the war – *Darro* and *Deseado* in 1942 and *Drina* and *Durango* in 1944.

As was usual so early in the war, the troop capacities initially given to the *Highland* ships were lower than in later stages. At first each could carry 1,200 people, mostly in converted hold space with little light or ventilation. For a time they sailed to Suez and South Africa. *Highland Chieftain*, in trouble again, spent the second half of 1941 at Durban undergoing repairs after colliding with Shaw Savill's *Dominion Monarch*. Then the *Highland* vessels carried Americans from the USA to North Africa. In 1943 they followed the Allied progress through Mediterranean Europe.

During 1944 *Highland Princess* moved to a new arena, one which quickly became a regular stamping ground for these ships – the Far East and Australasia. From Fremantle she returned by the Cape route, calling on the way at Mahé in the Seychelles, where meat was unloaded and was much appreciated as the town's freezing plant had broken down. Capt. J.W. Carr wrote of Mahé: 'The ship approached from the north through anything but an easy channel and anchored in a sort of pool off Mahé with not too much room for the *Highland Princess* to roam around'.

By the summer of 1945 attention was turning to South East Asia, and in September *Highland Brigade*, with troops from Burma, and *Highland Chieftain*, from India, were at Singapore for the re-occupation of Malaya; the old *Almanzora* took part in the same operation. Later in the month *Highland Monarch* reached Singapore, too, from Bombay, Madras and Rangoon, and then sailed to Hong Kong where prisoners-of-war were embarked. More joined at Singapore and Colombo for the voyage home to England.

This happier duty was now the main task of the *Highland* ships. After taking Indian PoWs home from Singapore, *Highland Brigade* returned to Singapore and embarked Australian released prisoners for Fremantle, Melbourne and Sydney. She then made a round of the Pacific islands, picking up Indians at New Britain, Rabaul and other island ports and returning them to Bombay. By the New Year she had visited Borneo and Bangkok, and halfway through January was near Singapore again when a mine exploded beneath her engineroom.

The damage was severe, especially serious as rising seas pummelled the ship. Her troops were transferred to other vessels and a tug eventually brought her to port. After more than two months in drydock she sailed across the Java Sea to Sourabaya, Indonesia's second-largest port. Later she embarked nearly 1,500 African troops for Lagos – that was her last voyage as a military transport.

After the surrender in Malaya *Highland Chieftain* set off with many Australians on board, through the Indonesian islands to Timor and on to Darwin on Australia's northern coast. Many of the servicemen returning to Australia were injured, some with lost limbs, and at Darwin a volunteer medical force came on board for the voyage down the east coast, inside the Great Barrier Reef, to Brisbane and Sydney. A right royal welcome greeted *Highland Chieftain* as she steamed into Sydney harbour.

Like *Highland Brigade* she then sailed out into the Pacific and took released Indians off the islands. On her way to Bombay she passed through the Malacca Straits, which were fouled by floating logs and trees. One snagged a propeller and a blade was lost – the remainder of the voyage, made at reduced speed, was uncomfortable.

Highland Princess ended the war by repatriating troops nearer home. In February 1945 a full ship of Russian troops was taken to Odessa in the Black Sea. During the voyage Capt. Carr had one nasty moment because, due to bad weather, he missed a briefing session at Malta. He was merely advised, without the reason behind it, that by the Dardanelles he should pass close to a certain buoy. He did so.

'Suddenly, in the moonlight,' he recorded later, 'I saw some black objects like drums on the starboard bow. They formed the end of the boom defence. I managed to get through the gates with the drums playing a tattoo on the port bow.' He learned later (as he should have learned at Malta) that the space was 120ft wide, allowing barely 25ft on each side. Later she took released troops to Middle East ports.

During 1946 the last *Highland* was returned to RML, and after necessarily extensive refits they were placed again on the London-River Plate service.

Final Years

It was probably at this juncture that their intermediate accommodation was abolished and the passenger complement of each ship reduced from 499 to 443, now comprising 105 first class and 338 third. Parts of the main accommodation housing now became third class public rooms.

The ships were rarely in the public eye after the war as they provided a steady second-string service in support of the Southampton-based mail steamers. Their large capacities for meat cargoes, added to the four 'D' ships of around 9,800 tons, built during the war, provided financially successful voyages as England clamoured for foodstuffs during those years of austerity. It seemed that the *Highland* ships would plod on for ever, so much a fixture were they; there was nearly always one to be seen discharging meat at London's Z shed, Royal Victoria Dock, or loading outward cargo at No.3 shed King George V Dock – and because of their outward similarity, their 'permanent fixture' status seemed to be enhanced. They were simply 'the *Highlands*'.

Only one serious mishap occurred during those later years, when *Highland Brigade* suffered major damage to her port engine at Buenos Aires in March 1956. Facilities in the Argentine were not adequate for repairs, so the ship was brought home on the starboard engine alone. Because of the difficulty in navigating, she ran aground by the entrance to the River Plate and was stuck for four days; but the river bed here is soft and there was no serious damage.

A classic picture of Highland Brigade, *passing a Thames barge on her approach to Tilbury Landing Stage.*

During 1955 *Highland Monarch* witnessed a momentous event at Buenos Aires. After almost ten years of turbulent and repressive power, which had impacted heavily on shipping firms like Royal Mail (a matter looked at in Volume 1), President Perón was ousted in a military coup. The sudden and violent revolt caught the ship's company by surprise, and *Highland Monarch* slipped out of Buenos Aires at dawn, surrounded by units of the Argentine Navy. A British cruiser, guns trained on the Argentine ships, escorted the *Monarch* and other British ships from the port for a dash across the Rio de la Plata to Montevideo.

In the late 1950s several factors led to a decision to sell the *Highland* ships. While their first class rooms were appealing with their period splendour and comfort, the accommodation and facilities were outdated and lacked some of the conveniences expected by travellers at that time. The third class left even more to be desired, despite the post-war upgrade, and while they were not expected to be express ships, their 15 knots was now too slow. Finally, the costs of maintenance and overhauls for four veteran liners were escalating alarmingly.

First to go was *Highland Chieftain*; the decision to sell her was announced in the autumn of 1958 and her last voyage for Royal Mail ended on 1 January 1959, a year before the first of the replacement ships entered service. The cause of such an early withdrawal was a recession in trade which did not warrant all of the *Highland* class being retained. She was sold to the Calpe Shipping Co. of Gibraltar, which turned her into an accommodation and store ship for the whaling trade, based at South Georgia and renamed *Calpean Star*. During the off-season she would carry whale products back to Europe. Her new career, however, was short. In March 1960, having sustained rudder damage in Antarctic waters, she was taken to Montevideo for repairs. Presumably the work couldn't be carried out, for on 1 June she was taken in tow by the tug *Atlantic*, en route for the UK. When she had reached Montevideo's entrance channel there was reportedly 'an explosion', or a failure in a seawater valve, and the engineroom rapidly flooded.

All power was lost and the vessel was abandoned by her crew and fifty-six 'passengers'. None of the latter apparently were humans – they included seals and penguins. *Calpean Star* settled with the weather deck just awash, gradually sinking deeper and more or less on an even keel. So gradual was this that by 1968 the topmost part of her superstructure, funnels and masts were still visible. Despite reports that she would be removed and broken up, she remained submerged, her entry in Lloyd's Register closing in September 1962.

Highland Brigade and *Highland Princess* were sold during 1959 to Greek shipowner John S. Latsis. They were reportedly expected to operate to Australia, where there was still strong migrant traffic (not least with another Greek owner, Chandris Line, which began a 'no frills' service with *Patris*, ex-*Bloemfontein Castle*). The Latsis service, however, did not eventuate. *Highland Brigade*, handed over to Latsis in London and renamed *Henrietta*, departed on 25 September 1959. After several months at Piraeus undergoing conversion, she emerged during 1960 looking outwardly similar except that her two squat funnels had been replaced by a single streamlined one. Soon she was renamed again, becoming *Marianna*. Part of her career with Latsis was spent in the Mediterranean; they were years dogged by collisions and breakdowns. With Piraeus as her home port, she was seen at Eleusis and Skaramanga Bay a little to the north and was a frequent visitor to Tripoli in Libya. For a time she carried pilgrims, on their way to Mecca, to Jeddah in the Red Sea.

A collision in October 1961 put her out of commission until the following year; another in July 1963 saw her laid up at Kynossoura into 1964. I am uncertain if she traded again or remained idle for the whole of that year. During 1965 Latsis sold her to Formosan (Taiwanese) shipbreakers and she reached Kaohsiung on 29 June 1965.

The unmistakeable profile of a Highland *ship sunk in shallow water off Montevideo. She was* Calpean Star, *formerly* Highland Chieftain.

A group of third class passengers on Highland Princess, *probably in the 1950s.*

Highland Princess went to Latsis at the very end of 1959, leaving London for Piraeus, as *Marianna*, while the new *Amazon* was in the docks awaiting her maiden voyage. She received a similar conversion to *Highland Brigade* (except that her original funnels were retained) and later in 1960 she, too, was reportedly carrying pilgrims from Tripoli to Jeddah. If that was so it was only for a short time, for in the autumn of 1960 she was sold to Czechoslovak Ocean Shipping of Prague.

Landlocked Czechoslovakia was at that time steadily building a merchant marine. From about 40,000 tons dwt in 1959, the national tonnage had risen to 112,000 by 1961, when its merchant navy was just ten years old. Its genesis in 1951 was largely due to pressure from the Soviet Union, which required Czechoslovakia to supply arms from its Skoda works to mainland China, for use in Korea. A freight service was established between Polish ports (where the cargoes were loaded) and China. By the time the Korean War had ended, a substantial commercial trade had been established as a by-product of the arms shipments. There was little surprise, then, to find this former *Highland* ship – now named *Slapy* – operating in Chinese waters. For more than a year she operated between Hong Kong and Whampoa, near Canton on the Chinese mainland. Her service appears to have been solely in Far East waters at this time, and her ownership was transferred late in 1961 to the Republic of China; her name changed to *Guang Hua*.

After operating between Hong Kong and Whampoa for some time, she made more distant voyages. In May 1967 she was repatriating Indonesian Chinese to their homeland. The last report I had of her was at Singapore in May 1971, en route from Dar-es-Salaam to Whampoa – but that was well short of the end of her life. By 1980 her owners were listed as China Ocean Shipping Co. and she finally left the Register in 1987, at almost sixty years of age.

When *Highland Monarch* reached London in April 1960 there was no exotic future awaiting her. I watched at Tilbury as she passed inward bound for the last time. Later I walked around her empty public rooms, echoing with thirty years of history, while London's dockers took out her last cargo of Argentine beef. If her old-world grandeur was faded and a little neglected, she managed still to exude the same old Tudor charm.

It came as a bit of a shock to realise, when she had been delivered to the British Iron & Steel Corporation on the Clyde in April, for breaking up, that the familiar, peculiarly squarish *Highland* ships, which I had known since my childhood (and which people much older than me had known since *their* childhood) would be seen no more in the Thames.

Andes (II)

On 5 August 1932 the directors of the newly-formed Royal Mail Lines, Ltd had their first board meeting. Among the long list of agenda items was 'the question of the construction of a new passenger vessel for the South American trade'. What developed from that seed was described in the entry for *Asturias* and *Alcantara* – the re-engining of those ships as turbine steamers as a cheaper option than building a new ship. The prospect of a new vessel, though, remained in the background.

By February 1935 it was felt that within three or four years *Atlantis* would need to be replaced with a newer cruising vessel. RML contemplated the construction of a brand-new full-time cruise liner to replace her, but when the subject was next raised, in September 1936, they were by then looking at a ship for the South America service which would also be suitable for cruising – this idea of a combination ship had succeeded with *Asturias*.

Tenders were invited that November, from Harland & Wolff, Swan Hunter & Wigham Richardson, Hawthorn Leslie, Cammell Laird and John Brown. With a 21-knot service speed, the ship was to be for the South America mail service, but her design should 'permit of her being utilised for cruising purposes when found necessary'. Harland & Wolff's tender was the lowest, but at £1,365,356 was still 'very much in excess of anticipations'. Another £200,000 would be needed for various extras. The Company sought a loan guarantee of £750,000 from the Government of Northern Ireland through the Midland Bank, repayable at 2% over ten years – a saving of about £40,000. In the event, they achieved only a saving of about £10,000, while Frederick Rebbeck, Chairman of Harland & Wolff, reduced his price to £1,360,000.

The manoeuvring of such small amounts in an outlay of more than a million and a third pounds suggested that Royal Mail was at the extreme edge of its financial resources, but it was patently clear that a new, large and fast ship had to be built if Royal Mail was to remain a serious competitor. That point was driven home when Cie Sud-Atlantique announced its intention of building the 30,000-ton *Pasteur*, due for completion at the same time as *Andes*.

On 5 March 1937 the Company announced that its new ship would be named *Andes*. Heaton Tabb & Co. and Hampton & Sons were invited to quote for the outfitting and decoration – both were successful, the work being divided equally.

Construction

The keel of 'Ship 1005', a turbine steamer of about 26,000 tons, was laid on 17 June 1937. She was to carry 607 passengers in first and second classes. Originally the passenger arrangements were for first and third but this was changed during the early stages of construction. Cargo facilities followed the established pattern of being mostly refrigerated spaces for meat and fruit. Of her five holds, only No.1 was not insulated.

Improvements to passenger facilities were periodically proposed. In the autumn of 1937, for instance, it was decided to provide air-conditioning in the first class dining saloon and foyer, at a cost of £15,196 for Thermotank's installation and £6,150 for J. & E. Hall's refrigerating plant. Having opted for an 'intermediate tourist class' (second) rather than third class, Managing Director P.G. Mylne Mitchell stressed in December 1937 the need for accommodation improvements 'to make this somewhat better than that of the second class in *Alcantara* and *Asturias* to enable the Company to meet foreign competition'. Those improvements had a secondary purpose, for second class accommodation would be charged at the minimum first class rate when cruising, allowing the ship to be one-class for those voyages.

As construction continued, the political situation in Europe deteriorated. In September 1938 the directors invited the Duchess of Kent to launch *Andes* in the following March. She accepted, but on 7 March 1939 – the day of the launching – it was not the Duchess who named *Andes*. A month before the big day, it was learnt that the Duke and Duchess had postponed their visit on the advice of the Governor of Northern Ireland. There was discontent around Belfast with the vast number of unemployed. The Royal Ulster Constabulary and 'B' Specials were on nightly patrols. In short, the spring of 1939 was not the best time for a Royal visit.

The search for a new sponsor resulted in Viscountess Craigavon, wife of the Northern Ireland Prime Minister, performing the ceremony. It was a day of biting wind and torrential rain, but large crowds gathered to watch the christening at 11.30 and there were cheers as the liner glided into the water without a hitch.

After the launch, Lord Essendon (RML Chairman) spoke of the shipowner's difficulties in ordering new tonnage at that time. 'On the one hand,' he said, 'the re-armament programme is largely responsible for the advanced building costs, and on the other hand world conditions, which caused the re-armament programme, are the very things that are largely responsible for the depression in trade. The result is that at today's prices it is inevitable that any ships constructed will involve loss in operation, unless we have a revival of trade.' He believed more shipowners would order new tonnage if the price difference caused by the re-armament programme could be 'adjusted' by the Government.

He ended with these words: 'In a few months time your work will be finished, and that of the owners will begin. Our work will last longer than yours – probably twenty years – during which time the *Andes* will no doubt experience the many vicissitudes to which the industry is always subjected over a period of nearly a quarter of a century. But of one thing I am quite sure, and that is that we shall never have reason to regret having built this ship with the famous and renowned firm of Harland & Wolff'.

Launching of Andes *(II) at Belfast on 7 March 1939.*

The Ship

Andes was built under Lloyd's and Board of Trade survey. Her design included four complete decks (A, B, C and D), lower and orlop decks forward and aft of machinery spaces, a forecastle deck, lower promenade deck (E), upper promenade deck (F), boat deck (G), sports deck and sun deck.

Most passenger cabins were on B, C and D decks, with the remainder on A and E. The hull was divided into twelve compartments by watertight bulkheads extending to B deck, with the forepeak bulkhead reaching C deck. A double-bottom was designed to hold fresh water, water ballast and oil fuel; the forepeak tank would contain fresh water, and the aft peak tank oil fuel or water ballast. Further deep fresh water tanks were provided in No.1 hold, and between and at the sides of the shaft tunnels. Right across the vessel between the forward end of the machinery space and No.3 hold were still more deep fuel tanks.

There were three holds forward and two aft of the machinery space, with corresponding cargo 'tweendecks to the underside of A deck. No.1 orlop and lower 'tweendeck, No.3 lower deck and No.5 tunnel decks would contain ordinary cargo, and the remaining spaces were insulated. The hatches of Nos 1, 4 and 5 holds were served by electric cranes;

tubular steel derricks (between 3 and 7 tons) served holds 2 and 3. J. & E. Hall provided the refrigerating machinery, a mixture of air cooling machines and brine grids.

Electro-hydraulic steering gear controlled by a telemotor on the bridge operated the streamlined semi-balanced rudder. With gear of Hastie's design, the rudder could move from hard-over to hard-over in less than twenty seconds with the vessel at full speed. Single-reduction geared turbines, built by Harland & Wolff to Parsons' design, were chosen for the main engines. They drove twin screws. Boilers, with a working pressure of 430psi, provided a high degree of superheat. Each set of turbines allowed for three stages of steam expansion for 'ahead' propulsion and two stages for 'astern' operation. Individual pinions, with double helical gearing, linked the turbines to the main gear wheel. The condensers were two-flow Weir regenerative units, the condensate being delivered to the boilers at a temperature of 350° Fahrenheit. Four horizontal turbine-driven feed pumps were installed.

Each boiler had seven oil fuel burners and worked on forced and induced draught. Above the superheaters, which formed an integral part of the system, were Howden-Ljungström regenerative air pre-heaters through which products of combustion were drawn by induced-draught fans. The combustion air reached the furnaces at a very high temperature after forced-draught fans had delivered it through the air heaters and the air casings around the boilers.

The funnel being lifted on to Andes *(II) at the fitting out basin, 30 May 1939.*

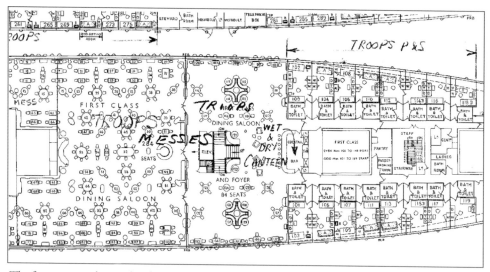

The first accommodation plan for Andes (II) *was produced in March 1939, six months before she was completed. It was never used, for the ship immediately entered war service and passenger arrangements changed when she eventually entered commercial service. A copy of that plan which has survived was used by the military authorities to identify accommodation arrangements for her role as a troopship. This is a small portion of that plan, showing the after portion of B deck, including the first class restaurant.*

All-electric installations included the laundry and engineer's workshop. Some 450 electric heaters, all cooking equipment, and nearly two dozen electrically-heated towel rails and drying-room heaters were installed. The gymnasium had electrically-driven horseriding, camel and vibrating massage machines. Connections were provided for a variety of purposes, among them a Suez Canal searchlight, vacuum cleaning plant and cinema equipment. Add to all those the usual passenger facilities like electric light, the Tannoy system and telephones, and you realise how extensive and complex was the electrical layout.

Fuel capacity was to be 'not less than 4,950 tons'; this high figure, required for the long return trips across the South Atlantic, stood the ship in good stead during her trooping duties. Her freshwater tanks held nearly 2,500 tons; in 1960 that was increased to 3,360.

The main construction material was high-quality steel made by the open-hearth process. High-elastic steel was used for the plating of D deck and for the superstructure above that level, reducing top weight while maintaining maximum stiffness. Rails and stanchions were given unvarnished teak tops. Wood decks and ladders were also of teak, and hatch covers and awning ridges were pitch and Oregon pine.

There were fourteen lifeboats – ten 30ft Fleming craft, two 24ft Flemings and two 30ft motor vessels capable of eight knots fully loaded. They were stowed in Taylor's gravity davits and had a total seating capacity of 1,174. The two steel masts were raked $1\frac{3}{4}$ inches to a foot, the foremast stepped on C deck and the mainmast on D. *Andes* had the usual navigational and other aids – Kelvite and Husun compasses, Brown's automatic helmsman, Stone's bulkhead door operation, gyro repeater, direction finder, smoke detector, Sal-log and so on. Radar was added during the war.

The first class galley had two double electric ranges containing fourteen ovens. There were fish fryers, charcoal grills, waffle irons, soup machines and egg boilers. The stillroom, vegetable preparation room, fish room, fruit room, butcher's shop, cold larder, bakery, oven room, pastry shop, cold pantry and dairy room were among the satellites around the main cooking area. Other facilities included laundries, printer's shop, lamp room, paint room, acid room, magazine, boatswain's store, carpenter's shop, plumber's shop, tank rooms, fan rooms, deck games lockers, drying rooms, linen rooms, blanket stores, barber's and shopman's stores, flour room, wine room, tobacco room, specie, mails, parcels and baggage rooms, garages, sewage plant, dispensing rooms and operating theatres, isolation and general hospitals, prison and padded mental room. Such features were needed to make *Andes* effectively a self-sufficient floating township.

Her First World – Wartime

Harland & Wolff worked full-tilt to finish *Andes* in time for a maiden voyage due to commence on 26 September 1939 – one hundred years to the day after RMSP's formation. As she neared completion, the situation in Europe worsened. Fitting-out continued and was almost completed late in August.

The Company prepared a brochure, and arranged special luncheons at Southampton for 21 and 22 September. Invitations and programmes were printed. The launching had been frustrated by troubles in Northern Ireland; now it looked as though her next special day was also to be spoilt. First came the announcement that her deep-sea trials, scheduled for 29-31 August, were postponed. When war was declared, the Senior Naval Officer at Belfast ordered them to be cancelled altogether.

Royal Mail agreed to accept the ship without trials, and Harland & Wolff handed her over at midnight on 24 September. Her crew was on board, among them barman Harold Isaacs, who still worked in *Andes* when she returned for her final refit almost thirty years later. On the latter occasion he pointed out of the large Warwick Room windows, towards grassy wasteland, and recalled that when he and *Andes* first saw that part of Ulster, the ground had swarmed with troops on training manoeuvres – a sight which left little doubt that, wherever her maiden voyage might take her, it was most unlikely to be South America.

She slipped quietly out of Belfast Lough on the morning of 26 September – the day she should have left Southampton in a blaze of glory. A considerable time passed before the authorities changed her Royal Mail livery to battleship-grey. As yet, in fact, she had not been requisitioned – that formality took place on 21 November at Holy Loch, where she had been lying-up since leaving Belfast. She was taken over as a troop transport, and on 26 November reached Liverpool where some of her finery was taken off – she made three voyages before most of the fittings and panelling were removed. What remained was covered with plywood; blast screens were erected, and there were even bricklayers at work.

At 9.15 a.m. on 9 December 1939 *Andes* left Liverpool for Halifax, NS, under the command of Capt. R.G. Clayton DSC, RD, RNR. Untried and untested (much the same situation as RMS *Queen Elizabeth*), the vessel sailed into a wintry North Atlantic. Capt. Clayton reported that in the circumstances, which included some bad weather, the average speed of 15.2 knots was fully up to expectations. Two fresh gales were encountered, through which *Andes* proved completely seaworthy, shipping little water, maintaining her speed and showing only a minimum of motion in high seas. The machinery worked without a hitch. The Canadian Seaforth Highlanders, who occupied the ship on her return from Halifax, were very happy with her; they were the first of many passengers to say so.

For the anxious directors in Royal Mail House, Capt. Clayton's report was particularly welcome, and it did not go unnoticed that *Andes* had just brought to Britain the first Commonwealth troops of the war. During the voyage, which was largely unescorted, her total armament comprised a single ancient Hotchkiss cone-feeding gun on the monkey island. This splendid-looking veteran of about 1898 was deprived of much of its dubious qualities against modern naval gunnery by a distinct shortage of ammunition.

She was ideal for trooping – fast, new and spacious. With enormous fuel and fresh water capacities she could travel many thousands of miles without a stopover. For long voyages, largely made alone, her crazy original armament had to be radically improved. Harold Isaacs recalled years later the tally of her final gun-power, as far as he remembered it: four twin-Bofors, fourteen Oerlikons, depth charges, two twelve-pounder guns and one each of 4.5in and 6in. In addition she carried a parachute and cable, a somewhat hopeful method of bringing down aircraft. Notwithstanding this collection, she never fired a shot in anger.

Her maiden voyage was an ideal duration for a liner denied her normal proving trials. Thirty days after returning to the Clyde, she left Gourock for a much longer journey – 32,859 miles, calling at Marseilles, Port Said, Colombo, Singapore, Hong Kong, Lyttelton, Fremantle, Capetown, Sierra Leone and back to Britain. She was now under the command of Commodore Purcell-Buret, her original captain-designate. At about the time *Andes* ended her career, the former Commodore – then ninety-one years old – explained to me why he missed the maiden voyage:

> *Nothing else being available, I went away in the* Highland Chieftain *and landed up in the Battle of the River Plate, bringing home the released prisoners and writing out their accounts of the battle, which are now in the National Maritime Museum at Greenwich. I arrived home just in time to take command of the* Andes *for her second voyage. We made a wonderful voyage to China and New Zealand…*

In earlier years, reminiscing for *Eight Bells*, he had written that *Andes* caused a great deal of excitement and curiosity wherever she went. 'On two occasions,' he added, 'I was asked quite seriously if this was a captured German vessel. Evidently it is unusual for an English vessel to have such a fine outward appearance.'

She returned from Australia in the mightiest of convoys – sailing with her were *Queen Mary*, *Empress of Britain*, *Mauretania*, *Aquitania*, *Empress of Canada* and *Empress of Japan*. HMS *Hood* was the escort leader from 300 miles west of Finisterre. 'I do not think there has ever been such a convoy before,' wrote Commodore Purcell-Buret. 'It is true that there were much larger ships, and some faster, than ourselves, but we were easily the best troopship; none of the others had anything like our range of action, not only in fuel, but in that which is almost as important – fresh water'.

The nearest that *Andes* came to an action was in September 1940 when bombing occurred at Suez while she lay at anchor. During that voyage she chose to show her paces, on several occasions exceeding her designed 21 knots for lengthy periods. On the 6,907-mile run home from Capetown she averaged $20\frac{1}{2}$ knots and reached 24 knots at times. Including crew, *Andes* carried about 3,400 people on the outward leg of that voyage. The numbers were already 500 above the official limit; a further 100 joined at Capetown and many slept on deck. Troopship conditions worsened as time passed. In 1941 the accommodation was re-arranged to provide for greater numbers; afterwards she often carried over 4,000 passengers. Those of us who knew her only in happier times find it difficult to visualise the Princess Lounge packed with four tiers of bunks.

Of the voyage through the Red Sea, the Commodore wrote: 'The work of the kitchen staff was very hard and I do not know how they endured it. The heat in the Red Sea during August is fearful, and during the blackout, when everything is closed on board, is unendurable. One of the ships with a less up-to-date system of ventilation than ourselves had several deaths, it is alleged due to the heat'.

In a 1941 springtime convoy, carrying around 80,000 men, one of *Andes'* running-mates was *Pasteur*, the French liner (but now flying the British flag and managed by Cunard-White Star) intended as a competitor to Royal Mail in the South America trade. At this period *Andes'* voyages were generally lengthy, frequently round Africa, doubling back across the Atlantic, via the West Indies, to Canada and back to Britain. She carried out her duties as smoothly as wartime conditions allowed. There was a conspicuous lack of complaints about ship or service; people were writing to Royal Mail years later about the troublefree voyages they made in her. This was the period when her quite unique character began to take shape.

Between 8 December 1941 and 11 May 1942 she sailed about 38,000 miles around the world – her first circumnavigation – showing off her massive fuel capacity in the process. Nearly 14,500 men were carried and two million meals served. On her way home *Andes* was drydocked in America, at Boston. Her commander then was Commodore Ernest Bridges, who was knighted shortly after his retirement in June 1943. Her predominance of long voyages was broken in 1943 by several months at the height of the North Africa campaign operating a shuttle service between New York, Halifax and Casablanca, bringing nearly 22,000 troops to Morocco.

After she had been pounding her way at high speeds through the ocean for a few years, the propeller shaft brackets began vibrating badly. Harland & Wolff designed and fitted two enormous struts as supports between hull and bracket. Fitted in drydock at Liverpool, the struts remained with her for the rest of her life. After a refit during the late summer and autumn of 1943, she returned to service at the end of October.

Cargo spaces were often used for their designed purpose. Cotton came from Suez, hundreds of tons of bacon from Canada, frozen beef and pork from New York. Wine was shipped from South Africa to Canada; nearly 50,000 cases of oranges and many tons of copper came from South Africa to England. Sometimes the cargoes were, from a monetary point of view, more valuable. Fine gold bars worth $7,750,000 accompanied a full complement of troops from New York in the winter of 1944.

A month or two later the recently-acquired radar proved its worth by locating ice in the liner's path while she was crossing the North Atlantic. Wintry conditions were no stranger to *Andes*, designed though she was for warmer climes. On one occasion at Halifax her mooring ropes had to be hacked from the bollards to which ice had bonded them. She suffered heavy weather damage *en route* to New York early in 1944. Repairs to the forecastle head, forward deck fittings, lifeboats, forward deck wash-house and toilet and the forecastle accommodation amounted to about $46,500.

On Voyage 29 she was four days out from Capetown, on her way to Liverpool, when news came of the cease-fire in Europe. Dressed overall with the flags of the United Nations, she fired a twenty-one gun salute. Peace in the Pacific that August she celebrated mid-way between Fremantle and Karachi with another twenty-one gun salute and a fireworks display. Ironically, it took the end of the war to allow her to try out at least a little of her armament. Between the VE and VJ festivities she was chosen to carry the Norwegian Prime Minister and most of his Cabinet from England to Oslo. Their return triggered a tumultuous welcome as she steamed slowly up the Oslofjord, carefully making her way to the landing stage between an armada of small boats.

The voyage that followed was a tremendous one for *Andes*. She broke the record for a circumnavigation of the world by covering 26,012 miles in 72 days, 8 hours, 55 minutes. Her time beat *Mauretania's* record by more than nine days. At the end of the voyage, on 10 September 1945, she steamed proudly into Southampton – the first time her Hampshire home port had seen her. At the end of the voyage it was reported that during hostilities she had steamed about 520,000 nautical miles and carried 350,000 troops.

Not yet satisfied with marathon voyages, she made another record passage on her next voyage, from Southampton to Melbourne via Suez. Her time of 23 days, 7 hours, 47 minutes again beat a record held by *Mauretania*, this time by five days. On board were 2,500 Air Force officers, 1,500 of them New Zealanders and the remainder Australians. From all accounts, the departure was memorable with a great deal of cheering and official send-offs for the ship and her passengers. Among those on board was Wg Cdr D.R. Hammond DSO, DFC, the New Zealander who sank the *Tirpitz*. The RAF's No.1 band played the vessel away from Southampton, while Meteor, Lincoln and Sunderland aircraft escorted her down the Solent.

She was now sailing under Capt. Clayton, who had commanded her maiden voyage. He was newly-returned from naval duties as Commodore of Ocean Convoys. When the trooping service of *Andes* came to an end, he retired after forty-two years with the Company, commanding no less than twenty-six of its ships. His exceptional ability was reflected in a percentage mark of 99.6 when he gained his extra master's certificate in 1911 – the highest mark ever recorded up to that time.

After 1945, still in Government service, *Andes* sailed mainly through the Suez Canal to Bombay, occasionally calling at Singapore, Aden, Naples and Piraeus, and once each at Saigon and Colombo. In the early part of 1946 she claimed a third record, from Singapore to Southampton in 16 days, 15 hours, 31 minutes, averaging 21.66 knots – this cut almost three days from the record held by *Winchester Castle*.

In January 1947 the RAF Central Band, Uxbridge, gave *Andes* a send-off on her last Government voyage, when she took 400 civilians and 2,600 service personnel to the Far East. The visit by the band was in appreciation of her services as an RAF transport for part of the war. She returned to Southampton on 7 March 1947 and a week later was on her way to Belfast. Until the following January she remained in the hands of her builders.

Her Second World – South America

Passenger accommodation in *Andes* was to have totalled 607 – 403 first class and 204 second. With the changed conditions of 1947, the Company opted to lower the number of first class, in the process creating more room for crew members. The forward cabins on A deck were never used for passengers, which reduced her overall capacity to 528. Much of the ship's furniture and fittings was remade, wartime bombing having destroyed the Company's principal stores.

The absence of third class passengers, and little more than 500 all told, provided *Andes* with a great deal of flexibility. Exceptionally wide open promenades were examples of the way in which her space was used; apart from creating an impression of size, those long decks, dipping noticeably with the vessel's sheer, helped to keep temperatures bearable in the tropics.

The accommodation layout was as follows: A deck (lowest of the passenger decks) second class cabins aft; B deck, first class cabins, first class dining saloon (seating 368) and foyer forward, second class dining saloon (seating 196) and second class cabins aft; C deck, main first class embarkation entrance and entrance to the orchestra balcony over the first class saloon; also first class cabins from midships forward on the starboard side and from two-thirds aft on the port side. Right aft were open stairs leading to the second class lounge and smokeroom. D deck had first class cabins on both sides from the Purser's Office aft to the point where stairways led to the second class upper promenade deck and open-air swimming pool aft. Four luxury suites were on D deck, together with hairdressing salons, ladies beauty parlour, chiropodist, shop, children's playroom and second class gymnasium.

More first class cabins, many opening onto those broad promenade decks, were on E deck. A cocktail lounge led out to the Lido Café and first class swimming pool. Right aft was the second class sun deck. A wide promenade on F deck, part of it fully enclosed, surrounded the three main first class public rooms – the Smokeroom, Grand Hall and Observation Lounge. The Grand Hall was a general facility, a lounge with a permanent stage and dance floor, which could also be used as a cinema. The library and writing rooms, gymnasium and a sports deck overlooking the swimming pool were on F deck as well. Above was the boat deck, used by the more energetic passengers, as was the sports deck, higher still on the same level as the wheelhouse.

The passenger accommodation was well-furnished and comfortable, but changes in design philosophy since the days of *Alcantara* and *Asturias* meant that the kind of breathtaking period-style décor which had created such a fine reputation from the 1920s was absent. It was a more subdued age; not to mention a time of austerity in which quality materials and artisans were not always easy to come by. If the décor was less flamboyant, in line with the art of the time, it still contained some little gems. There were, for instance, two-tone blue designs along the sides of the main body of the first class dining saloon, metal relief wall designs, and engraved and sand-blasted mirrors.

The great oval ceiling-bowl in the Grand Hall possessed concealed lighting, and a short promenade through to the Observation Lounge helped to make a big room appear even larger. In her early passenger days there was comparatively little carpeting

– none in the Observation Lounge, whose surface underfoot was rubber composition. In the Grand Hall were loose Persian-style carpets and an oak parquet dance-floor in front of the stage. The Smokeroom had rubberised flooring whose design incorporated heraldic motifs which complemented the Tudor flavour of weathered oak beams, stone and old plaster. Concealed lighting was built into crusted ceiling plaster, but in the main the room's illumination was from period-style wrought iron fittings.

Large French windows from all three of the main rooms led onto promenade decks. The centre of the smokeroom held an enormous fireplace, opposite which was an alcove containing a large painting in tapestry style. An original tapestry, of hare coursing in the Middle Ages, was boarded up during the war but disappeared. Hampton's arranged for a replica, painted on canvas by P.A. Staynes, which was fastened to a raised mount on the wall.

Between the Smokeroom and Grand Hall on the starboard side was the first class Library, with off-white plush panelling, soft green carpet and pale gold curtains. One end could be turned into an altar for Divine Service. A similar room on the port side, fitted out as a Writing Room, had English chestnut and burr panelling and walnut furniture.

The first class Dining Saloon was panelled in natural and weathered sycamore, with cross-bandings of bleached zebrano. The restaurant foyer was originally to have been used as part of the restaurant so that all first class passengers could be accommodated at one sitting; now that numbers were reduced the foyer became a useful adjunct to the Dining Saloon. Both areas were air-conditioned, selected ahead of other rooms because of their low position in the ship and the natural heat level of a restaurant area. The saloon spanned the full width of the hull, and the ports on both sides were screened by inner vertically-sliding windows of tinted and sand-blasted glass. The foyer contained a cocktail bar – with eight high stools, concealed lighting (which, by now, it will be realised was a feature of *Andes*) and wood and metal craft around the façade, the foyer bar was a popular venue for cocktails before lunch and dinner.

First and second class cabins were of a high order in terms of size, comfort and décor. Apart from four suites-de-luxe there were no ostentatious apartments – the clientele on the South America route would typically include businessmen, diplomats, British and European families living in South America, service personnel and South American ranchers and farmers, together with – seasonally – wealthier Britons bent on whiling away an English winter comfortably on the South Atlantic.

Every first class cabin had its own private bathroom or shower and care was taken to maximise ventilation. There were twelve bed-sitters in which the beds could be raised into the bulkhead to provide day-rooms. Heaton Tabb decorated each of the four suites in a different style. The most individual was known as 'Chinese Chippendale', a gold lacquer coating, standing out in relief, of Chinese motifs in a style used by Thomas Chippendale 200 years earlier. The second suite was in walnut, the third in figured mahogany and sycamore, and the fourth in bird's-eye maple.

Though formal entertainment was not a feature, *Andes* provided passenger activities along the lines of organised deck games, fancy dress dinners, aquatic sports, bingo, horse-racing, betting on the day's run and so on. Much of the time, passengers simply wanted to sit on deck and read a book, watch the flying fish or sit around the swimming

Bedroom of the distinctive 'Chinese Chippendale' suite-de-luxe in Andes *(II).*

pool cooling off with a drink. It all sounds very modest in comparison with today's high-powered entertainment on cruise liners – it was a different age with different expectations but, perhaps just as much, these were people who wanted to enjoy an ocean voyage rather than a floating extravaganza. They were content whiling away an evening in the Grand Hall watching a new film release – a good selection was maintained through a West End film agency. On other nights the ship's orchestra played for dancing, and on warm tropic nights that activity would move out on deck. At some ports of call, local singers and dancers performed on board, adding a touch of latin character.

The second class put on dances and other entertainments themselves. In general, second class accommodation was similar to first, but smaller and without some of the trimmings. The cabins, in particular, had to conform largely to first class standards for, with the top berth removed, they became part of the first class-only accommodation for cruising. Mahogany plywood was the facia used in most cabins, which accommodated between one and four people.

Of the second class public rooms, probably the most interesting was the smokeroom aft on C deck. Over a false fireplace hung a magnificent map of the world and RML track chart, into which one of the ship's seventy Harlandic clocks had been fitted. An inside wall displayed a splendid tropical vegetation motif – features of this kind in wood, metal and glass were found at many points in the ship, elements of décor that provided intriguing features wherever you went.

Across the South Atlantic

Late in 1947 plans for her peacetime debut, departing Southampton on 22 January 1948, were completed. An innovation in booking practice involved the reservation of 100 first class berths for round-voyage passengers. The ship could be used as a hotel during her week in Buenos Aires at an extra charge of £10. One-way first class fares ranged from £160 to £300. Early in the New Year the last berth was sold for the first three round voyages – the ship was full both ways, both first and second class.

Following successful trials over the Arran mile (she achieved a mean speed of 23 knots) *Andes* anchored off Gourock to pick up Company guests and steamed round to Southampton. At long last she was receiving the bouquets owed to her. She was no longer a new ship; rather, a war veteran of more than half a million miles.

The usual 'maiden voyage' receptions greeted *Andes* as she sailed down the South American coast. The climax was a reception for Argentina's President Perón at Buenos Aires on 7 February. After nine weeks of negotiation, a British trade mission was on the point of returning to England in *Andes* after failing to gain a new trade agreement with the Argentine Government. Then, unexpectedly, an agreement was reached on 7 February. Among its principal clauses were a 14% increase in meat prices but a reduction in the price of maize.

Present at that meeting were Perón himself, Miguel Miranda (chairman of the Argentine National Economic Council), Sir Reginald Leeper (British Ambassador) and Sir Clive Baillieu (chairman of the British Trade Mission). These four (the British, at any rate, rather bewildered by their sudden success) were found a little later celebrating the agreement on board *Andes*. The reception for Perón had been arranged long before the talks began, but everyone welcomed the Ambassador's suggestion that the trade treaty should be called the '*Andes* Agreement'. Her holds contained the first cargo under the treaty – 1,900 tons of beef and 140 tons of canned meat. The euphoria of that moment was to be short-lived, as the Perón policies bit deeply into Britain's trade opportunities (a matter looked at in Volume 1).

During *Andes*' second voyage to South America she picked up distress calls from the 8,268-ton Norwegian tanker *Fenja*, which had a fire in her engineroom. *Andes* reached the vessel and her people boarded the stricken tanker, which was later towed to Montevideo by another vessel. On 31 October 1948 she suffered a damaged stern gland and whipping tail shaft. The gland began to lose its packing and a radio message sent to London warned that the shaft would have to be re-aligned at Southampton.

So her first year of commercial service was quite eventful, but after that she generally operated with few out-of-the-ordinary incidents. Her average round voyage speeds were maintained with remarkable consistency. Designed to run at 21 knots when she was built, on her first four commercial voyages she averaged 20.88, 21.05, 20.94 and 21.04 knots.

At about that time the ship received from Lt Col. G.S. Gibson of the Canadian Army a bronze plaque to mark her maiden voyage in 1939, when she brought the first Commonwealth troops to the war in Europe. Among the guests at the ceremony was Capt. R.G. Clayton, who had commanded that voyage. The plaque remained in the ship until just before she went to the breakers, when some damage to the screws attaching it to

First class dining saloon in Andes *(II), and* (below) *first class smokeroom as they appeared when she first entered commercial service in 1948.*

the wall showed that someone was after a souvenir. It was taken off the ship for safe-keeping and later presented to the British Columbia Seaforth Highlanders Regiment, whose men had filled the vessel for her first voyage.

Shortly after that ceremony, *Andes* was involved in a collision outside Santos in thick fog. The other vessel was the Swedish Johnson liner *Colombia*. *Andes* received damage in the region of the bows, but it wasn't serious. *Colombia* was less lucky – when she returned to Europe she spent nearly three weeks in a repair yard. One of the great difficulties of operating to South America was to keep ships clear of the silt-laden bed of the River Plate. When *Andes* went aground late in 1950, during Capt. G.A. Bannister's first voyage in command, the incident was described as 'a light grounding'. However, an examination afterwards revealed that the starboard propeller had lost a triangular piece six inches by four from the leading edge of one blade, and other parts were bruised. No-one ever discovered the cause.

In June 1952, Royal Mail decided to renew her propellers. During the annual drydocking that year her rudder was also thoroughly overhauled. Her first serious engine defect occurred that autumn – a good record in thirteen years of service, but it had a permanent effect on the ship. Until then she had averaged between 20.5 and 21 knots. After this trouble, a defective IP turbine, the Company reduced her service speed to 18 knots.

That was the first real hint of age, and a sign of other things. A reduction of two or three knots was not to be taken lightly, and the directors must have felt confident that the ship would continue to attract passengers at the lower speed. They could presumably have made arrangements to keep her at least close to her original speed if they had thought it necessary. Some of the heat had been taken out of the long-running speed battle – aircraft were starting to seriously compete and their ability to carry people much more quickly when time was important took some of the competitive pressure off shipping companies.

Her first break from the mail service came in 1953 when she attended the Spithead Coronation Review. On 13 June, 404 passengers joined her at Southampton; she anchored for the night in Portland Bay while her passengers danced under the stars. Her passenger list was nothing if not illustrious, but two lesser known names were perhaps more interesting. One was Capt. F.G. Spriddell – back in the 1930s, as the Company's Marine Superintendent, he had approved the design for *Andes*. The other was Howard Jarvis, a senior member of the Society of Marine Artists. From the late 1940s to 1960s he was Royal Mail's contract artist, producing innumerable works for brochures, postcards and the like.

After the social extravaganza of the Review and a final fireworks display, it was back to ploughing the South Atlantic furrow. After two further voyages *Andes* was fitted with Denny Brown stabilisers. The rectangular fins each measured 78sq.ft. They were extended and retracted hydraulically from either the bridge or engineroom. Stabilisers were just becoming popular in passenger liners and *Andes* was the first on her route to have them. Work had begun in June 1952, when preliminary trunking was carried out. Her sides were then sealed and she continued her schedule until the fins were installed the following year.

Capt. H.H. Treweeks took command in 1955, and his duties included her first formal cruise, a 4,600-mile trip to the Mediterranean lasting less than three weeks. From that point – June 1955 – *Andes* spent a good deal of her time cruising to the Mediterranean and West Indies and rarely made more than two consecutive voyages to Brazil and the River Plate.

It was during this period that *Andes* began to fully realise that special character briefly referred to earlier, which grew from the fact that she retained to a remarkable degree a closely-knit crew who worked happily side by side year in and year out. There was growing evidence of this almost intangible dimension during the 1950s – an occasion, for instance, when she was among several ships chartered at Rio de Janeiro for accommodation and a short cruise for an International Eucharistic Conference. With the ship spending five days at Rio the crew hoped to have shore leave but, as she was in full service mode, Capt. Treweeks could allow them only half a day each. The crew co-operated splendidly. 'When I heard of the difficulties in the other vessels,' Capt. Treweeks told me in later years, 'I was very proud of my ship.'

Many well-known and influential people travelled in *Andes*. Their presence increased when the balance of service swung from a majority of South Atlantic voyages to a majority of cruises; and even more so when her life was totally devoted to cruising.

Prince Chula of Siam made several voyages in her to South America, and on one of them presented to the ship a silver bowl engraved with the Thai flag and the Red Ensign. During 1955 Field-Marshal Earl Alexander of Tunis and the Countess voyaged to Lisbon (and afterwards returned in *Alcantara*). Among her cruise passengers were Lord Birkett, Hannen Swaffer, singer Joan Regan and actress Margaret Rutherford. Entertainers David Nixon and Frankie Howerd each made a Christmas cruise during her later years. Then there was Alan Whicker and the full BBC *Whicker's World* crew, who provided for their programme a few controversial angles which would not have pleased the Company.

Andes made her first long Winter Cruise in 1958, a 17,000-mile voyage to Rio de Janeiro and Capetown – those voyages were a direct corollary of Royal Mail's long-standing popularity with winter-time round voyages to South America. As Britain's leading first class cruise liner, she became especially famous for those long sojourns, which occurred every year thereafter. In 1959, for example, passengers paid between £380 and £1,010 for a forty-five day cruise to the West Indies, Venezuela and New Orleans. One port of call was Havana – the missile crisis of 1962 put a stop to visits by a firm which had regularly visited Cuba since the very first ships in the early 1840s.

Her Third World – Cruising

Andes was settling into the cruising mould well before her conversion for full-time cruising. Most voyages were accomplished without incident, but there were occasional frustrations and highlights. During 1958 she had to omit Piraeus (for Athens) because of political disturbances and put in an unexpected appearance at Barcelona instead. In the same year her passengers had to be content with a view of Helsinki from the deck when high winds prevented anyone landing.

On the way home from a Mediterranean cruise in June 1959, passengers briefly found an unexpected face in their midst when Princess Margaret attended a cocktail party at Lisbon. Less than a month later the Princess was at Belfast to christen *Amazon*, first of the final group of liners for the Brazil and River Plate service. *Andes* made only two River Plate voyages in 1959, in the spring and autumn. On 23 November 1959 she closed the door on her second world when her last main line voyage ended.

Andes *(II) pictured during a cruise in the 1950s. At that period she alternated between cruises and South America mail voyages.*

For full-time cruising she underwent a major conversion. NV Koninklijke Mij. De Scheldte was awarded the contract, involving a two-part operation at Flushing at a cost of 5,285,000 Dutch guilders (about £500,000). After steadfastly supporting British builders and repairers for so long, Royal Mail went overseas reportedly through a combination of higher prices from British firms and an inability to gain from them a fixed price contract. From late November 1959 until early January 1960 the work focused on the construction of new cabins. There was a break while the ship made her Winter Cruise, then the remaining three-month refit took place.

Her profile was changed principally by an extension of the D deck superstructure, both fore and aft, to accommodate new cabins. With the after extension of D deck it was possible, on the deck above, to extend the lido area and build folding glass screens flanking the swimming pool so that a lido café, swimming pool and bar could form a focal point for shipboard life instead of being just another part of the deck area. That subtle change showed another aspect of *Andes'* cruising atmosphere. The two after deck cranes were taken out as the new *Andes* would not be carrying cargo. A kingpost and derrick for loading stores was placed abaft the E deck house (built to accommodate the lido refreshments facility and Mermaid Bar).

Above the forward D deck extension were two 44ft launches. More sophisticated than ordinary motor lifeboats (and canvas-covered in bad weather), they were designed to carry 118 persons each at ports of call where *Andes* could not berth alongside. If she was to remain Britain's number-one cruise ship it was essential to have the greatest possible choice of destinations. Small but quality destinations could be greatly increased if the ship had good facilities for ferrying ashore passengers who, in many cases, were elderly and not exactly sprightly. Other external changes were the loss of the deck cranes at No.1 hatch and a screen extension on F deck similar to that on E.

For all the external changes, it was inside that *Andes* became practically a new ship. The new cabins were built mostly into C and D decks. Aft on C deck they occupied what had formerly been the second class lounge and winter garden; bathrooms and an excursion office were also added there. On the starboard side of C deck more cabins were fitted in existing accommodation occupied earlier by engineer officers.

The new accommodation became known as the Dutch cabins. They had coromandel, zebrano and teak panelling and furniture. Part of the new D deck structure contained cabins where the second class swimming pool had been; there was also a new children's playroom, suggesting that the ship's cruising clientele was broader than many supposed. Every passenger cabin now had its own toilet and bath or shower. Some of the more expensive rooms had extra features like private refrigerators, and the suites were provided with complete cocktail cabinets holding fine cut glass; private parties were frequently held in the suite sitting-rooms.

The second class smokeroom right aft became, in reduced size, the Seahorse Inn, an L-shaped room whose bar was adorned with all sorts of nautical flotsam and became a popular haunt. It was later withdrawn from the passenger accommodation to become the officers' smokeroom. All of the passenger accommodation was now air-conditioned, except for the lido cocktail lounge, where it was thought that people coming inside after swimming or sunning themselves in the tropics might prefer to not suddenly find themselves shivering.

On F deck a large bar was added to the period-style smokeroom, designed in such a manner that you imagined it had always been there. There was about this room a quality which particularly attracted me; plush, period-style comfort with subdued lighting and dark wood hues oozed with an atmosphere which set it apart from the rest of the ship.

The provision at this time of names for public rooms added to the ship's individualism. The period smokeroom, for instance, became the Warwick Room, after the Company's Chairman, Walter C. Warwick, who was shortly to retire. The Grand Hall and Observation Lounge were merged into a single unit to become the Princess Lounge, in honour of Princess Margaret's recent visit at Lisbon. The Seahorse Inn acknowledged the seahorse component of Royal Mail's armorial bearings. The new bar by the swimming pool was the Mermaid Bar. The four luxury suites remembered earlier ships from the South America service with the names Araguaya, Alcantara, Asturias and Almanzora.

Another former ship was remembered. Inevitably *Andes'* predecessor as full-time cruise liner, the immensely popular *Atlantis*, had to be represented and her name was given to the restaurant. Part of the former second class restaurant was rebuilt as an exclusive small restaurant for private functions – it was given the name Galleon Grill (two galleons featured on the Company's armorial bearings).

Two cabins were removed on E deck to make way for a new bar in the lido cocktail lounge. The bar was curved and merged into an alcove panelled in dark wenge wood on which a colourful modern decoration was painted. A lowered ceiling created an atmosphere of intimacy, and its upholstery was in smart broken-white artificial leather.

Princess Margaret being greeted by H. Leslie Bowes, who would shortly become RML's chairman, on board Andes (II) at Lisbon in 1959. The occasion was a cocktail party in connection with a British trade fair.

The Atlantis Restaurant was enlarged so that all passengers could dine together, a feature which was always a strong selling point for the ship. In fact, so strong was the image of the ship's cuisine and the restaurant's environment that the passenger capacity was, to an extent, based on the restaurant's seating capacity. That, in turn, was limited by Ministry of Transport regulations restricting the length between bulkheads to 123ft. For the first time this room was now carpeted, in blue with red and yellow designs.

In the Galleon Grill (an interior room without windows or portholes, since its exclusive use was for private evening functions), the walls were panelled in olive ash and wenge wood, with some artificial leather. A large painting of a galleon on the dark wenge panelling, together with another painting in a recess, reflected the room's name. From the stern of the depicted Elizabethan galleon the artist chose to fly an enormous Royal Mail Lines houseflag. The fitting-out of this room was particularly distinguished, with a carpet designed to reflect the colours in the décor.

One of the biggest tasks of the conversion was the creation of a cinema-theatre out of a cargo hold. Wenge was used extensively in this new Ocean Theatre, which possessed full theatre lighting and acoustic equipment, and seated 260 people in great comfort. Plush gold-coloured carpet covered the stairway curving down from the balcony. The upholstery and stage curtain were also in gold, the walls grey and gold. Carpet at the front of the auditorium was deep blue. Who would have guessed that this sumptuous entertainment area used to be No.4 hold?

Other cargo spaces were used for the air-conditioning plant, extra refrigerating machinery and so on. The remainder were left empty except for holds 2 and 3, in each of which 250 tons of concrete blocks were kept as permanent ballast.

Into Service

Andes started and finished her cruises at Southampton. Mediterranean cruises lasted about eighteen to twenty-one days; West Indies cruises (usually in spring and autumn, when Mediterranean weather was less reliable) between twenty-three and twenty-six days; 'Northern Capitals' cruises (more accurately simply Scandinavian waters) around eighteen or nineteen days; a Christmas and New Year cruise, usually to Atlantic islands and perhaps west or north Africa, about sixteen or seventeen days; and the Winter Cruise, which might go anywhere that was exotic and warm, and lasted up to two months.

Not only was the ship changing her sphere of operation, a totally new routine was introduced for her turnround at Southampton. Her career was to become more rigorous than ever; the absence of cargo meant that she did not have to remain in port longer than was needed to make her ready for the next cruise. Frequently the vessel arrived from one cruise at eight in the morning and sailed again at lunchtime next day – little more than 24 hours to change linen, load stores, clean the ship, attend to routine maintenance and so on. Twice a year a longer stopover permitted bigger maintenance jobs, including her annual drydocking, but the general tightness of the schedule showed what faith the Company placed in the ship's reliability and in the qualities of its staff and contractors.

At the beginning of June 1960 *Andes* steamed down the Channel for a short shakedown cruise, the guinea-pig passengers being RML staff and their families, travel agents and others. Her passenger capacity was now about 470, but on occasion (especially if there were many children on board) the number could rise above 500 with top berths fitted.

The only port of call on that short weekend cruise was Guernsey in the Channel Islands. As the largest liner Guernsey had seen, she caused quite a stir. Islanders and holidaymakers filled every vantage point for a look at this grand ship whose white hull – repainted to follow the tradition of cruise liners – merged into the misty sunlight. She officially opened the third phase of her career with a three-week cruise to the Mediterranean. In command was Capt. Geoffrey Fletcher – except for three cruises he commanded her on every voyage until his retirement in March 1962. During that time he enjoyed great popularity with the cruising passengers, and the same was true of those who succeeded him. The captain of a cruise liner had to be something more than a good seaman.

After he retired, Capt. Leslie Peterson took over, and little time passed before he faced his first problem – the port propeller fell off at Lisbon. He brought the ship home a day late, having averaged 14 knots on one engine and allowing 12° of helm to counteract the single propeller thrust. A perplexed Capt. Peterson said: 'She handled beautifully. The accident was a profound mystery – nothing hit the propeller, it just came off while we were in the Tagus'. A very different event at this period involved the crew football team, which frequently played local teams in friendlies at Mediterranean ports. On this occasion they got slightly out of their depth during a call at the Soviet port of Yalta. The 'local friendly' became a match against the champion Crimean amateur team, attended by 5,000 paying patrons and watched by the Soviet Deputy President.

Andes provided kosher facilities for Jewish passengers, who made up a significant portion of her clientele. A larger number of Jews than usual were naturally attracted to a 1963 cruise which visited Haifa, during which a compliment was paid to Capt. Peterson 'in appreciation of his understanding of, and helpfulness to, his Jewish passengers on the cruise'. The testimonial took the unusual form of a grove of 100 trees to be planted in Israel's Herzl Forest in his name.

A broadening of shipboard entertainment began with the Christmas Cruise of 1963/64, when Crockfords, the gaming firm, placed a roulette table on board which was manned by croupiers from Le Touquet. Gambling apart, the Christmas cruise was popular with children. Santa always managed somehow to find *Andes*, and the ship was transformed into a shimmering fairyland of colour with seven Christmas trees, lametta, tinsel and more than a thousand metal foil decorations.

What would the nation's premier cruise liner load in the way of stores for a Christmas Cruise? I once had to make the calculation for the media. The figures, for 480 passengers on a sixteen-day cruise, were staggering: 3,500lb turkeys, 6,000lb chickens, 2,000lb ducks, 70 grouse, 80 partridge, 30 pheasant, 160 quail, 30,000 eggs, 1,500lb cheeses of twenty-four varieties, 600lb lobsters, 400lb prawns, 200lb scampi, 1,600lb salmon, 500lb trout, 70lb caviare, 300 tins paté de fois gras, 300 tins ravioli, half a ton of almonds, sultanas and currants, 3cwt icing sugar, 1,300 bottles champagne, 4,700 bottles other wine, 2,900 bottles spirits and liqueurs, almost a quarter of a million cigarettes, 1,800 cigars. What a different world from the shopping list for the Salisbury livestock market of 1841! It should perhaps be added that caviare was an optional extra at (in 1968, at least) 12s 6d per portion.

It was, though, her long Winter Cruises which built a special reputation for *Andes*. She visited a great many of the world's exotic places. In 1964, for instance, she voyaged 20,570 miles to India and the Far East. The most expensive accommodation, for two people, cost £3,300, and one of the 'shore excursions' alone, across India from Madras to Bombay, ran to several hundred pounds. Royal Mail's director in charge of passenger operations at the time, Cyril Matthews, commented early in 1963 that the demand for even longer winter cruises had increased after recent severe winters. Such was their popularity that a booking list for the following year was opened before the current voyage ended. Many passengers re-booked year after year.

What should have been her finest Winter Cruise was originally scheduled as a 25,000-mile, seventy-eight day voyage in 1968 to Africa and the Far East. The minimum single fare was £650 and a luxury suite for two cost £4,680. There were by then so many trouble-spots around the world that it was increasingly difficult to schedule a long voyage which steered clear of unwelcome areas. The voyage was to take *Andes* to Luanda, Capetown, Durban, Ceylon, Singapore, Hong Kong, Manila, Penang, Bombay, Suez, Israel, Lebanon and Gibraltar.

Well before the cruise began, apartheid troubles erupted in South Africa, the June war of 1967 closed the Suez Canal and communist Chinese sparked riots in Hong Kong.

Drastic modifications had to be made, though the situation in South Africa didn't, in the end, require changes. Omitting Asia, Suez and the Mediterranean, the ship instead visited Mauritius in the Indian Ocean, St Helena in the Atlantic and Rio de Janeiro.

So the rather affluent world of *Andes* rolled on. The affable Capt. John Fox reported in 1964 that at Barbados the ship had berthed next to the Royal Yacht *Britannia*. The Queen Mother was visiting the island, convalescing after an accident, and several times drove past *Andes* to the cheers of passengers and crew. A goodwill message was sent to their Royal neighbour before the ships parted company. Two years later the crew had a sense of déjà vu when they and the passengers cheered *Britannia* as she left Barbados. This time the Queen and Duke of Edinburgh were on board.

When the Pears soap company, which promoted a child beauty competition, decided to hold the finals on board a liner in 1964, RML agreed to use *Andes* on 9 June. Gracie Fields was persuaded to emerge from her island home in the Mediterranean to present the prizes. The day was a great success in spite of the enormous crowds which packed the Princess Lounge, probably the largest concentration of people in the room since her trooping days.

The mid-1960s proved the peak period of her 'third world'; a time of prosperity, a time when she had become well-known and accepted as a top-class cruise liner, a time when passenger lists were often full and there was sometimes a waiting list. New ports of call were added to old favourites. Akureyri in Iceland and Leghorn in Italy were new ports in 1966, while Mahé in the Seychelles made an exotic Indian Ocean debut in 1967. Also in

In June 1964 Gracie Fields was enticed out of retirement to crown the winner of the Miss Pears competition. The event was held on Andes *(II) and Gracie is pictured with the winner, and with Captain Leslie Peterson, whose cap she borrowed for the occasion.* (Author's photograph)

1967, *Andes* became the first large cruise liner to visit Tobago, her passengers ferried ashore at Pigeon Point to be greeted by a steel band and a barbecue.

For all that this was *Andes'* cruising heyday, several problems began to demand attention. New fire prevention regulations by the United States Government required ships to conform to strict rules before being allowed to enter United States ports. Those regulations were virtually a new international standard and few passenger ships, particularly older ones like *Andes*, conformed. Bringing the ship up to the required standard would be expensive, and with *Andes* approaching thirty years of age, the question of 'will we or won't we?' occupied the minds of the directors for some time.

Finally it was decided to go ahead and bring *Andes* up to the American standard. Faced with the same problem, Cunard Line decided otherwise with *Queen Elizabeth*. These two liners shared something of a bond, having been completed at much the same time and both being forced into war service after a dash across the Atlantic without undergoing trials. Now they were two grand old ladies of the sea; one about to gain a final facelift, the other destined for the shortest of new careers for she was destroyed by fire while being converted to a floating university.

Andes was starting to suffer some difficulties in the engineroom – the 1966 Christmas Cruise, for instance, was delayed for several hours by a sticking boiler-valve. Such things did not take long to put right, but with a tight schedule the vessel could ill afford even these irritating delays. She was also beginning to look her age inside and a certain amount of refurbishing was needed to bring her accommodation up to date without losing her special character.

The Rotary Clubs of Great Britain privately booked *Andes* for a cruise in May 1967. Through lack of support the cruise was cancelled, and Royal Mail used that opportunity to carry out the first part of her final refit. It took place at Harland & Wolff's yard at Belfast, the first time *Andes* had been there since her 1947 refit. The work was completed at the end of the year, with the Christmas Cruise cancelled. The duration of the work may have been short but for most of the time the ship looked like a cross between a construction site and the residue from a bomb blast. Matters looked particularly grim in the engineroom, not least because there had been a minor explosion. New boiler tubes and fire resistant bulkheads, doors and ceilings had been fitted. Much of the passenger accommodation had been refurbished, the most noticeable change being to the Princess Lounge, which was almost unrecognisable, resplendent in green, red, white and blue.

The Last Years

While *Andes* slipped easily back into her schedule, for the Company (now operating within the Furness Withy Group) the cruising waters were becoming increasingly choppy. With labour costs rising sharply, the one-to-one crew/passenger ratio (she carried 458 crew) was increasingly less viable. She had to maintain an ever-larger load factor before breaking even. By 1970 it was more difficult still because of matters like escalating oil prices and increasing competition from other operators. There seemed to be declining numbers of people drawn to the *Andes* style of cruising, and who could afford it, and so the balance relentlessly swung against her operation. News that she would be withdrawn from service, along with other Group ships, came out of the blue on 13 November 1970.

A study of Andes *(II) at the beginning of 1968. She was at Harland & Wolff's yard at Belfast for her final refit.* (Author's photograph)

Given only a few months more service, the old ship rather disgraced herself. The early part of 1971 was taken up with a combination of three winter cruises, scheduled so that passengers could join any combination or all three. The first was to South and West Africa, the second to Rio de Janeiro and the third to the West Indies. On the first cruise the ship was stopped twice with boiler trouble. Repairs were carried out at Capetown and her schedule went back by three days. On cruise two the centre boiler forced-draught fan shaft sheared, the start of a series of major engineroom mishaps. Then the steering gear failed as she left Rio de Janeiro.

On 4 April she departed for her final cruise; a cold, dull and slightly misty day. The ship was dressed overall and streamers formed a shredded curtain between ship and shore. Every berth was filled, mostly with regular patrons returning for a final nostalgic voyage. There were devotees who had made forty or fifty cruises in her. It took her to the West Indies, calling at Las Palmas, La Guaira (Venezuela), Antigua, St Lucia, Grenada, Barbados and Madeira. There was a touch of boiler trouble again, and then further engine trouble put her arrival back twenty-four hours. This time no-one seemed to mind.

On the morning of 4 May 1971 she reached 30/31 berth at Southampton with a 93ft paying-off pennant and a dressing line of flags which spelled out the message '*Andes* in opus per mare ubique 1939-1971 hodie recedere'. Literally: '*Andes* in operation by sea everywhere 1939-1971 today retires'. Behind her lay a career which had lasted 11,544 days and in which she had steamed about 2,770,000 miles – an average, had she travelled non-stop for those thirty-one years, of 240 miles every day. Her 285 voyages took her to 174 different ports.

Just two days later, with a skeleton crew, Royal Mail's largest liner made her final departure for Ghent in Belgium. Her sale realised £325,000. A Company memorandum stated: '*Andes* – The above-named vessel was handed over for breaking up to the purchasers, Etablissements Van Heyghen Frères Société Anonyme of Ghent, in Ghent at 14.00 hours BST on Friday 7 May 1971'.

Magdalena (III)

During 1946 the 17,547-ton *Magdalena* was ordered for the intermediate London – River Plate run, when the post-war travel boom was starting to escalate. She was a replacement for *Highland Patriot*, which had been lost in 1940. *Magdalena* has at times been compared with the three 'A' ships built about a decade later. A degree of similarity in external appearance is evident, including a return to the 'split bridge' concept (though the 'A' ships had a complete separation while on *Magdalena* one deck linked the two structures). They held similar amounts of cargo; *Magdalena's* insulated space amounted to 451,240cu.ft and general hold space was 43,093cu.ft bale. Her sixteen tubular steel derricks included two of 10 tons capacity; the rest were either 5 or 3 tons.

There were four complete decks, an orlop deck fore and aft of the machinery spaces except No.1 hold, a long bridge deck forecastle, promenade, boat and observation decks. The hull was divided into watertight compartments by eight bulkheads. A continuous double bottom held fresh water, water ballast and oil fuel. Total fuel oil and diesel capacity was 2,530 tons, and 2,077 tons of fresh water could be carried. Her principal dimensions were length overall 570ft 1½ in, length bp 540ft, moulded breadth 73ft and depth moulded to shelter deck 45ft.

A significant difference between *Magdalena* and the later ships was in propulsion machinery. The 'A's were given diesels, but *Magdalena* received double-reduction Parsons geared turbines, driving twin screws at an output of 18,000shp. By means of a bypass valve located on each hp turbine a continuous overload power of 19,800shp at 109rpm was maintained.

Cargo spaces were complex because of the variety of freights to be carried. Most meat cargo was chilled at fractionally above freezing point, some frozen meat and other frozen items were accommodated in No.1 lower hold, while in No.4 lower 'tweendecks there was a compartment for quick frozen produce at temperatures as low as -10° Fahrenheit. Slight variations in chilled space for certain fruits were also catered for.

Passenger capacities in *Magdalena* and the 'A' ships were almost identical – 479 and 475 respectively – but there was a major difference in that the 'A' ships catered for three classes and *Magdalena* two – 133 first class and 346 third. About 30% of the third class were in dormitories, sleeping up to ten and designed for Spanish and Portuguese migrants. With a crew list of 224, total accommodation was for 703.

First class passengers were offered staterooms, mostly with private bathrooms, for one or two people; a few took three or four. The cost between London and South America ranged from £135 to £173, while third class paid between £60 and £67 (there was a reduction of only £5 for dormitory accommodation).

Launching of Magdalena *(III) at Belfast in 1948.*

For the passenger accommodation, a mixture of traditional and modern styles were used. The war was no doubt partly responsible for that, for creative minds had had little chance to forge a new path of style and design since 1945, and neither would there have been an infinite range of materials. In spite of the austerity, however, they achieved attractive and comfortable, though not overly flamboyant, passenger rooms.

The principal first class rooms were, except for the dining saloon, at the forward end of the main superstructure, at different deck levels linked by a lift and surrounding stairwell. The lift operated from the shelter deck, at the dining room vestibule (below superstructure level). Two decks up was the smokeroom, then the main lounge, occupying the full width of the ship, on the boat deck. A large well in the lounge rose through the next deck which contained the observation lounge (surrounding the well on three sides), reading and writing rooms. First class passengers had a swimming pool and lido café on the promenade deck – this was similar enough in design and layout (though not as spacious) to the equivalent area in the later 'A' ships to suggest that theirs were modelled on *Magdalena*.

In a particularly convenient arrangement, all provedore and cooking facilities, and all principal third class public rooms and crew mess facilities, were laid out on the shelter deck abaft the first class dining saloon.

The first class lounge was cleanly modern, particularly the ceilings, light fittings and wall-to-wall carpeting. Some wall panelling, a Cippolino marble mock fireplace and the relief mural above it, were more in keeping with pre-war concepts. They formed the focal point of the lounge, with the mural rising through the well to the observation deck above and surrounded on three sides by glazed screens. The mural panel, in fibrous plaster, was the creation of Norman Cornish and depicted South American fauna and flora, including llama, alpaca and vicuna. The international flavour extended to a pair of Chinese Kylins in coloured porcelain. The lounge could be adapted as a cinema, using Gaumont equipment.

The observation lounge possessed tall windows which offered uninterrupted views of the sea. The room's design was light and airy, and contained a mural treatment in pale green formica trimmed with sycamore.

At first glance the smokeroom simply seemed to be in period style, with an arrangement of wooden roof beams, but the bar, with curious curved hatchways, offered the best clue to its design origins in the Austrian Tyrol. It was effectively a Germanic development of the equivalent room in *Andes*, with the designers freely adapting 16th century Tyrolean styles. Some wall surfaces had hand-textured plaster and stone niches, while those flanking the bar were adorned with tapestries. The unusual ceiling treatment included grey-oak beams supported by oak corbels and stone piers. There were painted motifs in Tyrolean character, wrought-iron pendants and wall brackets. Furniture was grey-oak with chip carving and some introduced colour. Easy chairs and settees were covered in various coloured hides and tub chairs were upholstered in tapestry. The rubber-surfaced floor was dotted with oriental rugs. In all, this room was among the most unusual and innovative found on a Royal Mail ship.

Pastel colours dominated the first class restaurant, which seated 164 at tables for two to eight people. It was panelled in walnut and sycamore – two stalwarts of the maritime décor world – and had a central dome two decks high. The brightest colour in this room was coral. The side walls of the dome were adorned with two bas relief motifs depicting incidents from ancient Greek mythology, while similar panels in lower parts of the room portrayed events from the ancient Olympic Games – including running in armour and mule-cart racing. Sand-blasted glass panels covered the area occupied by grouped side lights, and were set off with pale gold satin curtains.

Third class passengers were placed in the after half of the upper deck. Though wash basins in cabins had only cold water, bathrooms and showers were fitted with hot and cold water (a mixture of sea and fresh water), and there were wash troughs in the style migrants had been used to in the *Highland* ships. Cabins and dormitory spaces were mechanically ventilated.

Their dining saloon, seating 174, was panelled in plywood with pastel finish, with pilasters and detailing in mahogany. The smokeroom panelling was oak veneer, and the furniture was oak. Armchairs and settees were upholstered in tapestry fabric. Mahogany panelling was featured in the lounge, where seating was upholstered in hide. A piano was provided in the lounge, which could also be utilised as a cinema.

For her size *Magdalena* provided a good quality of accommodation, with sufficient space on a limited passenger capacity to allow her patrons room to breathe. She was the first UK-based liner with design-built air-conditioning throughout the first class spaces.

The unique style of the first class smokeroom in Magdalena *(III). It was a free adaptation of old Tyrolean design.*

Medical facilities were very comprehensive, not least because of the many European migrants she would carry. General hospitals, with male and female wards, operating theatre, dispensing and consulting rooms were all aft. In fact the operating theatre, surprisingly, was almost directly above the port screw. Isolation hospitals for infectious diseases were also at the stern but in an upper deck house. There was a special ward for maternity cases. English, Spanish and Portuguese surgeons were carried.

Into Service

Launched at Queen's Island, Belfast, in May 1948, *Magdalena* was ready to enter service the following March. On trials she reached 20 knots, two more than her designed service speed. Members of the Press who sailed in her from Belfast Lough to London were full of praise, one report describing her as 'an outstanding example of British shipbuilding craftsmanship – and in that we include design'.

Despite that, machinery problems delayed her maiden voyage from Tilbury from the scheduled departure on 26 February until 9 March. It was announced then that a new shaft would be fitted and modifications made to the funnel after the first voyage. While the former Nelson Line *Highland* ships had always operated from the Thames, *Magdalena* was the first custom-built Royal Mail passenger ship to be based at London.

Magdalena (III) on trials early in 1949.

The southbound voyage, under Capt. Douglas Lee, was as uneventful as a fine liner's maiden voyage can be. In the River Plate she loaded a large quantity of Argentine meat and sailed north to Santos to take on the first Brazilian oranges of the season, a consignment of 20,000 cases. She left Santos on the afternoon of 24 April and throughout the passage to Rio steamed in fine conditions. However, she was continually set northwards of her course, though whether that was caused by a current or compass error was later in dispute. Just under fourteen hours after leaving Santos, and travelling at a moderate 13 knots, she grounded at 4.40 a.m. on the 25th, on a reef half a mile south of the Tijucas Islands and twenty miles from Rio. She rested in the vicinity of No.3 hold; the hull was torn and No.3 quickly flooded to a depth of 20ft.

An SOS was sent at 4.45 a.m. and passengers were ordered to emergency stations, but the boats were not lowered until rescue craft arrived. In fact, Britain's traditional 'stiff upper lip' was evident if the local British Press attaché was to be believed. 'At eight o'clock,' he reported, 'breakfast was served as usual in the dining saloon before the passengers were disembarked'.

During the day, as salvage negotiations took place, the weather deteriorated and a heavy swell developed. At 7 p.m. the engine was shut down for fear of an explosion – the turbines were being shifted several inches by the contorting hull. Thus the use of engines to assist refloating was ruled out.

Shortly before midnight the wind and sea did the job without mechanical help. *Magdalena* was lifted free by a wave and was anchored in deep water. The sea quickly entered No.2 hold now, and some also went in No.1. Though well down by the head, she was afloat and awaiting the assistance of tugs for the short journey to the safety of Rio de

Janeiro's naval drydock. That news heartened the marine insurance market in London as they closed their offices that night, for the payment hanging over them, more than £2,250,000, was believed to be the largest ever claimed for a marine casualty.

Next morning the underwriters went to their businesses in a very different frame of mind. As they slept, all hope of avoiding a total loss was dashed. *Magdalena* had broken her back. They wondered, understandably, how this could be when she was safely afloat a few hours earlier. That the liner had been most unlucky probably brought greater frustration than if she had never been refloated. The tow to Rio had begun at about 7.30 a.m. She was sluggish and unwieldy, the forepart deep in the water. Large crowds lined the waterfront to watch. When she was at the entrance to Rio bay she touched bottom – apparently not heavily, but on the harbour bar, and the strain was taken by the portion of the hull damaged in the original stranding. The resulting weight on either side of the 'pivot' was too great for the weakened hull and she broke in two in the way of No.3 hold, between the bridge section and main accommodation.

The forepart was anchored and later sank. Her more valuable midship and stern section drifted across the harbour entrance and grounded about a mile away. For some time Santos oranges were being washed ashore on Copacobana Beach. Drastically revised salvage plans were discussed, but in the event very little of commercial value was saved. At least there was no loss of life, and injuries were minimal.

Within three days the underwriters had parted with the £2,250,000. The stern portion was sold to Brazilian buyers for £50,000 for breaking up and salvaging what they could. There were reports that the forepart was blown up because of its danger to navigation.

Magdalena (III) under tow after her initial grounding. It was during this episode that she touched bottom and broke her back.

*The fore and after portions of
Magdalena (III) after she had
broken her back and the two
sections had drifted apart.*

Crew and officers were commended for their efforts, and cash awards were made by the underwriters. The Company's Superintendent Engineer praised them thus:

For several weeks some of the officers and men strived to the limit of physical endurance, under most discouraging conditions, to retrieve as much as they could from the wreck, frequently taking risks without regard to personal safety... Although the attempt to refloat the after part failed, the efforts of the personnel should not, in my view, be allowed to pass without suitable recognition. Although the conditions in the engineroom were appalling, the engineer officers carried out modifications and repairs to pumps and pipe lines etc with considerable skill and ingenuity.

For Capt. Lee it was a devastating way to bow out of his seagoing career – he had been scheduled to make one further voyage before retiring. After a fine record of forty-three years at sea, holding a master's certificate for nearly thirty, Douglas Lee was found at the Board of Trade enquiry to have shown 'grave dereliction of duty', principally on the question of the ship being northward of her course line and not taking account of compass error; his certificate was suspended for two years. The first officer received part of the blame and had his certificate suspended for a year. (The Enquiry is discussed in Volume 1.)

Amazon (III), *Aragon* (II) *and Arlanza* (II)

After its misfortune with *Magdalena*, Royal Mail did not replace her. The reasons – in essence changed trading conditions and the advent of the Perón regime in Argentina – are looked at in Volume 1. These new 'A' ships took a little of their lineage from *Magdalena*, but they were replacements for the four *Highland* ships and also incorporated elements from the Southampton mail service.

In view of their short RML careers it is worth considering the business climate of their time. The broad canvas of the 1960s suggests it was the most crucial decade for shipping in a very long time. The traditional break-bulk freighters which dominated the seaways were, in a short space of time, ousted by container ships, specialised carriers and ever-larger bulk carriers. It was the period when air travel came of age and sent most passenger shipping line services to the wall. The 'A' ships were caught in both situations.

Who was controlling the Company when they were built? There was Walter C. Warwick (the 'Grand Old Man of Shipping', they called him) – chairman until 1960. He had been in shipping since about 1895, for many years working closely with Lord Kylsant, and was on the original Board of Directors of Royal Mail Lines in 1932. His successor as chairman was H. Leslie (later Sir Leslie) Bowes, whose service harked back to 1911, again covering the Kylsant era. Another senior director was Cyril Matthews, who had been Assistant Accountant for RMSP in Lord Kylsant's later days. A further Board member with decades of involvement was Frank Charlton – in fact his links with the Kylsant era and its aftermath were immensely wide-ranging. Initially an accountant with Price, Waterhouse, he began his influential work in shipping during the First World War and was later a director of White Star, Cunard, Royal Mail and The Pacific Steam Navigation Co.; and in 1959 he became chairman of Furness, Withy.

Those were some of the decision-makers who controlled Royal Mail's destiny. Mr Warwick and his colleagues were people who watched the *first 'A'* ships entering service before the First World War – small wonder that they were reluctant to embrace the rapidly changing world by 1960. The criticism would be that they did not acknowledge those changes and give more power to those better suited to coping with it.

If there is justification for a charge of stagnation during the early to mid 1960s, it would be unfair to tar the 1950s with the same brush. There was far less reason to believe at that time that such enormous changes would be wrought in the following decade. A hint, perhaps, but not certainty. That was reflected in a comment, referring to the new 'A' ships, made by RML's new chairman, H. Leslie Bowes, about his predecessor: 'It required a good deal of courage to build splendid ships of this kind at this time, an act of faith in the continued growth and prosperity of the South American nations in which all concerned have the greatest confidence'.

At the time these ships were ordered, the industry was not seriously in a state of flux. They would have been advanced on paper by 1956 and 1957, well before the kind of factors which would destroy line services had firmed as a serious threat. Along with ten conventional break-bulk freighters built in the 1950s – cumulatively a massive investment, with the 'A' ships requiring a large bank loan – this was a calculated gamble that the ships would remain viable throughout a normal lifetime. Conversely, the long-term future for such vessels was sufficiently uncertain that a decision left until the future was set in concrete would probably never be made. That was Walter Warwick's 'courage'.

In the event, their withdrawal late in the 1960s was not simply a matter of inadequate cargo or passenger earnings. Staff wages became increasingly important; labour costs caused headaches in many an industry, and the more labour-intensive an industry was, the more difficult the problem became. There were escalating fuel costs; greater difficulty in gaining adequate cargoes because of flag discrimination; increasing competition from airlines; and a reduction in meat cargo quotas from South America. Ordering the 'A' ships, then, was – depending on your point of view – an act of faith or a calculated gamble.

I came to know them intimately and became very attached to them. They were ships which grew on you – they didn't possess the instantaneous breathtaking appeal of *Alcantara* and *Asturias*, but over time each created its own character. The first, *Amazon*, seemed to reflect her slightly older status (and, perhaps, the fact that she was the only one to have a Royal sponsor, Princess Margaret), by a certain aloofness, an aura of efficient independence. In contrast, *Arlanza* was renowned as a sociable vessel, with a more carefree atmosphere than her sisters. The middle ship was *Aragon*, probably between the others in character, too; thought by many to have the nicest layout and décor and, at least at times, the best food. These were subtle differences, though, for you could board any of them and be immediately enveloped by their sense of relaxed comfort. Not for nothing were they christened 'the three graces'.

When the order was placed with Harland & Wolff, the Company announced its re-shaping of the mail and passenger services. The express mail line from Southampton would, after more than a century, be abolished. *Alcantara* was to be broken up and *Andes* converted for full-time cruising. The new ships would be London-based, replacing the *Highland* ships, but they would also absorb the former express Southampton mail service.

In terms of passenger capacity, there would be a drop in availability, approximately 1,400 being the combined total. This seemed a balanced decision reflecting expected growth in air travel against confidence that ships would maintain a fair share of the market. They would maintain the mail service. Perhaps most important, though, was the provision of almost half a million cubic feet of refrigerated cargo space in each. For so long the concept of a dual-purpose liner was the key to success, but with the coming changes, that was ironically one of the factors which went against them after a few years.

The entry for *Magdalena* highlighted similarities and differences between that ship and the new ones a decade later. The two most significant variations were that the 'A' ships were given diesel engines and three classes of passenger accommodation. *Magdalena* and the *Highland* ships had carried only first and third class passengers. It was probably the composite role of the 'A' ships – replacing both the *Highland* ships and the Southampton service – which led to the provision of three passenger classes.

Tourist class offered at a cheap rate a standard of accommodation which must have been a revelation to migrating Spaniards and Portuguese. It was a perfectly acceptable level of comfort for any travellers on a tight budget. No cabins contained more than four berths and each had wardrobe space and hot and cold water. Though the tourist public rooms were functional rather than luxurious, they were large, airy (all passenger spaces were air-conditioned), bright and comfortable. A separate galley adjoined the tourist class restaurant, where Portuguese staff cooked very different meals from those served in the other restaurants. Tourist passengers had to make do mostly with deck spaces abaft the superstructure, in the way of the after hatch, but they succeeded splendidly in turning the area into a vibrant Latin quarter. Often at night the sounds of singing, laughter and guitar music would draw other passengers to tourist class territory where an impromptu fiesta was in progress.

First and Cabin class passengers were housed in the main body of accommodation. Though each class had its own public rooms, various squares, lifts and stairways were common to both. The central point was known ubiquitously as 'C deck Square'; into this area all passengers except tourist class embarked, choking arteries to other parts of the ship. Here, too, was the Purser's Office and bank, the entrance to cabin class areas and a subsidiary entrance to the tourist class restaurant, the corridor leading to the first class restaurant and officers' quarters, and lifts and stairways to just about everywhere else.

Lounges, smokerooms and other amenities for first and cabin class were all above C deck. Notable for the cabin class was the smokeroom bar, an unusually shaped room (varying slightly in each ship) which was so welcoming and full of atmosphere that regular travellers in first class at times abandoned their larger and more luxuriously carpeted bar in favour of it. *Aragon's* smokeroom, where a curved screen of bamboo and flourishing cacti led to its nick-name of the Bamboo Bar, was particularly attractive.

First class public rooms naturally left the most indelible memory. In the 'A' ships they were very fine; a quiet touch of class. Memories dwell largely on their comfort – thick-pile richly coloured carpets and the kind of easy chairs into which one seemed to sink into soft oblivion. The first class restaurants were splendid. Their simple but inspired design ran the width of the ship and had a curved appearance as they followed the contour of the superstructure front. Glass screens inlaid with unobtrusive gold tracery formed an effective break and helped hide the entrance doorways and the waiters' doors to the galley.

The aesthetic appeal of a large mirror fitted behind the captain's table was lost on me when I battled with its reflective qualities while photographing after-dinner speakers. There was, then, a uniqueness about these rooms, helped by their comparatively small size, which made them particularly pleasing.

Services to South America were conservative in terms of entertainment, films and dancing to taped music being the principal offerings. The 'A' ships showed films in all classes, but with no cinema on board, the respective lounges were used. The first class lounge had remote control wall panels which slid back to reveal a screen, and there was a projection box behind the opposite wall.

The first class smokeroom bar led out to the lido deck and swimming pool, an area which looked particularly fine on warm nights with concealed underwater lighting and coloured lights around the lido deck. Cabin and tourist class passengers had their own pools, and a toddlers pool was forward in the bridge housing. The 'A' ships were given the 'split bridge' design, where an open deck and hatchway separated the bridge structure from the main passenger accommodation.

The generally unobtrusive décor possessed attractive feature items. A mural was the decorative focal point of each first class smokeroom. In *Arlanza* it was a splendid painting in oils by Claude Muncaster of the Iguazu Falls; *Aragon* had a photomural of an engraving depicting London shortly before the Great Fire of 1666; and *Amazon* had a painting of South American wildlife, treated 'in a stylised manner' by Dolf Reiser.

Wood panelling was widely used. The most interesting effect was in *Arlanza*'s cabin class restaurant, in which Waring & Gillow (who shared the majority of décor with Heaton Tabb) created two large scenes in traditional Chinese marquetry. A large mirror in the same room continued the theme with black decorations and motifs in Chinese character. The same ship had marquetry panels depicting the five oceans and the sea god Poseidon.

Aragon's first class gallery contained an unusual leather wall map showing the world's shipping routes. In her first class lounge were sprays of gilded orchids against a black leather background, and illuminated perspex panels displaying the Coat of Arms of the Duchy of Aragon and its capital city, Saragossa. Nine original watercolour studies of orchids were found near the bar in the first class smokeroom. Among *Amazon*'s features the most notable was a series of delicate colour and line drawings of dances of the world on ivory plastic panels in the first class lounge.

Each vessel had five holds and four 'tweendecks, most spaces catering for meat and fruit cargoes. There were forty-five separate chambers and trunks, each isolated from the others to avoid cross-tainting of produce. They also utilised a recent development to deodorise cargo spaces after discharge – ultra-violet lamps irradiating an air stream from fans, which converted oxygen to ozone. Many derricks and posts, rigging and winches influenced their appearance. Their profiles were also affected by high-sided hulls – this, together with a broad beam (78 feet) and 'Belfast bottom', was to combat the ever-present difficulties of the River Plate.

Their length was 583ft overall and 540ft bp, moulded breadth 78ft and gross tonnage 20,350. Of the half a million cubic feet of cargo space, 435,000 was insulated for chilled and frozen cargoes. Cargo handling equipment included two 15-ton, four 10-ton, two

7-ton and twelve 5-ton tubular steel derricks. Thermotank plants provided air-conditioning to all accommodation and public spaces; first class cabins had individual controls for temperature and airflow.

First class accommodation was for ninety-two passengers and cabin class eighty-two, with an additional fifteen interchangeable cabins. Tourist class, on D and E decks, accommodated 275. Crew members, who had their own galley, lived in single and double cabins.

Propelling machinery consisted of two single-acting Harland & Wolff/Burmeister & Wain six-cylinder, pressure induction, two-stroke diesel engines of opposed piston design, with exhaust pistons controlled by eccentrics on the crankshaft. It was a type of machinery in which Royal Mail and Harland & Wolff had gained experience during the 1950s with many new cargo liners. The main cylinder bore was 750mm. Though designed for heavy-grade fuel oils, the engines could use diesel grade if required. There was particular interest with the electrical installation, for these liners were the first British ships to use alternating current throughout.

From Slipway to Seaway

The three ships were ordered from Harland & Wolff at Belfast. At first it was planned, I believe, that they would follow their predecessors in having black hulls; I have seen no explanation as to why they were, in the event, painted white, a colour previously adopted for the South America service for only a couple of years after 1900.

Amazon was launched by Princess Margaret on 7 July 1959; *Aragon* by Lady Snedden (wife of Sir Richard Snedden, Director of the Shipping Federation) on 20 October 1959; and *Arlanza* by Lady Dorothy MacMillan (wife of the then Prime Minister, Sir Harold MacMillan) on 13 April 1960. As the first of the group, *Amazon* naturally absorbed the bulk of their early publicity. Upwards of 20,000 people flocked to the shipyard to watch her enter the water, and the 400 official guests included Government representatives and dignitaries of South American nations.

Speaking after the launch, Princess Margaret said:

> She is the first of a new class and I am sure that she will uphold all the proud traditions of the Royal Mail Lines, whose reputation for fine ships has been established for over a century. The close ties between our country and South America go back to the early 19th century, and I am glad that the bond of friendship will be further strengthened by the opportunities that the Amazon and her sister-ships will provide for increased commerce and passenger travel. I feel it is most important that even today, in this age of air travel, we should continue to build great ships. We are a maritime race and our merchant navy is as important to us now as it has ever been.

For three weeks during January 1960 *Amazon* – by then in London's Royal Docks – received wave after wave of visitors – foreign and British government officials, City Livery clubs, bankers, port officials, shippers and the media. In the midst of all this, on 12 January, Princess Margaret inspected the ship from top to bottom. She expressed most interest in the kitchens, and especially the two sets of escalators – a novel feature for ships then – which linked the galley to the first and cabin class restaurants one deck above.

Amazon *(III) enters the water at Belfast in 1959 after being christened by Princess Margaret. Note the stylised houseflag with a rope circle adorning the bow. This nice touch (on all three ships) was the only time bow decorations had appeared since the days of clipper bows and figureheads.*

The launching of Arlanza *(II) in 1960 occurred in squally conditions and there was a lengthy battle to get her under control. She is seen with the tug* Audacious *shortly after entering the water.*

Arlanza *(II) pictured off Southend in September 1960, approaching London from the builder's yard to start her career. (*Author's photograph*)*

It is, of course, a tradition that the owner presents a gift to a vessel's sponsor. Royal Mail's choice for Princess Margaret (and to Lady MacMillan after she had christened *Arlanza*) was a postage stamp. These, though, were no ordinary stamps; they were among the last known survivors of the special stamps issued by RMSP in 1875 as legal postal currency, mostly in Caribbean areas where drastic cuts in the Post Office subsidy had forced a curtailment of services. Lady Dorothy's ceremony with *Arlanza* came to the verge of being postponed on a day of sunshine, heavy showers and violent wind. The squally conditions had Harland & Wolff's experts in two minds up to the last moment. Finally they said the launching could go ahead. A band played enthusiastically, its music all but lost against the platform's canvas cover flapping noisily. When *Arlanza* entered the water she got into difficulties, for her high hull was caught by the wind, and waiting tugs battled to secure lines. It took an hour to get her under control.

Aragon, which had entered the water without problems the previous October, was conveniently ready for her voyage to London in time to bring guests returning from *Arlanza*'s launching. Belfast's weather rather upset this plan as well, and she did not reach the Thames until 16 April. On the 29th she departed for her maiden voyage under the command of Captain T.W. Stevens RD, RNR.

At Vigo on 2 May, Señor Antonio Zubiri, President of the County Council of Saragossa, presented the ship with a replica of the Arms of Aragon. In *Amazon*, Commodore Harry E. Sang received a testimonial from a group of passengers during her second voyage, prompted by no greater reason than that a group of passengers had enjoyed their passage. This was a ballet company, under the Marquis de Cuevas, en route to Buenos Aires, who presented a framed photograph of the forty-one strong company, surrounded by their signatures.

Among regular travellers with Royal Mail were many Ambassadors, but probably there was no ambassadorial voyage like *Arlanza*'s homeward trip in September 1961, when the

Princess Margaret touring Amazon *(III), the ship she had launched in January 1960. With her is RML's chairman Walter Warwick, and behind them Commodore Harry Sang and H. Leslie Bowes, who was shortly to become chairman after Mr Warwick's retirement.*

British Ambassador to Uruguay, the Danish Ambassador to Portugal and the Uruguayan Ambassador to Holland all travelled to London in the ship. It was a good voyage for passengers all round – on the southbound voyage she carried no less than 1,030, a figure made possible by separate coastwise and transatlantic bookings.

At much the same time *Amazon*, Capt. Gilbert S. Grant RD, RNR, docked at and sailed from Rio de Janeiro without the aid of tugs or port labour during a strike. As she left, the Italian liner *Guilio Cesare*, which was ferrying passengers to and fro by launch, sounded three siren blasts in recognition of Capt. Grant's fine seamanship. *Amazon* had an eventful crossing late the following year – the ship's surgeons performed two appendicitis operations, then she rendezvoused with *Arlanza* in the Atlantic to transfer a stowaway.

Next voyage, Capt. T.W.F. Bolland in *Arlanza* returned Capt. Grant's courtesy by accepting a stowaway from *Amazon* by sea transfer, this time off the Brazilian coast. The two operations succeeded so well (and provided entertainment for passengers) that stowaway sea transfers became an 'A' ship speciality. Virtually every voyage turned up anything from one to four unofficial passengers, who became expensive items. When two ships were not conveniently passing, stowaways were landed in Police custody at the first port and later picked up by the next 'A' ship travelling the opposite way. They were regarded by officers, as I was told once, as something annoying that had to be lived with, 'like scavenge fires in the engineroom'. They were to be expected as long as visitors were allowed on board at the ports. In South America visitors provided a traumatic time. One captain estimated that 900 people swarmed on board at Buenos Aires on one occasion, while Capt. Bolland wrote in 1963: 'As I have reported before, the behaviour of visitors at Montevideo is appalling. This voyage articles were stolen and ship's fittings damaged'.

Royalty became involved with another 'A' ship in 1962, when the Duke of Edinburgh visited *Arlanza* at Buenos Aires. The British Ambassador, Sir George Middleton KCMG, greeted the Duke, and the biggest reception ever held on the three ships was under way, with 880 members of the British community in Buenos Aires on board. Later that year *Arlanza*, at Vigo, was presented with a plaque of the Arms of the Arlanza family by the Marqués de Arlanza.

Teething troubles on the ships were soon ironed out, the only lingering problem being a long chapter of minor irritations in *Arlanza*'s engineroom. At one period, cracked piston liners were in vogue, sometimes two or more in a single voyage. Passenger totals varied enormously. *Arlanza*, as mentioned earlier, carried 1,030 southbound on voyage five. On a later passage, northbound, she had little more than a hundred, only eleven in first class. Traffic was seasonal and during the northern hemisphere winter many round-voyagers occupied first class. They remained on board in the River Plate, being charged only £3 a day for the pleasure (as expressed by many) of watching meat-loading operations at the frigorificos.

Officers looking after cargo had a difficult job. Freights of all kinds were carried and they were shipped and discharged in a complex series of permutations – London to Buenos Aires, Vigo to Santos, Lisbon to Las Palmas, Las Palmas to Montevideo and so on. Some needed chilled accommodation, some frozen and some general stowage. There were shippers from South America who were not happy with the spaces allocated, and

Chilled and frozen meat cargoes were crucial aspects of Royal Mail's South America trades in the twentieth century. Refrigerated beef is here being unloaded from Aragon (II) *at London's Z Shed, Royal Victoria Dock during the 1960s.* (Author's photograph)

others who booked cargoes which failed to eventuate. What did they carry? A short answer might be 'machinery out, meat home'. Manufactured products (though much more varied than machinery) formed a high proportion of southbound freight. This was supplemented (some seasonally) by cork (from Lisbon), chestnuts (Vigo and Lisbon), melons (Vigo), frozen fish (Las Palmas), bananas, tomatoes and frozen shrimps (Santos).

After a week or more loading meat, the ships began the northbound voyage, picking up extra cargoes en route – bulk peanut oil, tung oil, apples and pears, oranges, grapefruit and other citrus, gluten feed, frozen horse meat, coffee, sawn timber, castor oil (in deep tanks, loaded by pipeline), peanuts, tomatoes, cucumbers, potatoes, frozen fish and preserves.

'A' Ship Tales

Willie Repetto, patient and dignified, sat a little in front of fifty other islanders from Tristan da Cunha, listening gravely to Nigel Fisher from the Colonial Office. It was March 1963 and the islanders were on board *Amazon* at Tilbury, about to fulfil their dream of returning to a home they had hurriedly left in the wake of volcanic eruptions. This advance party had the task of making the island habitable again – but first they faced the more daunting experience of an onslaught of Fleet Street reporters and television cameras. It wasn't easy for them, for these people belonged to a different world. It was the islanders' unique heritage, more than anything, which characterised the quiet dignity of Willie Repetto in *Amazon*, and the patriarchal figure of a bearded William Glass – a direct descendent of Tristan's first leader – as he stood on deck and gazed with creased eyes down the narrow reaches of the Thames. In that direction lay the sea and Tristan da Cunha. There were few more interesting or worthy passengers who set foot on the 'A' ships.

Amazon had cameras on board again soon afterwards. A film about Trinity House pilotage was being made in Rank's *Look at Life* series. Called *Pilot Aboard*, it covered aspects of the pilotage service around Britain's coast. The camera team joined *Amazon* with the pilot off Gravesend to film the passage upriver to the Royal Docks. No-one, I suspect, had thought through the logistics of hauling nine people and a considerable tonnage of very expensive camera and sound equipment onto the slowly-moving ship.

Early in 1965 *Amazon* was host ship for the finals of the first Ocean Princess contest. During its short life this promotion by Ocean Travel Development was popular. Any beauty contest was likely to gain the interest of the media, and especially so with the line-up of judges assembled in *Amazon* – they included actor Ian Hendry and his actress wife Janet Munro, producer/director team Betty Box and Ralph Thomas (they were responsible for the early Carry On films), actress June Thorburn and pop star Brian Poole.

Ocean Travel Development (OTD) was established to promote the concept of voyaging by sea at a time when aircraft were beginning to carry all before them. In that sense, as we discovered, it was a lost cause. It was a joint venture by major British shipping companies to boost the image and awareness of ship travel, and it operated under the chairmanship of the redoubtable Coard Squarey. The major venture created by OTD was Ocean Travel Fortnight, when passenger ships were opened to the public. Whichever 'A' ship was in London annually received its quota of visitors. They were popular events; many people had never set eyes on a large ship before, let alone been on one. How many, though, were

A familiar silhouette off Tilbury Landing Stage in the mid-1960s as one of the 'A' ships is manoeuvred to the Stage to embark passengers. (Author's photograph)

The only occasion all three 'A' ships – Amazon (III), Aragon (II) and Arlanza (II) – were seen in one photo. It occurred in London's Royal Victoria Dock during July 1966 and was the result of a seamen's strike. The other ship in the picture (with black hull) was also a Royal Mail ship, either Loch Avon *or* Loch Garth. (Author's photograph)

A first class cabin in Amazon *(III).*

A corner of the first class lounge in Aragon *(II). The rooms in these ships enjoyed a touch of class and great comfort without much of the flamboyance evident in many ships from earlier in the century.*

persuaded to book a voyage was probably never calculated. The whole OTD business mirrored the situation in which passenger shipping then found itself – it was an exercise that had to be mounted, but as the 1960s progressed it became clear that nothing could halt the slide in line services.

During 1965 and 1966 the 'A' ships went through a variety of happenings. The most notable belonged to *Aragon*, in London's King George V Dock, when she was visited by that king of entertainers, Charles Chaplin (he wasn't yet knighted). He was searching for a suitable ship in which to film scenes from *A Countess from Hong Kong* – in the event, I believe, he filmed in the studio, but his informal Saturday afternoon visit to *Aragon*, when he toured the ship and had afternoon tea, was greatly enjoyed by everyone who met him.

The saddest story occurred in September 1965 when a barman in the homeward-bound *Amazon* became ill with asthma. It was decided to divert to Plymouth to land him, but so much oxygen was being used that the ship's supply would not last. Naval authorities agreed to provide a high-speed air-sea rescue launch. Escorted by a Shackleton aircraft of Coastal Command, it rendezvoused with *Amazon* at 10 p.m., the launch having covered 130 miles in five hours. With the oxygen on board, the naval dockyard supplied another fast launch, which was standing by at 3.30 a.m. to take out a stretcher party and the Shipping Federation doctor. By then fog had taken a hand and it was six o'clock before the ship anchored; by 6.45 a.m. the launch, with patient, had left the ship and he was in hospital soon after seven. What an immense combined exercise! And how devastating, after such effort, to record that the man died shortly after reaching hospital.

Inevitably, illness, accident and death were encountered in the ships. An idea of the problems and occasional crises may be gained from the following examples, from both crew and passengers: severe nervous breakdown, epilepsy, glaucoma, thrombosis, alcoholism, acute appendicitis, attempted suicide, duodenal ulcers, broken kneecap, spinal injuries, syphilis, heart attacks, kidney stones, phlebitis and bronchial pneumonia. Crew members were injured in shooting and knifing attacks; a pilot suffered a hernia; a seaman was landed and taken to hospital with 'anxiety neurosis'; another fell through three decks in No.1 hold but emerged without serious injury.

During *Arlanza's* southbound crossing of the Bay of Biscay on Voyage 8, a seaman was reported missing. The ship retraced her course, and eventually he was found – fast asleep in the officers' toilet. Later that voyage the ship hosted the party attended by Prince Philip referred to earlier. *Arlanza* then took on board over 3,000 tons of meat and tried to depart. She was firmly aground at her berth and had to wait four hours for the tide to refloat her. Between Montevideo and Santos Capt. Bolland took on board a stowaway from *Amazon* in one of the sea transfers at which the crews were so adept. Homeward earnings were high on that voyage, with 4,500 tons of freight and 446 passengers for the transatlantic crossing. On the outward trip 460 passengers had been carried.

Aragon's eighteenth voyage was also eventful, and again the incidents began during the southbound crossing of the Bay of Biscay – No.2 alternator failed, causing the automatic helmsman and stabilisers to fail too. As a result, in poor weather she broached-to for 'a sufficiently long period to break a considerable amount of crockery and glass'. A day later, while leaving Vigo (where no tugs were available), a buoy rope parted and the wind brought *Aragon* into contact with the quayside, damaging the starboard quarter. The captain's unhappiness wasn't helped by the presence on board of the Chairman, H. Leslie Bowes. At Las Palmas an officer was landed to hospital with an injured hand, sustained during boat drill, and a steward was discharged 'on the grounds of mental instability'.

In the River Plate she loaded meat at Armour's Wharf and moved on to Swift's. The lines were ready for running ashore when the fresh breeze suddenly whipped into a Force 8 gale. The underpowered tugs couldn't hold the ship and she drifted across the water towards a loaded tanker. Capt. W.S. Thomas reported later: 'I told the pilot I was "getting out". Tugs were immediately slipped and "full ahead" rung until vessel was not only clear of the tanker but also a collection of small craft'. In Santos Bay a heavy swell made the ship roll heavily and bump bottom five times, causing minor damage. Throughout the voyage an unwelcome epidemic of cockroaches roamed the ship, reaching as far afield as A deck cabins.

At Montevideo there was a problem which mirrored one of the most frustrating situations through the 1960s. Capt. Thomas recorded that 'the customary and fictitious claims were made by the stevedores for loading into gaseous and damp spaces. These claims were substantiated by the Government inspector who is completely dominated by the men'. Virtually every voyage by an 'A' ship recorded some such problem at South American ports. Montevideo's labour situation was so consistently bad that a twenty-four hour lightning strike was treated as an everyday occurrence. November 1964 found them working half hour on/half hour off, immediately following a two-day strike, and when they *were* working, the performance brought comments like 'shamefully slow'.

One of the less graceful moments for Amazon *(III) after she struck the wharf at Vigo in August 1963.*

The Uruguayan port was not alone in causing freight-handling difficulties, and some situations were more serious. They were encapsulated by an event at Buenos Aires in 1962. A shipper was allocated No.2 lower hold in *Arlanza* for part of its meat quota. The firm refused to use those spaces and insisted that if its chilled beef was not given room elsewhere it would be loaded in an Argentine vessel instead. In official circles this kind of thing was diplomatically referred to as 'flag discrimination'. Such ransom demands were serious enough in themselves, but one side-effect was potentially worse. *Arlanza*'s master wrote: 'Fortunately more frozen cargo was made available and other spaces were found, but if no frozen had come forward it would have caused a serious stability problem'.

When *Arlanza* was at Santos in May 1964 there was difficulty loading castor oil. Pumps broke down one after the other and all round it was 'the most inefficient operation' her captain had ever experienced. Two years later, at Buenos Aires, *Aragon*'s officers and crew supervised youths and scab labour to discharge freight during a port labour strike; the ship's personnel, in fact, did much of the work themselves. At Recife 'a large number of stevedores lay about doing precisely nothing' – which was put down to 'the Carnival spirit'. In contrast, at Lisbon near the end of the voyage, cargo work was completed in record time: 'The stevedores got a move on so that they could attend a football match'. On her next voyage *Aragon* suffered at Rio de Janeiro, where loading of frozen meat 'could only be described as scandalously slow'. There was a dispute at Las Palmas on one occasion, between a shipper and consignee, as to whether 125 tons of frozen fish should be loaded with or without their heads. When *Aragon* departed – minus the fish – the argument was still raging.

With its peculiar current flow and steeply-dropping seabed from the Continental Shelf, the Bay of Biscay often provides a rough ride. I experienced that in *Arlanza* – an astonishing display of ferocity with the ship rolling far and wide for hour after hour. I was distinctly peeved that in his voyage report Capt. Gibbons, with all his years of storms at sea behind him, dismissed the whole affair with the trite words 'Gale and storm force winds were experienced on leaving Vigo until arrival in Southampton'. To me it had warranted Conradian hyperbole. Probably the fiercest Biscay conditions were encountered by *Aragon* in October 1964, when winds increased to Force 12. Speed was reduced to lessen pounding and propeller racing. In that scenario *Aragon* answered a distress call from the Spanish freighter *Vincente Suarez*, with nineteen men and a woman on board. The tanker *Esso Bremen* was already standing by. Little could be done for the apparently foundering ship in such enormous seas. Thus the steamer's crew remained on board and *Esso Bremen*'s master told *Aragon* that he was confident of coping. Satisfied that he could do nothing further, Commodore Thomas resumed his uncomfortable passage. He heard later that *Vincente Suarez* reached Brest under her own power.

One of the 'A' ships in 1966 took the ground on her port side while moving downriver from La Plata; she 'pushed heavily for about two kilometres until refloating' and suffered no damage. It says something about the nature of the River Plate that a responsible shipmaster in command of a 20,000-ton liner will 'drag' his ship over the mud for more than a mile. Wind also caused problems in the Plate. One occasion was at Interseccion, Buenos Aires, where in December 1963 *Aragon* was damaged on the port quarter when the motorship *Waterland* struck her while leaving the quay. Another problem area can be the Tagus bar, approaching Lisbon. In March 1963 *Aragon* experienced a bad crossing. The rolling and yawing occurred during breakfast, 'but since the staff had ample warning, breakages were slight'. The biggest roll was described as 'more in the nature of a heavy list'.

Between Vigo and Lisbon, *Arlanza* once closed on a ship which was 'burning so fiercely that it was impossible for any humans to be alive on board'. Trawlers were steaming around the stricken ship and *Arlanza* could clearly do nothing to help. During her next voyage *Arlanza* herself was threatened by fire – several blazes were deliberately started in the third class accommodation, but were put out before serious damage could occur.

On voyage thirty-four she intercepted distress calls from the German steamer *Arenberg*, on fire and being abandoned in the Bay of Biscay. *Arlanza* raced to the scene, where smaller vessels were already searching for survivors. *Arlanza* approached close to *Arenberg*, to make sure that no-one remained on board. She then helped with the search for survivors in the middle of a January night. One of the other ships eventually found a lifeboat with *Arenberg's* crew on board, and *Arlanza* was able to resume her passage.

It was rare for the 'A' ships to vary their itineraries, though there was some musical chairs with French ports – originally Cherbourg outward and Boulogne northbound, but after a time the calls were reversed and eventually no French port was visited on the homeward passage. Their original schedule was London, Cherbourg, Vigo, Lisbon, Las Palmas, Rio de Janeiro, Santos, Montevideo, Buenos Aires; northbound the same ports were visited in reverse except for Boulogne *vice* Cherbourg.

The biggest itinerary change was the addition in 1964 of Rotterdam as a port of discharge. The ships now called at Southampton homeward to disembark UK passengers before proceeding to Rotterdam, thus for the last few years Southampton was again part of the Company's mail service. After the call at Rotterdam, they departed for London's Royal Victoria Dock. Very rarely did they depart from the schedule, though once in a while they were seen at Recife, and in June 1963 *Arlanza* called at Salvador. That unheard-of diversion was at the request of the Governor of the State of Bahia, so that four passengers might embark – His Eminence Cardinal Augusto Alvaro da Silva and three of his staff.

Reports reached Capt. W.A. Kennedy on one occasion that a man with a gun was 'on the loose' in *Aragon*. The master soon apprehended 'a disreputable looking character carrying a revolver'. The Brazilian gentleman, it seems, was 'some sort of plain clothes investigator of the Alfandega engaged upon a special mission'. He was permitted to continue his mission, but without the aid of his revolver. Someone of his ilk could perhaps have been useful in *Arlanza* in December 1963, though, as it turned out, Capt. Bolland was a more than adequate investigator. At Lisbon, southbound, Capt. Bolland became more and more perplexed as the passengers' baggage was loaded. During recent calls, the tourist class baggage seemed to increase with each successive voyage without a similar increase in passenger numbers. On this occasion, in addition to the usual motley collection of bags there were over 100 cases, all the same size. There was no time to check during loading, but when the ship was at sea an investigation was made. One by one the suspect cases were opened. Each contained a barrel of wine.

Outward bound on her final South America voyage, *Amazon* was involved, off the coast of Brazil, in a medical rescue. A lady passenger on board the Houlder Bros. freighter *St Merriel* decided to give birth prematurely and a doctor was urgently requested. *Amazon* altered course, but turned back when it was learned that a Russian ship was closer. However, the baby arrived before either ship could have reached *St Merriel*. There were post-birth complications, and when the Russian doctor arrived he could do little to help as he had injured a hand. *Amazon*'s help was again sought and as she raced towards the freighter her carpenter was busy knocking up an improvised incubator of plywood and perspex. As dusk approached, passengers crowding *Amazon*'s rails saw *St Merriel's* mast lights ahead; the motor lifeboat was lowered into the swell. After ninety minutes the returning boat was spotted bobbing between the waves and was soon back in the davits after a successful mission. The baby, a girl, was christened Merriel.

At the end of the voyage, reporters boarded at Tilbury Landing Stage to interview three British climbers who had made the voyage home in the ship. Ian Clough, his wife Niki and Gordon Hibberd were among a team which conquered the previously unscaled 10,000-foot Fortress peak in the Patagonian Andes. They disembarked from the ship on 14 March 1968, together with the remainder of *Amazon*'s last complement of passengers from South America. *Amazon* was to be transferred, within the Furness Withy Group, to Shaw Savill Line, converted to an all-tourist class ship and placed on a round-the-world service. Before the conversion she made a voyage to South Africa under charter to Union-Castle Line, bringing home a large fruit cargo.

Despite the reinstatement during 1968 of Argentine meat shipments after a ban imposed because of Britain's foot-and-mouth outbreak, the overall quota for Britain had been cut and the future was too uncertain for Royal Mail to maintain such expensive ships on the route. With a mail contract to maintain and passenger bookings to honour, they had to keep a strict and tight schedule, which became even tighter during the final few voyages as a day or more was cut from voyage times. Late in 1968 the Company announced that *Aragon* and *Arlanza* would follow *Amazon* into the Shaw Savill fleet. *Arlanza* made her last voyage to South America in the winter of 1968/69 and *Aragon* closed the service a few weeks later. There you have the bones of an event which, almost without a whimper, ended nearly 130 years of mail voyages by Royal Mail. (*Aragon's* voyage which closed the mail service is described in Volume 1.)

A reasonable amount of work took place at Belfast to make the 'A' ships suitable for the round-the-world service, but it involved little structural alteration. The main tasks were to convert them from three-class ships to tourist class only, and to cater for the longer duration of the voyage, particularly the long haul across the Pacific. Much of the accommodation appeared little different. Cabins were altered to minimise the quality difference, but according to some passengers the result wasn't very satisfactory – a gulf remained between the highest and lowest standards without an appropriate price difference. Passengers at least had the run of the ship as far as amenities and public rooms were concerned.

Shaw Savill was lucky in having a wide range of rooms at its disposal; it was possible, for instance, to plan noisy rooms for teenagers well away from the more sedate lounges enjoyed by older travellers – the ships were now to handle a different range of clientele.

The former tourist class swimming pool became a children's paddling pool and the other two were retained for adults. The tourist class lounge on C deck became a cinema. Further forward on C deck were the three restaurants. Only the first and cabin class ones were now used (which also caused friction from time to time owing to the quality difference); the tourist class restaurant became a baggage room. Cargo spaces were well used, particularly for meat, fruit and dairy produce from New Zealand and Australia.

The new names for the ships were *Akaroa* (ex *Amazon*), *Aranda* (ex *Aragon*) and *Arawa* (ex *Arlanza*). They achieved a moderately popular following, sometimes supplementing *Southern Cross* and *Northern Star* and at other times holding the fort while the other two cruised. Generally there was little to record, though in April 1970 *Akaroa* suffered an engineroom fire which crippled her 1,200 miles from Bermuda. An SOS was sent and US Coastguard ships and planes and a dozen other vessels headed towards her. It had the makings of a full-scale emergency but, while far from being a false alarm, the fire proved less damaging than had at first been feared.

Not long after that, the winds of change again began to blow. Changes in economic management which resulted from the massive capital investment facing the industry for more advanced and specialised tonnage altered the whole structure of shipping companies. High outlays for new types of ship and freight-handling methods were added to crippling cost increases for fuel, wages, port charges and the like. The 'A' ships could no longer be profitably used by Shaw Savill; thus, after such a short time in their new role they were placed on the market.

They attracted buyers almost at once; ironically, the ease with which buyers were found was probably due to the very trend towards specialisation which was spelling the end of the line for vessels like the 'A' ships. All three were purchased by joint-venture Norwegian owners for conversion to car carriers. Unlike their previous change from Royal Mail to Shaw Savill, this conversion was a major affair, a complete rebuild above the hull, and large-scale changes below.

Epilogue

After working for Royal Mail for twelve years I left in September 1971, drawn by the mystique of some of the more remote regions of the world. In the early stages of my journey, travelling in a distinctly aged bus, I was in Yugoslavia heading for the Adriatic. We drove through Rijeka and skirted the Jadranbrod repair basin in its picturesque setting. My fellow passengers thought I was a touch eccentric, leaning far out of the window taking photographs of two ships moored at the basin. They were two of the 'A' ships. One was still easily recognisable but the other was, above the hull, a mess of uncompleted box-like appendages. Her new name was already roughly painted on the hull – *Höegh Traveller*.

What a prosaic final chapter to the Company's mail services. While I was still remembering 'the three graces' as they were in their heyday, that fleeting vision of what would become a hideous floating box was a jolting reminder of the suddenness and comprehensiveness with which the world of shipping had changed. This was just twelve years after Princess Margaret had commended Royal Mail for its faith in the future, continuing to build great ships, 'even today in this age of air travel'.

The former Aragon *(II) at Rijeka in September 1971, undergoing conversion to a car carrier. She became* Höegh Traveller. *Astern of her, awaiting her conversion, is* Arawa, *ex-*Arlanza *(II).* (Author's photograph)

Aranda, ex *Aragon*, emerged as *Höegh Traveller* and *Arawa*, ex *Arlanza*, as *Höegh Transit* (quickly renamed *Höegh Trotter*), both owned by Leif Höegh A/S of Oslo. *Akaroa*, ex *Amazon*, underwent a similar conversion, becoming *Akarita*, owned by J.M. Ugland of Grimstad (the two companies operated a joint service). The radical changes reduced their tonnages, which had previously dropped from about 20,000 gross to 18,000 under Shaw Savill, to just 10,900.

In the late 1970s they went to a group in Monrovia, becoming *Hual Traveller*, *Hual Trotter* and *Hual Akarita*. The word 'Hual' was later dropped from their names; and by the early 1980s they had vanished from the Register, delivered to shipbreakers in the Far East.

Other ships
Esk (I), *Prince*, *Camilla*, *Mersey* and *Arno* (I)

From the start of South America services until *Douro* inaugurated the through service to Buenos Aires in 1869, these ships successively operated a feeder service from Rio de Janeiro to the River Plate.

Esk was purchased to replace the schooner *Lee*, which had been lost in the middle of 1848. Her early service would therefore have embraced local routes in the West Indies. Purchased during construction at Menzies' yard at Leith, she was a 231-ton schooner

There are no known contemporary illustrations of Esk *(I), RMSP's first feeder ship between Rio de Janeiro and the River Plate. This drawing was made by Howard Jarvis in the 1960s, based on available information.*

supported by an auxiliary screw. This made her the first screw steamer in the Royal Mail fleet. Her trials in the Firth of Forth on 27 June 1849 were regarded as 'very pleasing'.

By the time 89 tons had been deducted for engine spaces, *Esk*'s net tonnage was a mere 142. Her main saloon, with eight berths opening from it and a 'large skylight' above, measured 12ft by 9ft 9in, with a height of 6ft 6in. A further five berths were off the Ladies' Saloon (which was 16ft 3in by 8ft) and the remaining sixteen berths adjoined the forward saloon, the most spacious at 12ft 3in by 18ft 10in, and 7ft high. The passenger capacity of twenty-nine comprised, apparently, twenty-four males and five females, an imbalance which would have caused great difficulty filling the ship.

At a directors meeting in October 1850 there was discussion as to whether *Esk* should be used for the River Plate feeder service or whether a steamer called *Prince* should be purchased instead. It was decided to use *Esk*, but she proved too slow, and her accommodation was inadequate. In April 1851, therefore, the Court decided to purchase *Prince* for £16,500. Other than that she was a new Sunderland-built 398-ton iron paddle steamer (having only made 'one or two experimental voyages'), and was purchased from Capt. Andrews, nothing more is known about her. *Prince* was the first iron vessel to enter RMSP's fleet. *Esk* was then despatched to the West Indies, 'where she will probably be employed hereafter, to improve some branch of service hitherto served by sail alone'.

Prince proved adequate for a time, but by 1853 she, too, needed to be replaced. The iron paddle steamer which took over was *Camilla*, purchased that May from G. & J. Burns, for whom she had operated the Glasgow – Liverpool service. There was a considerable size increase, to 539 gross tons.

Camilla filled the role for six years before being replaced by *Mersey*. An iron paddle steamer, *Mersey* was almost double *Camilla*'s size at 1,039 gross tons, and was the first ship custom-built for the feeder service. Her builder has not been positively identified – the centenary history has a question mark against Thames Ironworks at Blackwall and the only tenderer named in the Court minutes was Wigram & Sons. Maudslay & Co. built the engines, which increases the likelihood that she was built on the Thames. Early in 1864 RMSP made plans for *Mersey* to return to England for an overhaul and re-boilering. Rather than provide an existing ship as a temporary replacement, they elected to build a new ship for a stint on the feeder service and then, when *Mersey* returned, to enter the West Indies intercolonial trade.

The ship was built and named *Arno*, departing from Southampton on 13 September 1865. Another iron paddle steamer, she was built at Greenock by Caird & Co. *Mersey* returned for her refit, but while that was going on the directors decided to reverse their roles: *Arno* would remain in South America and *Mersey* would go to the West Indies. *Arno* remained on the feeder service until withdrawn late in 1869 when the through service began. She was then refitted and despatched in March 1870 for the West Indies intercolonial service.

A brief look at the later careers of those ships: on the return of *Esk* to the West Indies in September 1851, she operated inter-island routes. Small and unpopular, she was withdrawn and brought back to England, where she was sold in 1854 to Thomas Hill of Southampton. He made major changes, including lengthening the hull by more than 30ft. After a further change of ownership she was lost in April 1856 in the Black Sea.

Prince, also transferred to the Caribbean, was sold there in 1862. *Camilla* remained in South America after her withdrawal from the feeder service, sold in 1859 to the Buenos Aires Government. *Arno*, almost the same size as *Mersey*, remained in service in the West Indies until 1882. While there is no doubt that she was sold that year, there is uncertainty as to what happened to her, for Lloyd's Register recorded her owner as unknown but Spanish until she left the Register in 1885.

Mersey, too, transferred to the West Indies station, where she remained for a decade or so. The decision to sell her was taken in 1876 and the Company's superintendent in the Caribbean was to sell her for what he could get without reference to London. Two offers were received, £650 and £700. Then came a telegram, in August, saying that '*£1,000 is offered for the* Mersey *by Mr Adamson, passenger in the* Larne'. B. Adamson, then, bought her and registered the ship in London; about three years later she went to W. Moodie. In 1881 or 1882 he removed her engines and turned her into a four-masted barque, then sold her in 1884 to A. Major.

During the late 1880s, Major changed her rig to what *Lloyd's Register* described as a four-masted barquentine. This caused some confusion which later brought *Mersey* to the attention of maritime historian Harold Underhill – he described her as one of only a handful of four-masted jackass barques – square-rigged on the two forward masts and fore-and-aft rigged on the after two. Around the early 1890s she spent some time in the Antipodes, bringing home wheat cargoes from South Australia and filling in with Australia – New Zealand voyages. At that period there were a couple of quick sales to other London owners, then just after the turn of the century she was sold for the first time outside Britain. Her new owner in Grimstad, Norway had her only briefly before she left the Register in 1903.

Solent (I)

Solent was unique as the only composite steamer in the fleet. She and the *Medina* of 1841 were the only ships built for Royal Mail by T. & J. White at Cowes, Isle of Wight. An 1,804 gross ton paddle steamer, *Solent* was built with iron frames and timber planking in 1853. That mode of construction was reputed in some quarters to make her more buoyant than her consorts. She was also considered to use less coal.

She was launched, controversially, by the daughter of exiled Buenos Aires dictator Manuel de Rosas, who had been banished from his homeland and spent the remainder of his life as a farmer near Southampton.

Regarded as a particularly handsome ship, her most distinctive feature was the paddle box design, bearing a rising sun motif with the Royal crown at its centre. She was designed for West Indies intercolonial service but operated to Brazil for two voyages; these were in 1855,

Solent (I), built at Cowes, Isle of Wight, in 1853. She was probably the only Royal Mail ship to incorporate the Royal crown in her paddle box design.

filling in while another ship was chartered for Crimean War service. Capt. J.H. Jellicoe was in command and these were the first transatlantic voyages as captain for a man who enjoyed an extraordinarily long and successful career with RMSP (looked at in Volume 1). *Solent* then returned to Caribbean services and remained there until her sale in 1869.

Danube (I)

Danube was ordered in 1863 for West Indies intercolonial services. Her construction was the most protracted and trouble-plagued newbuilding the Company ever had to contend with, for she was not completed until at least the middle of 1866. Admiralty surveys on behalf of the Post Office during 1864 were very critical – the longitudinal strength was not adequate and there were problems with bulkhead and compartment construction.

The nature of the subsequent dialogue between RMSP and the builders (Millwall Ironworks Co.) is not known, but it can be fairly surmised from the fact that, in July 1865, RMSP received legal opinion that the Company was at liberty to reject the ship and recover payment instalments already made if *Danube* had not been constructed in accordance with the contract. The response of the directors was 'that without foregoing any legal rights the Company possess, an endeavour be made to come to some amicable arrangement for carrying out such alterations as may render the ship serviceable to the Company'.

That aim was achieved, but during 1865 and 1866 RMSP displayed growing frustration with the delays. Finally in service in Caribbean waters during the second half of 1866, she remained in that region except for two unexpected transatlantic voyages to Brazil in 1868. She was a true white elephant, for after three years under construction, she was in the fleet for only around six years before becoming so outmoded that she was sold. The idea of a new ocean-going steamer using paddles in the mid-1860s was quite extraordinary. She was the last Royal Mail paddle steamer to be built, and measured precisely 2,000 tons gross.

Her two Brazil voyages were in the latter months of 1868. Capt. West wrote from Lisbon to report the satisfaction of passengers with 'the table accommodation, ventilation and general comforts of the ship'. During the voyage, however, things appeared to become *too* comfortable – reports reached Head Office that Capt. West had indulged in a game or two of cards, and while card playing among passengers was accepted (providing it didn't become serious gambling), captains weren't supposed to join in. Capt. West was severely reprimanded and wasn't in *Danube* for her next voyage.

In 1871 she was sold to the Union SS Co. That company (one half of what would become Union-Castle) felt it was worth spending the money to buy her – £14,250 – and then convert her to screw propulsion. She was sent to Day, Summers yard at Northam for the conversion, which included other changes like replacing her twin funnels with a single one. Despite her elegant clipper bow and counter stern, she ended up anything but a handsome ship – there was virtually no sheer aft of the foremast and the only deck housing was a small structure supporting a raked but spindly funnel.

One of the earliest photographs of an RMSP ship, the 2,000-ton Danube *(I). It was taken, probably at Southampton, between 1866 and 1871.*

Her passenger accommodation was also changed, reducing her first class capacity by about a third. Now she was to travel in cooler climes, a new feature was 'central heating' with hot water circulating through two-inch pipes through all cabins flanking the saloon. According to *The Times* this was the first use of such a 'novelty' in any ship. Union Line sold her in 1888 and she was broken up shortly afterwards.

Don and *Para*

A pocket of exceptionally high quality ore from Scandinavia was used for the construction of the iron screw steamers *Puno* and *Corcovado* for The Pacific Steam Navigation Co. Both were built by Cammell Laird at Birkenhead, *Corcovado* in 1872 and *Puno* a year later. For a short time they were used in PSN's west coast of South America trade, but in 1875, following the loss of *Boyne* and *Shannon*, they were purchased by RMSP. *Puno* became *Para* and *Corcovado* became *Don*.

Purchased for Caribbean services, they were fine ships and popular on the route. For a few years they were the largest vessels in the fleet, and were also RMSP's first ships with steam steering gear. *Para*, later in life, was fitted with a new form of refrigerating equipment – it involved hermetically sealing the chambers and pumping in low-temperature carbon dioxide. During her second voyage with this equipment it exploded, killing its inventor, Mr Lawton, and two assistants. It also badly damaged some public rooms.

Para did not visit the South Atlantic, but *Don* made about five voyages to South America – four in 1889/90 and a fifth in 1894. The first closely followed the installation of triple expansion engines which were provided by Earles Shipbuilding Co. at Hull. Her

The sleek lines of the 4,028-ton Para, *purchased together with her sister-ship* Don *in 1875 from The Pacific Steam Navigation Co.*

accommodation was improved at the same time. PSN listed both ships as 3,805 gross tons, but Royal Mail's fleet list credits them as 4,028. The increase was caused by those accommodation changes (*Para* underwent the same changes after *Don*).

This was the *Don* of Kipling's poem referred to elsewhere. However, though he called her a 'great steamer white and gold', she didn't sail to South America in those colours, which were not introduced until years after her last visit; indeed, she was sold to the French Government for breaking up in 1901, shortly *before* Kipling's poem was published.

Para followed her to France two years later. Their high-quality hulls were melted down and used for armour plating.

Trent (II) and *Tamar* (II)

These ships were bought in 1878 as an outcome of an enquiry into 'the injury done to the Company's operations by quarantine in the fever season'. The presence of yellow fever in parts of South America meant that RMSP's ships faced quarantine on their return to Europe. To overcome this, additional ships were provided to maintain separate schedules.

Trent and *Tamar* could be used for other routes outside the quarantine periods, but in the event virtually all of *Tamar's* sixty-seven voyages and *Trent's* sixty-five were to South America on one or other of the schedules. They were sister-ships built by Hendersons at Renfrew in 1873 for China Trans-Pacific SS Co. of London, as barque-rigged iron screw steamers named *Vasco da Gama* (renamed *Trent*) and *Vancouver* (renamed *Tamar*). Their

Trent (II), bought by RMSP in 1878 for a new South America service to counter delays through yellow fever quarantine. She remained in the fleet for almost twenty years.

gross tonnage was about 2,920. Engined by Henderson, Coulborn & Co., they were given compound machinery producing 530hp.

Trent's entry into RMSP service was particularly troublesome. Her first voyage departed from Southampton on 27 December 1878 – she and *Tamar* (which had departed a month earlier) at this time inaugurated a direct service to the River Plate to avoid the fever country in Brazil. *Trent* became disabled in the Atlantic and was towed to St Vincent by the Allan liner *Manitoban* (which earned £2,500 for her services). Eventually the voyage continued, but at Bahia on 8 April 1879 she suffered a fire in her coal bunkers. That problem over, she arrived back in Europe – only to take fire again at Antwerp on 7 May.

In the following May she was in trouble at Rio de Janeiro where a damaged stern tube had to be replaced. All this time her sister-ship was settling in with no mishaps. Soon both became good, reliable 'plodders', principally carrying cargo. They didn't have the plush accommodation of the mail steamers and were more inclined to carry steerage migrants. Perhaps 'plodders' is the wrong word, for they could average 11 or 12 knots, no mean speed for second-string ships of that era. Their best performances were remarkably close, for *Trent's* fastest round voyage average was 12.46 knots and *Tamar's* 12.44. Accessories added in the late 1880s included electric light and stores refrigeration. Both ships had their yards removed in 1891.

With replacement ships entering service during the 1890s, *Trent* and *Tamar* were placed on the sale market. *Tamar* went to shipbreakers in Holland during 1897, while *Trent* was sold and given the name *Luigi*, but ended up with Italian breakers a year later.

Derwent (II), *Humber* and *Avon* (II)

These were not sister-ships, but are linked for a couple of reasons – they were purchased with a view, like *Tamar* and *Trent*, to relieving the quarantine situation, and also because they were bought while on the stocks with builders who had laid them down as speculation ships to keep workers employed, a common situation in the late 1870s.

Derwent was built by Robert Thompson Jr at Southwick, Sunderland. Royal Mail agreed to buy her on 15 October 1879, presumably very close to her original specifications for she was in service by January. Her gross tonnage was 2,466. In twenty-three years of RMSP service there was little to record – in fact, she warranted no mention in the Company's centenary history outside the fleet list. An unexceptional freighter, her designed speed of 9 knots was rarely exceeded, though she *did* maintain 11 knots on one occasion with all sail set. The yards were removed in 1899.

The first of her seven voyages to South America began from London on 1 November 1881, under Capt. C.W. Hanslip. The use of London as a freight port had first been discussed a year earlier, and in January the directors approved the Royal Albert or Victoria docks for use by *Avon* on West Indies service. The November sailing by *Derwent* was almost certainly the first occasion London was used as a loading port for South America. It was a shortlived arrangement, however, and though Royal Mail periodically used London from then on, many years passed before it usurped Southampton as the major terminus port.

At this period the Company began thinking about voyaging to Brazil, West Indies and New York. It had been tried on a single voyage earlier by *Rakaia*, and it was approved as a new schedule in March 1884. *Derwent's* last voyage to South America followed this itinerary early in 1885. She did not sail the South Atlantic again. In 1892 she was overhauled and reboilered at a cost of £10,300. On 10 January 1899 she collided with the barque *Edith & Mary* in the Thames, inflicting some £30-worth of damage on the sailing ship.

Derwent became a victim of the Company crisis of 1902 which culminated in the arrival of Owen Philipps the following January. She was put on the sale market during 1902, after her September voyage had been cancelled 'as prospects of satisfactory business had fallen off', and in October was sold to G.P. Walford of Cie de Navigation Extrème Orient for £6,600. They renamed her *Lilia*. No longer a modern ship, she nevertheless had many years of service ahead of her, under a swag of owners, and did not leave the Register until 1931.

Humber was purchased by RMSP when she had just been completed on the Clyde by the London & Glasgow Engineering & Iron SB Co. The decision to purchase was made at the end of January 1880. A month later she was waiting at Gareloch for the voyage to Southampton. She was an iron screw steamer of 2,371 gross tons.

Her short career included three voyages to South America, but before that she got into a little trouble by grounding on the Culebra Bank in the Caribbean during her second voyage. In February 1881 she was chartered by the British Government to carry a West India regiment to Africa in connection with the Ashantee War. It was a tight squeeze to fit 1,492 soldiers into her. Later that year she made her first voyage to Brazil and the River Plate, the second ship on the route to load in London. There was a second voyage to South America in 1883, and her third began on 1 December 1884. It took her initially to Lisbon, Pernambuco, Maceio, Bahia, Rio de Janeiro and Santos.

From there she sailed north to Rio, Barbados, St Thomas and New York, arriving in the Hudson on 8 February. She departed from New York on the 15th on a cargo-only voyage, bound for England. Two days later, at 11.30 a.m., she was sighted by the steamer *Atlantique* in latitude 40° 20' N, longitude 68° 15' W. That was the last that was heard of her. Two letters from relatives of people on board claimed the interest of the directors, for they described the very bad weather through which the ship had travelled on the way to New York. Whether that weakened the ship will never be known. Hitting an iceberg was another possibility.

Third of these similar but essentially unconnected ships was *Avon*. Purchased near completion at the yard of James Laing at Sunderland, she was a touch smaller than the others at 2,162 gross tons. The decision to purchase was made in October 1879 and she had a long and unexceptional career with the Company. During the early years, while extra schedules to overcome quarantine were in force, she made seven voyages to South America.

Like *Derwent*, her time with the Company ended in the wake of the boardroom upheavals of 1902; in February 1903 she was sold to John Ellerman for £4,300. She appeared in the ownership of Cedardene Steamship Co., under the management of Ellerman Lines' Fred Swift. Over the ensuing years ownership devolved simply on Ellerman Lines and she left the Register in 1917.

Dart (I)

The 2,641-ton *Dart* was launched at the Middlesborough yard of Sir Raylton Dixon & Co. in 1883 and departed for South America on her maiden voyage on 1 December that year. She was either being built on speculation or was purchased from her intended owner, for it was not decided to buy her until late May 1883, at which time she bore the provisional name *Cavio*.

Her second voyage took her to the West Indies but in August 1884 she returned to South America for the new route to Brazil, West Indies and New York. On 11 September she left Santos for Rio de Janeiro and at 10 p.m. that night, during a tremendous thunderstorm, hit a reef off San Sebastian. She quickly heeled over, but officers and crew remained by her all night after the passengers had been landed at Rio from the boats.

During the following afternoon the ship broke up and was abandoned. The chief officer was lost, but there were no other casualties – except to this short-lived service, to whose demise *Dart's* loss contributed.

Nile (I)

Nile was ordered shortly before *Elbe* and, like her, was built for the new through-service to Colon as part of RMSP's involvement in a new mail service to Australia and New Zealand.

Built by Day, Summers & Co. at Southampton (launched on 7 September 1869), she was to have been a sister ship to *Neva* if the plans could be obtained from Caird's, but it seems likely that she was built to a new, if similar, design. Initially 2,994 tons, that figure rose to 3,039 in 1878 when her original 600hp direct-acting engines were replaced with compound machinery.

During a long career which began with her maiden voyage departure on 2 February 1870, she operated to South America on only a couple of occasions. In May 1887, under Capt. Brander, she sailed to Brazil only (that was her 80th voyage) and there was a further voyage a year later.

Nile's career was less than auspicious, being well peppered with incidents and accidents. In February 1872 she collided with the cutter *Surprise* and sank her, three months later ran into HMS *Sirius* at Barbados, and four months later again collided with a ship named *Yokohama*. There was a major fire on board at Barbados in December 1874, in the aftermath of which Capt. Revett was recommended for the Albert Medal. Within a few months *Nile* was in trouble again, grounding near Le Havre through what the Court decided was 'an unfortunate error of judgement' from Capt. Revett.

She was next in the news – now commanded by Capt. Bruce – after grounding on the Haitian coast late in 1879. In July 1881, under Capt. W.W. Herbert, she suffered an explosion and fire, and in June 1882 Capt. Dickinson put her ashore on Beacon Shoal near Port Royal, Jamaica.

That litany of accidents – eight in ten years – was probably unparalleled for a single ship – and she survived them all. In 1889 the decision to sell her was taken. Capt. Robert Woolward suggested that after her withdrawal early the following year she should be used for a cruise ('yachting trip') to the West Indies, but a sale was quickly made that May to the Union SS Co. for intermediate services to South Africa. Renamed *Roman*, she was described in a Union-Castle history as a 'bad buy' and within a year she had gone to shipbreakers.

What constituted a 'bad buy'? As indicated above, her last RMSP skipper was Capt. Woolward, who was given command of her temporarily while his own ship, *Don*, was being fitted with triple expansion engines. He described her as:

…not at all equal to the service required of her, but she was considered one of the strongest ships afloat, and was comfortable. She was a caution, certainly, to have anything to do with. Short of speed from her birth, she could not carry either the coal she burnt or the cargo that offered. We always arrived after time, and were obliged to remain longer in port than the time allowed to get the little cargo she carried in and out, as her hatchways were too small…

La Plata (III), *Minho* (II) and *Ebro* (II)

These steel screw steamers of 3,445 gross tons were built by the Napier yard at Glasgow in 1896 for the intermediate, or 'B', service to South America. They were among RMSP's 'slow boats' on long itineraries, unhampered by the tight scheduling of mail voyages.

In the overall scheme of things, they hid somewhat in the shadow of their larger and more glamorous contemporaries. That they were not successful is borne out by the sale of one after four years and the others by 1903 – and yet, on the face of it, they seemed right for the job. Each carried some 4,000 tons of cargo, had refrigerated stores chambers and electric lighting, and could accommodate large numbers of third class passengers.

Perhaps their scheduling was made *too* flexible. *Minho's* maiden voyage, for instance, lasted nearly three months, a time frame which would only be profitable if there were significant inter-port freights within South America. After leaving Southampton on 22 October 1896, she called at Coruña, Leixões, Vigo, Villagarcia, Las Palmas, Pernambuco, Maceio, Bahia, Ilia Grande, Rio de Janeiro, Santos, Montevideo, Buenos Aires, Montevideo, Santos, Rio de Janeiro, Bahia, Maceio, Pernambuco, Las Palmas, Lisbon, Southampton and Antwerp. In addition to cargo, the ships carried migrants from Peninsula ports to Brazil and the Argentine.

During *Ebro's* maiden voyage she was aground for six hours near Maceio, but their brief years of service were, in the main, not newsworthy. *La Plata* was sold in 1900 to Booth Line, who renamed her *Clement*. At this time the other two were used as transports in the Boer War. They were then sold to H.F. Swan (W. Petersen Ltd, managers) in 1903, *Minho* becoming *Halifax* and *Ebro* the *Quebec*. They were almost immediately re-sold, at which time *Halifax* was renamed *Montreal*. The new owners, from 1904, were French Line (Cie Générale Transatlantique), and the ships, registered at Le Havre, operated principally as freighters on the North Atlantic. They left the Register in 1916.

Clement remained with Booth Line until 1915, when she became *Freshfield* in the ownership of H. & C. Grayson of Liverpool. In 1918, she passed to R. Lawrence Smith Ltd and was registered at Montreal; a year later she left the Register.

Severn (III)

Several ships were sold during 1897 and this vessel was part of the replacement programme, ordered from Sir Raylton Dixon in July 1897. She appears not to have been designed for any particular service; at 3,760 tons she was suitable both for South American cargo services and intercolonial trades in the Caribbean.

Most of her voyages were to the West Indies, but the first year or more saw her in the South Atlantic. Her maiden voyage, taken by Capt. Thomas Pearce, began in November 1898. Her South American voyages were a mixture of Brazil and River Plate and Brazil only, and there was at least one further Brazil voyage, in 1902/03.

At the turn of the century she was briefly taken up as a transport for the Boer War, and having delivered her troops to South Africa, crossed to South America to load home.

Hers was an incident-free career but with a slightly unusual end. In April 1913 it was stated that 'the steamer *Severn*, which under another name has been on a prolonged charter, has been sold'. That 'other name' was *Fernando Poo*, which she had borne since about 1910. By 1913, still bearing that name, her owner was given as Cia Trasatlantica of Cadiz. She left the Register about 1917.

Teviot (II) and *Tamar* (III)

Craig, Taylor & Co. built the 3,200-ton *Teviot* and *Tamar* at Stockton in 1902, steel screw ships for freight services to South America. Their timing was fairly crucial in the RMSP story, for they were the last ships built before the arrival of Owen Philipps. The fact that the directors were aware of the need for flexibility with general cargo tonnage which could load and discharge at many ports helps place the matters of that time in perspective; it may have been a case of 'too little, too late', but strategies *were* being put in place.

As well as the usual port range, the ships initiated calls at a variety of outports like Rosario, San Nicholas and Villa Constituccion, while at the European end their range was even wider, taking in Antwerp, Rotterdam, Le Havre, Newport, Swansea, Cardiff, Middlesborough and Hartlepool.

During 1911 *Tamar*, homeward bound from Rio de Janeiro, ran short of coal and had to burn ship's fittings in order to reach port. Some £500-worth were used, and her chief engineer was subsequently suspended for three months. In January 1913 her propeller worked loose towards the end of a long, trying voyage with a particularly recalcitrant crew; five days were spent at Southampton undergoing repairs. *Teviot*, too, endured an exceptionally long voyage – it was to Brazil only, in 1906, and lasted over four months.

During 1915, homeward-bound from Santos, *Tamar* became the second RMSP ship in a short time (the first was *Potaro*) to be captured by the German raider *Kronprinz Wilhelm*. Her crew was taken off and the ship scuttled.

Teviot *(II), a cargo ship built by Craig, Taylor at Stockton in 1902 and used on various routes.*

For a while during the war *Teviot* was used as a transport for the British Expeditionary Forces being taken to France. Few voyages to South America occurred after that and in 1923 she replaced *Caraquet* (which had been wrecked) in the Company's Canadian service. Because this route was not expected to continue much longer, no new ships were built for it. Indeed, 1927 saw an end to this enterprise, and *Teviot* was broken up at Danzig a year later.

Catalina, Conway (II) and *Caroni*

These small steamers, of about 2,650 tons, were built in 1904 by Armstrong Whitworth at Newcastle. Owen Philipps ordered them for the West Indies cargo service but, by 1906, *Catalina* and *Conway* were both sailing to Brazil and continued to do so sporadically until 1914. *Caroni* made a single Brazil voyage in 1913/14; thereafter only *Conway* continued on the service, loading and discharging at such unexpected ports as Northfleet, Higham Bight, Hole Haven, Dartmouth and North Shields. The developing structure of freight diversification brought these ships to South America, for during 1905 they underwent alterations to accommodate limited amounts of chilled fruit.

In September 1915 *Caroni* (serving as a transport) was sunk by submarine gunfire off the French coast. *Catalina* was sold in 1922 and *Conway* in 1930, but despite their reasonable ages neither went to the breaker's yard. *Catalina* was sold to Matsuoka Kisen KK, renamed *Nisshin Maru* No.3 and registered at Shikitsu. Her name and owner were later slightly modified, listed as *Nissin Maru* No.3 owned by Matuoka Kisen KK. In that guise she saw out the Second World War and left the Register in 1948.

The disposal of *Conway* began quite a merry-go-round. She was bought by Pentwyn SS Co. of London and renamed *Pentusker*. In 1935 she was sold to Dah Loh Industrial Co. of Shanghai and renamed *Dah Sun*. In 1938 she went to G. Stamatelatos of Greece and was renamed *Pipina*. After the war she reverted to her former name and ownership – *Dah Sun*, with Dah Loh Shipping Co. – and left the Register in 1958.

Pardo (I), *Parana* (II) and *Potaro* (I)

The first ships which Harland & Wolff built for Royal Mail – starting a long and enduring association – were *Pardo* and *Potaro*. *Parana* came from Workman Clark, so all three were Belfast ships. At around 4,500 tons (*Potaro* was a touch smaller) they held importance as the first RMSP ships designed for the carriage of meat, earlier vessels having had cool chambers installed in existing spaces. Together with the smaller 'C' class ships they were the first fruits in terms of newbuildings to come from the appointment of Owen Philipps as Chairman.

The 2,650-ton cargo steamer Conway (II), built in 1904 for Caribbean trades but used later to South America. She is pictured at Kingston, Jamaica in 1920.

Pardo (I), one of three meat carriers built in 1904. The picture seems likely to have been taken at Belfast before she left Harland & Wolff's yard.

Parana (II) of 1904, one of the first three custom-designed meat carriers built for RMSP. She came from Workman Clark and the other two from Harland & Wolff.

They carried many migrant passengers from Spain and Portugal. It was becoming increasingly common among non-mail ships to visit many ports beyond the familiar ones of earlier years. In the UK these ships normally loaded and discharged at east and south coast ports, at times as far north as Hull and Newcastle. On other voyages they were seen in South Wales. In the River Plate they loaded at La Plata and Ensenada, and steamed beyond Buenos Aires to Campana. Migrants were embarked at a number of ports, particularly Vigo, Coruña, Bilbao and Santander.

Potaro did not survive the First World War, for in January 1915 she was captured by the Norddeutscher Lloyd liner *Kronprinz Wilhelm*, operating as a raider. Her crew was taken off and she was used as a scout ship for a while before being scuttled. Capt. T.J.C. Purcell-Buret was awarded the DSC after *Parana*'s hour-long battle with a submarine when the Royal Mail ship suffered engine trouble while in convoy in September 1917.

Parana and *Pardo* continued in service until 1933 and 1934 respectively, during which time they inaugurated a new service. When, in 1918, the first of the 'N' class ships (*Navasota*) entered service, she replaced *Pardo* on the River Plate meat run. *Pardo* then loaded in South Wales, sailed to the Plate and then continued southwards to load meat in the wild and lonely regions of Patagonia; at Rio Seco, Gregory Bay, Punta Arenas, Rio Gallegos and San Julian. For years this cattle country in the deep south kept *Pardo* and *Parana* occupied; at the time of the Depression, however, the trade tailed off and they were laid up. Following the creation of Royal Mail Lines in 1932, the two old ships were sold for breaking up and the Patagonian service ceased except for occasional general cargo voyages to Punta Arenas.

Manau and *Marima*

Owen Philipps' plans for South America services were insatiable for some years after his appointment as Chairman. To boost the Brazil cargo service he proposed the purchase, in 1906, of the 2,740-ton freighters *Zulu* and *Transvaal* from Bucknall Bros. Renamed *Marima* and *Manau*, they were steel screw steamers built in 1892 by Sir Raylton Dixon at Middlesborough.

Before entering RMSP service *Manau* was drydocked at Antwerp for an overhaul and repairs. When some of the lower hull plates had been removed, the drydock was accidentally filled and the ship submerged. The ensuing problems were cleared up and she left the Belgian port on 22 March 1906 to load at Newport and Swansea. Her first voyage for the Company took her 6,833 miles to Bahia. Close to this port, ten minutes after midnight on 22 May, she struck a submerged rock and broke in two.

After an initial voyage to the Caribbean, *Marima* began her links with Brazil and the River Plate. Over the years her South Atlantic voyages took her to unexpected British and European ports, including Sligo Bay and Wallsend. Early in February 1908, en route from Middlesborough to Newport, she grounded on Cross Sands near Great Yarmouth. After refloating and a brief stopover at Yarmouth, she made her way to Tilbury and spent a week in the Thames under repair. When she at length got away from South Wales, bad weather forced her back and she spent ten days awaiting calmer weather.

In 1911, after only five years in the fleet, she was sold and renamed *Marika*. Her new owner was George Coulouras; she was now under the Greek flag, with Andros as her port of registry. During the First World War she was sold to Hannevig Bros of Christiania, Norway, and foundered in April 1916.

Alcala (ex-*Vauban*) and *Vandyck*

With the Brazil and River Plate trade growing rapidly early in the 20th century, new tonnage was needed faster than Harland & Wolff could complete the final four 'A' ships. In 1912, therefore, RMSP chartered from Lamport & Holt *Vauban* and *Vandyck*. They were modern passenger-cargo liners of 10,660 tons, sufficiently comparable with the 'A' ships to fit in well. *Vandyck* made three voyages for RMSP before returning to Lamport & Holt.

Vauban made four voyages between July 1912 and March 1913; then she briefly entered the RMSP fleet and was renamed *Alcala*, and in that guise made four further trips to the River Plate. She left Southampton again on 28 November 1913, and on completion of her outward voyage at Buenos Aires was handed back to Lamport & Holt, immediately resuming her original run between the River Plate and New York.

In January 1913 *Vauban* picked up wireless distress calls from the steamer *Veronese*; she turned back, sighted *Veronese* ashore near Leixões and stood by the stricken vessel all day. Bad weather, however, prevented her from providing assistance.

Vauban, *Vestris* and a later *Vandyck* were chartered in 1922, this time for a single voyage each during a busy period on RMSP's North Atlantic service.

Essequibo (II) and *Ebro* (III)

The 8,489-ton twin-screw steamer *Essequibo* and her sister-ship *Ebro* were built at Belfast by Workman Clark in 1914 as the last of the transatlantic West Indies mail steamers. Though smaller than the 'A' ships, and designed for different requirements, they were clearly modelled on them, not least with the split bridge design.

The First World War cut their operation short, and after the Armistice mail and passenger services to the West Indies ceased. They remained in the Royal Mail fleet until 1922 but operated for The Pacific Steam Navigation Co., at which time they were 'exchanged' for three PSN liners which Royal Mail wanted to use for its North Atlantic service. *Ebro* did not make any voyages to Brazil and the River Plate, but *Essequibo* made two in 1915, filling in for an 'A' ship which was on war service. *Essequibo* was then requisitioned as a hospital ship. *Ebro* was used as an armed merchant cruiser with the 10th Cruiser Squadron.

From 1922 PSN used both ships in their Chile-New York service, via Panama, and it was on board *Ebro* that Harland & Wolff chairman Lord Pirrie died while undertaking a work study tour for RMSP (looked at in Volume 1).

In 1930 they were laid up in the River Dart, and five years later were sold. *Ebro* went to Jugoslavenski Lloyd, who renamed her *Princesa Olga*; in about 1942 she went to Portugal's

Ebro (III) (above), built in 1914, and Essequibo *(II) were designed for the West Indies mail service.*

Companhia Colonial de Navegacao, who renamed her *Serpa Pinto*. She survived until 1955. *Essequibo* was purchased by the Soviet Union, which was desperately in need of good ships. They renamed her *Neva* and operated her in the Black Sea for many years. She left the Register in 1960.

Deseado (I), *Demerara* (II), *Desna*, *Darro* (I) and *Drina* (I)

Like the 'A' and 'P' ships of the early twentieth century, the twin-screw 'D' ships were strategic elements in the development of South America services. In their case, the dominant factor was large refrigerated spaces for meat – they could carry 40,000 carcasses per voyage.

They carried many passengers, too. Each accommodated ninety-five first class and thirty-eight intermediates, with 800 (more, according to some sources) in steerage. The steerage accommodation was 'unrivalled' for some time, but that was comparative – by the standards of later years the accommodation amounted to no more than the bare essentials. First and second class were quite adequate, but plainer than in the 'A' ships.

Their gross tonnage of around 11,480 was astonishingly large for such ships, especially with five operating together – they were larger than the early 'A' ships. Their home port, for the first time in RMSP history, was Liverpool, allowing quicker access for meat cargoes consigned to butchers in the north of England.

The 'D' ships were built at Belfast by Harland & Wolff, entering service between July 1912 and January 1913. They had scarcely become familiar with their schedule when the First World War began. To a large degree the trade was so important that they were left to continue it for much of the war. *Drina*, the last to be completed, was an exception, for she was one of the first British merchant ships requisitioned; on 1 August 1914 she was taken over and fitted out as a hospital ship. By 1916, though, she had also joined the River Plate route.

Two 'D' ships were not initially owned by RMSP but by Elder Dempster group companies, though from the start they operated RMSP's River Plate service. Through an arrangement within the RMSP group, *Darro* was built for Imperial Direct Line and entered the RMSP fleet only in 1916/17. *Drina* was built for Elder Line and transferred to RMSP in 1914/15.

Darro was involved in a catastrophic accident in February 1917. Its failure to appear in the Company's war history was perhaps because it was not an act of war but, for all that, the wartime ban on lights probably contributed. She was in the English Channel in foggy conditions when she was in collision with Elder Dempster's *Mendi*. The latter vessel, carrying South Africans, sank in a few minutes and over 650 lives were lost. I have not seen reports of *Darro's* losses and damage, but she was back in service by May.

On 1 March 1917 *Drina* was torpedoed and sunk three miles off Milford Haven, with the loss of thirteen lives. Four months later *Demerara* was torpedoed off La Rochelle, but remained afloat, and was beached and later repaired.

The four surviving ships continued their voyages to South America until the formation of Royal Mail Lines in 1932. With economic conditions so bad they were laid up at times.

Darro (I), one of five 'D' class passenger and meat cargo ships for the River Plate service. Ownership was originally vested in Imperial Direct Line; she entered the RMSP fleet about 1916.

A group of migrant passengers on one of the 'D' ships, most likely in the 1920s.

A glimpse of the eating facilities offered to steerage passengers in Darro *(I) around the period of the First World War. She was 11,493 tons and carried some 800 third class passengers.*

In 1933 and 1934 they were sold for breaking up, the last to go being *Deseado*, which went to shipbreakers in August 1934.

In marking the sale of the last 'D' ship, Liverpool's *Journal of Commerce* had this to say:

Having been specially designed for the carriage of a large number of emigrants, which trade is now dead, through no fault of their owners, the 'D' class of the Royal Mail Lines have not had such long lives as such fine vessels would merit: the Desna, Demerara *and* Darro *were sold to Japanese scrappers last year, and now the* Deseado *has gone to the same purchasers, a change in the usual routine for such transfers being that delivery was accepted in Liverpool...*

When she came out she was noted for having the most complete refrigerating plant and best steerage accommodation afloat. Captain S.J. Corbould was put in command and she left Liverpool on her maiden voyage inaugurating the Company's new passenger service, between the Mersey and South America, early in July 1912. On that voyage she was the largest ship to load frozen meat at the port of Ensenada, and she brought home a very big cargo.

Shortly before the war she was one of the Royal Mail liners selected for the protective armament of a 4.7 inch gun, but no ammunition was provided until after the actual outbreak.

Within a few weeks of that she was taken up as a Transport for the Expeditionary Force and also carried a number of Indian troops before she was paid off at the beginning of 1915. Early in 1917 she beat off the attack of a German submarine off the south-west coast of Ireland in a very meritorious fashion, and at the end of the year she had a narrow escape from no less than four enemy submarines in heavy weather in the Bay of Biscay. She then had 1,149 people on board and was commanded by Captain G.S. Gillard, who had been placed on the German 'black list' for his successful resistance of a previous attack.

After the Armistice she was the first Royal Mail ship to resume the Vigo call, and was received with a 21-gun salute, taking her place on the Liverpool – Buenos Aires trade, on which, within the limitations of changed conditions, she was as successful as before the war.

The Shire Ships

Royal Mail first bought an interest in Shire Line in 1907, and by 1911 owned the company outright. Among the ships to enter the RMSP fleet through the 1907 deal were *Monmouthshire* and *Denbighshire*. The latter ship became, in March 1913, the first Shire vessel to visit South America – a voyage in which her propeller was lost off the Portuguese coast, forcing her to be towed into Lisbon by a German ship.

Early in the First World War two freighters, *Carmarthenshire* and *Pembrokeshire*, were built by Workman Clark for Shire's traditional Far East service. However, the war changed the plans and their maiden voyages were to Brazil early in 1915. By the end of that year they and *Denbighshire* had between them made nine voyages to South America.

After a further trip by *Denbighshire* in January 1916 there were new ships on the service, which was operating monthly. That February *Carnarvonshire* was seen for the first time on the South Atlantic, then *Cardiganshire* followed in April. They were sister-ships, built by Workman Clark in 1913 and described as being among the finest freighters of their day, twin screw steamers with deadweight capacities of 13,500 tons and accommodation for twelve cabin passengers. In addition, 1,000 steerage could be carried in collapsible 'tweendeck accommodation. The old *Monmouthshire* made her first South America voyage in 1916, too.

During that year the new *Brecknockshire* neared completion at Belfast. Because of war work her construction occupied practically three years and she wasn't completed until January 1917. Later that month, under Capt. G.A. MacKenzie, she left Liverpool with coal for Rio de Janeiro. She was immediately pitched into ferocious storms, which lasted a week and left officers and crew injured and much of the ship's gear damaged. She continued across the South Atlantic and was close to her destination on 15 February when she was seized by the German raider *Möewe*. Her men were taken off and the ship torpedoed.

Two new vessels made their maiden voyages to Brazil in 1919 – *Radnorshire* (6,723 tons) and *Glamorganshire* (8,192 tons). Both were wartime standard ships – *Radnorshire* was an F-type laid down at Sunderland by J.L. Thompson as *War Diamond* and *Glamorganshire* in Yokohama as the C-type *War Armour*. When *War Armour* was completed in 1917 she was owned by the Shipping Controller and managed by RMSP; in 1919 she sailed to England via Java and Capetown. Sir Owen Philipps and P&O chairman Lord Inchcape between them bought a large number of the standard ships not allocated when the war ended, and these two were among the vessels taken by RMSP. As *Glamorganshire* and *Radnorshire*, they spent many years operating on a variety of routes. They were also chartered at times, and *Radnorshire* brought large amounts of cotton from Texas during a boom year in 1921.

Built in 1902 for Jenkins & Co., Monmouthshire *entered the RMSP fleet five years later as part of its purchase of Shire Line. She was later renamed* Tyne *(IV).*

Glamorganshire was sold for scrap in 1933. *Radnorshire* was sold to Edinburgh owner Henry Thomson in 1930, receiving the name *Sithonia*, and was torpedoed in July 1942.

Cardiganshire and *Carmarthenshire* were sold in 1929 to Christian Salvesen's South Georgia Co. for conversion to whale product factories. They were renamed *Salvestria* and *Sourabaya*. *Cardiganshire's* most significant drama occurred in 1924, when the schooner *Inspiration* got into terrible trouble during an Atlantic storm. Lightning struck and brought down a mast; then the storm completely dismasted her and tore away the rudder. Her crew, in the helplessly-drifting ship, were near exhaustion when the freighter reached them twelve days later. In getting the seven crewmen off the ship in heavy seas, *Cardiganshire's* boat was badly damaged and was half full of water when it returned to the ship.

Between the Wars

Many standard-design freighters entered the Royal Mail fleet in 1919 and 1920. Those which traded to South America included most of the 5,200-ton 'S' class – *Segura, Sabor, Sambre, Sarthe, Severn, Somme, Silarus* and *Siris*. Those First World War standard ships were invaluable as replacements for lost tonnage, and while *Segura* was soon sold (and reported to be a war loss in 1939), most remained with the Company into the 1930s. Some were still operating during the Second World War. Little was recorded about their inter-war careers, possibly more because of their modest status in the fleet than a lack of

Sambre, *a standard First World War freighter of 5,260 tons completed in 1919, a typical acquisition by RMSP to replace war losses. She, in turn, was lost by torpedo in 1940.*

The motorship Araby *(I), built for David MacIver & Co. and absorbed into the Royal Mail fleet following the Scheme of Arrangement in 1932.*

The diesel cargo ship Gascony *was originally owned by MacIver & Co. and entered the Royal Mail fleet in 1932. She was the last survivor among the MacIver ships, being sold for scrap in 1958.*

occurrences. It is known, for instance, that *Sambre* had upper hull damage from a collision with *Maria Luisa* at Rio Grande do Sul in 1929.

A brief look at one Brazil cargo voyage by *Sabor* in 1939 provides a glimpse of how the surviving 'S' ships were faring at twenty years of age. Under Capt. A.E. Jones she left England in ballast on 25 August and returned on 1 January 1940 with a full cargo. The voyage was affected by wartime conditions, for Admiralty routes and zig-zagging added 2,621 miles to the journey. Her average of 8.84 knots was also affected by the war – coal consumption of 26.35 tons per day was described as low because of reduced speed, suggesting the restrictions of convoys.

Sabor was the last survivor among the 'S' ships, being torpedoed in 1943. *Sambre*, *Sarthe*, *Somme* and *Siris* were all torpedoed earlier in the war, also still in Royal Mail ownership. *Silarus* and *Severn* were sold to Greek owners in the early 1930s and *Silarus* appears also to have been a war loss. *Severn* left the register in 1935.

During the inter-war years Royal Mail made its last foray into the North Atlantic trade with ships of about 15,000 tons which came from The Pacific Steam Navigation Co. (in exchange for *Ebro* and *Essequibo*). They were on a par with the later 'A' ships, like *Almanzora*. One was *Orbita*, which was in RMSP ownership between 1923 and 1926. Several years earlier, however (while still under PSN ownership), she had made the occasional voyage under Royal Mail operation to Brazil and the River Plate.

Freighters scheduled at times for South America services included *Larne*, *Vologda*, *Brittany*, *Gascony* and *Araby*. *Larne* was a bit of a curiosity, a 3,800-ton cargo ship purchased in 1916 and kept for only two years. She made a single voyage to Brazil in 1918 and returned via West Africa. Her short stay in the fleet wasn't as unusual as the idea of buying a ship which was already over twenty years old. Built by Robert Napier at Glasgow in 1894, she was one of the lesser-known units of a famous fleet – George Thompson's Aberdeen Line. They named her *Nineveh* and she remained with them until 1907 when she was purchased by the Eastern and Australian Line to cover the loss of *Australian*.

E&A renamed her *Aldenham* and kept her until her sale to RMSP in 1916, presumably acquired to compensate for war losses. She was given the name *Larne*. RMSP sold her to the Zurbaran SS Co., whose managers were MacAndrews & Co.; as MacAndrews was within the RMSP group she effectively remained in the family until sold in 1923 to Schiffswerft Unterelbe AG, a German shipbuilder which dismantled her to re-use her steel for new tonnage.

Brittany, *Gascony* and *Araby* entered the fleet in 1932 as part of the RMSP Scheme of Arrangement – they were originally part of the David MacIver fleet, a wholly-owned subsidiary of RMSP from 1919. The MacIver family's links with steamship operation harked back to the early 1830s, and by 1840 David MacIver & Co. was intimately involved with Samuel Cunard in the formation of Cunard Line. This, however, was not the David MacIver & Co. which entered the RMSP group. The original partners from the 1830s were the brothers David and Charles MacIver. Charles's son, another David, was made a partner in the 1860s. During the mid-1870s, David Jr. left the firm to start up on his own, and so a new David MacIver & Co. was born.

He started with general cargo ships which were either chartered or operated as tramp ships. Later he gained a foothold in the River Plate trade, and then Brazil. This was the company which

RMSP purchased. Six MacIver ships were inherited by Royal Mail in 1932; as general traders they were utilised on a range of routes, those principally involved with Brazil and the River Plate being *Araby*, *Brittany* and *Gascony*. At less than 5,000 gross tons they were useful carriers to complement the larger refrigerated ships. They had been built between 1923 and 1928, all by A. McMillan & Son at Dumbarton, and were given diesel machinery. In that respect they were remarkably cost-efficient, averaging about 10 knots on a little less than 10 tons of oil per day.

Araby and *Brittany* were sunk during the Second World War, while both were on South America voyages. *Araby's* loss in December 1940 was particularly frustrating – she survived a voyage from Brazil via Freetown, Oban, Methil and Hull, only to fall victim to acoustic mines by the boom defence six miles below Southend on her way to London. 'The vessel was stopped to pick up the pilot', wrote her Chief Engineer, A.R. Bunday, 'and the mines exploded on starting up the engines… The explosion broke the ship's back just on the forward engineroom bulkhead…' *Gascony* served Royal Mail until 1958, by then well over thirty years of age.

After the Russian Revolution a number of countries which opposed the communist regime seized Russian ships in their waters. Of those seized by Britain, twelve were placed under the management of RMSP. *Vologda* was one of them. She had been built by J.L. Thompson at Sunderland in 1913 for Harris & Dixon's Century Shipping Co. of London, a steamer of 4,784 tons. Her name then was *Mottisfont* and she was sold around 1916 to the Russian Volunteer Fleet Association. Renamed *Vologda*, her new home port was Petrograd. By 1918 her ownership was given as The Shipping Controller, with RMSP as managers, and this remained so until about 1923. At that point she appeared as *Tideway*, owned by St Mary SS Co. of Cardiff. In 1933 they sold her to I. Margaronis; she was renamed *Nellie* and left the Register in 1943.

While *Vologda* may have been the only Russian Volunteer Fleet ship to trade to South America for RMSP, another ship operated in similar circumstances made a voyage to Brazil and the River Plate in 1919. She was *Meteor*, a steel steamer of 3,617 gross tons built by Blohm & Voss at Hamburg in 1904 for Hamburg-Amerika Line. It seems that she was seized by Britain as reparations, for by 1919 she was owned by The Shipping Controller, with RMSP as manager – hence her voyage to South America. In 1921 she was sold to H. J. Jewell of London, then in 1923 went to Bergen Line. She remained with them for many years, finally leaving the Register in 1946. During Bergen Line ownership she was painted white and operated as a cruise ship, and retained her original name throughout.

Navasota, Nagara, Nariva, Natia, Narenta, Nictheroy, Nebraska, Nasina, Nalon, Nela and Nogoya

These cargo liners (some of whose origins were as Standard ships from the First World War) emphasised how rapidly the meat trade escalated during the first two decades of the 20th century. First the *'P'* ships, then the *A's* and *'D's*, provided enormous capacity. The *'N'* ships, while to an extent helping to replace war losses, further boosted the capacity.

Navasota, first of the 'N' class meat ships and the only one completed before the end of the First World War – hence the dazzle painting which adorned the ship when she entered service.

Not only was their advent a new departure, providing purely freight operation (mostly refrigerated), they initiated the creation of a new owning company – RMSP Meat Transports Ltd. Most were large, solid-looking ships and RMSP's first with cruiser sterns. Some were twin screw steamers of about 8,700 tons and others were smaller at about 7,200. They operated at around 10-11 knots. Crew numbers varied, but some required exceptionally large crews of eighty or more (a large proportion of them stokers).

The outbreak of war delayed the construction programme and only one, *Navasota*, was completed during the war. Her maiden voyage, in March 1918, was to the River Plate, and she was resplendent in Norman Wilkinson's dazzle-painting creation. What a variation in painting techniques that was for Wilkinson, a respected marine artist. In fact, late in 1904 RMSP took up an offer from him to produce a painting of the first of the 'A' ships, *Aragon*, which the Company purchased for £75. A year after *Navasota* entered service she was joined by *Nagara* (both built by Swan Hunter & Wigham Richardson); then came *Nariva* and *Natia* from Alexander Stephen & Son in 1919/20.

Slightly smaller at 8,260 tons were three G-type standard ships which were on the stocks at Belfast with Workman Clark when the war ended. Completed as turbine-powered refrigerated ships, they were given the names *Narenta*, *Nictheroy* and *Nebraska*. Only one appears to have been allocated a name prior to completion – *Narenta* had been laid down as *Neganti*.

The remaining four 'N' ships entered the fleet much later, following the advent of Royal Mail Lines in 1932, for they had been part of the Nelson Line fleet. Three of them, the 7,200-ton *Meissonier*, *Murillo* and *Molière*, were the only Nelson ships not to have the *Highland* prefix, for their names had not been changed after being purchased from Lamport & Holt in 1930. They were built in 1915 by Russell & Co. at Port Glasgow. The fourth was *Highland Warrior*, another G-type, completed by Barclay, Curle in 1920. They became *Nasina*, *Nalon*, *Nela* and

Nogoya respectively and (like the other 'N' ships) not only traded to South America but also to the west coast of North America, South Africa, Australia and New Zealand. Originally intended for Brazil and River Plate service, their eventual use on other services mirrored the uncertain trading climate of the 1930s. More than other ships in the fleet, they were affected by the downturn in trade, being periodically laid up, generally for a few months at a time, at Southampton, Barry, Rotterdam and other centres.

All of the G-type 'N' ships purchased to fill the gap caused by tonnage lost during the First World War were sunk by submarine torpedoes during the Second World War. Only one of them, *Nebraska*, was still in the Royal Mail fleet by then; she was sunk during a voyage to Buenos Aires in 1944. *Narenta* was owned by a Japanese whaling company and named *Kosei Maru* when she was sunk by a US submarine in 1943. *Nictheroy* had been sold in 1936 and, as *Cuma*, was sunk off Sicily in 1940. *Nogoya*, also sold in 1936, and renamed *Marlene*, was torpedoed off the West African coast in 1941.

The first 'N' ship lost in the Second World War was *Navasota*, torpedoed off the Irish coast on 5 December 1939. The following appeared in *Sea Breezes* in November 1947, written by R. Byrne, who was serving in the destroyer HMS *Escapade*.

> *…The* Navasota, *abreast of us, was struck by a torpedo just by the bridge. She cracked up immediately and within five minutes stood like the letter V upon the water. We raced around her and found we could do little to help… Soon afterwards the stern half slid beneath the waves, the bows floating perpendicularly. Before the stern half sank a man scrambled along the deck, hoisted the ensign and plunged overboard… We then sped away after the U-boat and depth-charged it successfully…*

Escapade picked up thirty-four survivors and looked after them well. Byrne continued:

> *The Royal Mail Line presented the ship with a cheque for £50 as a fund, and £3 10s per man for, as they said, 'a very gallant rescue'. Nothing could have been more gallant than the action of the man of the* Navasota *who hoisted the ensign. The Royal Navy was very proud of the Merchant Navy.*

Navasota
sinking after being torpedoed in December 1939.

In the autumn of 1940, *Natia* was a victim of the German raider *Thor*, posing under the name *Vir*, while voyaging to Buenos Aires. *Thor* probably wouldn't have discovered *Natia* if it hadn't been for vast volumes of smoke emitted by a coal-burner steaming at full speed. The unequal encounter was soon over, with *Natia* disabled and subsequently sunk. Her people were taken on board *Thor* and spent sixteen weeks in her (including the occasion when she was chased by RML's *Alcantara*). The full story of *Natia's* loss, in *Eight Bells*, was based on the diary of Capt. J.W. Carr. One of the remarks in the diary was this: '*Thor* was commanded by Kapitan-zur-See Otto Kähler, a resourceful officer. Unlike most of his compatriots, he was careful to maintain, so far as he was able, the best traditions of the sea'.

That observation had a sequel, for in 1961 the retired Capt. Carr wrote:

> Early in June, my wife and I went over to St Malo in Brittany to join in the Annual Congress of the International Association of Master Mariners-Cape Horners. We had a wonderful time there amongst 500 sailor men of various nationalities – Belgian, Dutch, French, German, Scandinavian and 22 British... The German party was a large one and amongst their names I saw one which caught my eye at once – Otto Kähler... I promptly enquired of the German leader if this could be he; it was.
>
> As soon as possible I got another German captain to take me along to him, for although he sank my ship, his treatment of us while we were what he now calls his unwilling guests was as good as could be expected under the circumstances. I was very interested to meet the man who had caused such an upheaval in the lives of my ship's company.
>
> He knew me at once, greeting me with open arms and even knowing the name of my ship... Next day we were his guests on board the Gorch Fock, a beautiful full-rigged cadet ship recently built... That night I had the pleasure of entertaining him and his wife to dinner – and what a wonderful lot of things we had to talk about. He told us of his encounter with the Alcantara and, of course, of his part in the fight with the Carnarvon Castle.

Pardo (II), *Pampas* (I), *Potaro* (II), *Palma*, *Pampas* (II), *Paraguay*, *Parima* and *Pilcomayo*

Urgently-needed merchant ships built during the Second World War included this group of general cargo liners for RML, between 7,400 and 7,600 tons gross. Known collectively as the 'P' ships, two were lost during the war (*Pampas* [I] and *Palma*) and *Pilcomayo* was built as a partial replacement. Having given their tonnage range, it should be mentioned that those figures were used for much of their trading careers but initially (due to shelter deck status) they were much smaller.

First to enter service was *Pardo*, during 1940. The following year saw *Pampas* [I] and *Potaro*, then came *Palma*. By 1944 *Pampas* [II], *Paraguay* and *Parima* were in service. *Pilcomayo* followed in 1945.

They were designed principally for the Brazil freight service, but were employed on a variety of routes. These unpretentious break-bulk freighters gave excellent service. The odd occasions when they were in the limelight were mostly through wartime exploits. The first *Pampas*, after a brave push to Malta with vital supplies in 1942, was bombed and sunk in Valetta Harbour. In the same campaign *Potaro* led the port column of a convoy from Port Said to Malta, while a second convoy approached the island simultaneously from the west. *Potaro's* cargo included high explosives and 100-octane spirit. On the way her convoy met some of the fiercest opposition in the Mediterranean theatre of war; several bombs exploded a few feet from *Potaro's* hull, causing serious leaks and a complete lighting failure.

She continued to limp along with the other ships, but the increased mileage steered, due to evasion tactics, forced the convoy to turn back through lack of fuel. Part of the east-bound convoy got through to the beleaguered island.

Palma was torpedoed in February 1944 while carrying military equipment from Colombo to Madras. That October the new *Pampas*, already a veteran of the Normandy Landings, emerged from a refit as HMS *Persimmon*, and was made a headquarters ship in the Far East. She must have created something of a record, for she had three names within her first year, as she was launched as *Parramatta* before the directors chose to rename her *Pampas* in memory of the ship which had made such a courageous journey to Malta. As *Persimmon*, the new *Pampas* acted as Commodore ship for the re-occupation of Malaya in 1945; the terms of surrender for Sumatra were conveyed and accepted on board her.

Though *Parima* entered service late in the war (July 1944) she was initially used by the Ministry of War Transport and visited the likes of New York, Aden, Beira, Zanzibar, Colombo, Bombay and Fremantle before entering commercial service.

In December 1945 *Pilcomayo* symbolised the cessation of hostilities when she began her maiden voyage after emerging from Harland & Wolff's Govan yard; this was a cargo voyage to Recife, Bahia, Rio de Janeiro, Santos and Rio Grande do Sul. At the latter port a full cargo of canned meat and timber was loaded for Europe. Post-war commercial services to South America had begun.

For the rest of the 1940s and the 1950s Brazil was most often the destination for the 'P' ships. In September 1959 an agreement with The Pacific Steam Navigation Co. saw a change of schedule. From Brazil some of the ships, starting with *Potaro*, travelled further south to Buenos Aires and the Magellan Straits port of Punta Arenas; thus she revived echoes of a route pioneered over fifty years earlier by the first 'P' ships, though as general freighters these vessels did not carry chilled and frozen meat.

So rare were merchant ships in the remote Magellan Straits that the 'P' ships found themselves in unexpected situations at times. *Parima*, for instance, in 1960 entertained the British Ambassador to Chile at Punta Arenas during an official tour of the southern province. During the same voyage she took a Chilean naval lighthouse keeper to his post. The courtesy was returned by the Chilean patrol ship *Laturno*, which put men on board *Parima* to assist in repairs to electrical gear. Capt. J.F. Anderson of *Pilcomayo* was asked by the lone Salvation Army outpost at Punta Arenas to arrange for a portrait of Queen Elizabeth II to be supplied, a request RML was happy to grant.

Pampas *(II) was taken over by the Admiralty while under construction and radically converted to an Infantry Landing Ship, carrying 650 troops and eighteen landing craft. 'A very pretty blue and light grey camouflage which made the Red Ensign look somewhat incongruous' was how her captain described the hull paintwork. The ship and her troop mess are pictured, probably photographed before leaving the Belfast builders. Though she missed the D-Day landings on 6 June 1944 through engine trouble, she was landing troops on the French beaches a few days later.*

Pilcomayo, *last of the 'P' ships to be completed, entered service in 1945 and operated in various trades until her sale twenty years later.*

Changing trade conditions and the age of the 'P' ships saw the fleet of six on the sale market in the mid-1960s. All but *Parima* left the fleet for further trading in 1965; *Parima* was sold in 1962. None survived very much longer, the last, *Potaro*, leaving the register in 1971.

Darro (II), *Deseado* (II), *Drina* (II) and *Durango*

These were further products of wartime Britain. With gross tonnages of around 9,700, they were twin-screw motorships built in 1942 and 1944. Just as the earlier 'D' ships were invaluable during and after the First World War, so these ships had enormous refrigerated capacity which was important during and after the Second World War. The most obvious difference between their concepts was that the new ships accommodated only twelve cabin passengers.

They were generally bracketed as a group of four but were quite distinctly two pairs of sister-ships. *Drina* and *Durango* comprised one pair, the principal external differences from the other two being a split bridge design and the presence of a massive, raised goalpost kingpost between holds one and two.

All were built at Belfast by Harland & Wolff. Their voyages were at first varied and sometimes long; in 1944, for instance, *Darro* sailed eastabout around the world, picking up a hundred survivors from a torpedoed British India ship near Aden, and loading 6,000 tons of meat and butter in New Zealand. June 1945 found *Drina* at Plymouth, disembarking the port's first passengers since 1939. The naval tender *Camel* was used to bring ashore twenty-five passengers. Her voyage from Montevideo had been completed in the quick time of sixteen days and she brought 7,000 tons of meat for the British Army in Germany.

When peacetime services were restored, the *'D'* ships began their proper commercial careers, initially on the River Plate run. Outward general cargo (often machinery, vehicles and the like) was limited; frequently they took only a thousand tons or less, but it was a satisfying sight, voyage after voyage, to watch them return to London loaded down to their marks with meat, fruit and dairy products.

During the 1960s, freight conditions became unstable. When there was nothing offering from South America they sometimes made charter voyages to New Zealand for Shaw Savill, and at others they loaded fruit cargoes on America's North Pacific coast. In 1964 *Durango* voyaged to Australia. After leaving Aden revised orders were received, sending her through Torres Strait to Brisbane, a region for which the ship had no charts. The resourceful officers, under Capt. J.A. Phillips, acquired some from an Australian naval ship a thousand miles out to sea – in exchange for a few bottles of Scotch. 'I often wonder,' *Durango's* third officer, Philip Smith, commented recently, 'what the Australian Navy men thought of the mad British, sailing the world with plenty of Scotch, but without charts!'

By then their passenger accommodation was closed down, but in *Deseado*, from 1964, it was re-used for a purpose new for Royal Mail, adapted as an engineer cadet training unit. After three years of land-based training, the cadets spent their first six months of sea service in *Deseado*.

When meat shipments from the River Plate declined during the early 1960s, some *'D'* ships, under charter to Shaw Savill, brought New Zealand meat to the UK. In 1965 *Drina* was sold to Shaw Savill, for New Zealand and Australia had become a more reliable trade area. She was

Darro (II), built in 1942, seen in the grey dress of wartime shortly after completion. Her voyages at that period took her to many parts of the world.

renamed *Romanic*. *Durango* joined her early the following year and was renamed *Ruthenic* – she left the Register in 1968. *Romanic* was later sold to a Panamanian company, Embajada Cia Nav SA, and renamed *Sussex*. RML sold *Darro* direct to the same firm in 1967; she was renamed *Surrey*, and almost at once both ships were re-sold to Taiwanese shipbreakers.

That left *Deseado*, whose most unusual voyage was left to the end of her career. For a time in 1966 *Darro* and *Deseado* had lingered in mothballs in the River Fal. At the beginning of December Capt. Miles (now Capt. Sir Miles) Wingate KCVO FNI was given the task of bringing her back into commission. She was drydocked and repaired, and rumours began spreading about where the voyage would take her. When the destination was revealed the secrecy was explained: she was to make a charter voyage to Vietnam.

Sailing early in the New Year, *Deseado* first visited Buenos Aires, where 1,500 tons of pork (probably the most pork Royal Mail had ever loaded in the Plate) was taken on board. The next leg was a non-stop passage across the South Atlantic and Indian oceans to Singapore. It lasted twenty-eight days and was, Capt. Wingate believed, the ship's longest passage since the Second World War. 'In the Malacca Straits,' he reported later, 'we fell in with ships of P&O, Blue Funnel and Ben Line – vessels only normally seen when we are in London Docks. As we passed, one could almost hear them say, "My God, they've lost their way!"'.

During the final passage to Vietnam she was buzzed by US aircraft and questioned by American destroyers, and when she finally rounded the headland of Cap St Jaques, her crew's hearts sank to find twenty-seven vessels at anchor, awaiting (as some had done already for nearly a month) a river passage to Saigon. However, *Deseado* was lucky, for after three days a cable from the charterers' agents welcomed them to Vietnam (nice thought), and advised that a berth was available.

Strict precautions during the passage of the Mekong River forbad anyone to go out on deck, but there was no shooting from the banks and she safely reached the Naval Dockyard.

> *Our berth* [said the captain] *turned out to be a small jetty alongside which we could only work two hatches at a time. Repeated requests over the VHF and whistle blasts failed to raise any spark of interest in anything resembling a mooring party; however, something had to be done quickly, as mooring is only possible at the change of the tide, which reaches a speed of four or five knots. The bow was manoeuvred alongside the knuckle and a heaving line was hopefully thrown at a Vietnamese army private quietly fishing on the jetty, accompanied by the usual polite request, "Would he mind putting it on the post he was sitting on?"*
>
> *Keeping the bow on the quay, a pilot ladder was put over the side and some of the men sent ashore to moor the ship to palm trees along the riverside.*

Two brothers from Tel Aviv were in charge of trying to sell the pork to the citizens of Saigon. Because so little could be put in cold storage ashore, *Deseado* acted as a storeship for a month until the remainder of her cargo could be discharged. Her stay lasted nearly two months, and then she was moved to Nha Be to await the down-river passage of the Mekong. The day she left Nha Be, a tanker moored near to her was mined.

That much was recorded at the time in the Company's house magazine. In a recent letter to me, Sir Miles described just how hair-raising the story of the mined tanker really was. 'On the way down the river from Saigon, of course, there were no aids to navigation, and as darkness descended it behove us to find somewhere to tie up for the night.' A tanker berthed at a small wharf allowed *Deseado* to moor second-off with the aid of fenders, friendly relations extending to the skipper enjoying a nightcap aboard the tanker.

Deseado cast off just before dawn. 'About an hour to an hour and a half after departure Sparks appeared on the bridge with a message which stated that our friendly tanker had been mined, and warning me that we may well have one of these things stuck to our side or bottom.' What a fascinating dilemma! There might be a mine on the ship and there might not; and no chance of acquiring a diver to check. Capt. Wingate elected to continue his passage: 'We can't stop the ship and take to the lifeboats and just sit around waiting for something to happen.'

His decision was influenced by a matter which is referred to frequently in these pages – the shallows of the River Plate and consequent groundings and draggings: 'Experience of the River Plate immediately came to mind where, more often than not, you are sniffing the bottom at frequent intervals. So I thought that if there was something there, then it had been brushed off by now'. The ship reached Singapore safely but, just to make sure, the captain had a diver there check the hull. We will never know whether or not *Deseado* carried a mine along the Mekong.

Having been safely extricated from Vietnam, *Deseado* sailed south to New Zealand and brought a cargo home to Britain, but by July 1967 she was laid up again, this time at Belfast. Without making any further voyages she was sold to Hamburg shipbreakers early the following year.

Deseado (II), 9,641 tons, was built in 1942 for the River Plate meat trade. The last of the quartet of 'D' ships to leave the fleet, going to shipbreakers in 1968, she is pictured arriving in London's Royal Docks during the 1960s with a full meat cargo from the River Plate.

Liberty ship in convoy. The value on the world's trade routes of these rapidly-constructed ships during the Second World War was inestimable, and their value as replacements for lost tonnage after the war equally so. A number bolstered the Royal Mail fleet.

The easily recognisable hull lines of a Liberty ship. This is Balantia *(II), photographed in November 1952 at Itajai, Brazil, where she loaded timber.*

246

Liberty Ships and Others

Ship losses during the Second World War were in part made up with wartime standard newbuildings, among them *Beresina, Berbice, Barranca, Balantia, Teviot* and *Tweed*. Many were periodically seen in South America. The four 'B' ships were American-built Liberty ships which Royal Mail managed through the later war years. One, at least, visited South America at that time, for *Beresina* was at Buenos Aires during her second voyage.

At that time her name was *Samspring*, and her original master, Capt. J.N. Duncan, provided some recollections which told a little of the remarkable story of the Liberty ships; not least the astonishing rapidity with which they were built. Capt. Duncan travelled to America to take over *Samspring* while she was still on the stocks, initially bearing the name *Charles A. Young*. He wrote:

I attended the building of this vessel and was much impressed by the hustle and bustle of the American workmen. Work progressed throughout the twenty-four hours in three shifts of eight hours each. In no case was there any slacking, the full eight hours being worked by all, so much so, that I could not help but admire the American effort.

Men, women, boys and girls were all employed, and I spoke to many of them, finding out that quite a number came from inland, and had never been employed on ships in their lives. Each person had his own job to do and was never altered to another job. Many a time I saw fittings being put on the vessel which I would have liked in a different position, and when mentioning this to the Manager he told me that I could do just exactly as I wished after I had taken the ship over, but that he would alter nothing at all for me, and explained that he knew that some of the fittings were incorrectly placed, but that his whole organisation depended on one person doing one job, exactly the same on every vessel.

To give an example, all bell pushes were fitted by a woman who previously had been a farmer's wife in Ohio. She had a plan of where to fit these pushes in all vessels and went ahead on her own without future instructions at all. To have to alter any of these fittings would have meant loss of time, which could not be permitted.

The foregoing is merely an example of what I mean, and is only one of the many minor jobs done by wholly inexperienced folk. The vessel's future officers were allowed to wander round the vessel at leisure and view all the work going on, but we were not allowed to make any comments whatsoever.

The Charles A. Young *took 38 days to complete, but was ready for launching in 29 days. The launching day arrived without fuss, or any bother. Cold efficiency was the password. The Governor of Portland, Maine arrived down, together with his wife and youngest daughter, and at 14.00 hours the vessel took the water, after having been launched by the daughter…*

The next day I went to the yard to see the fitting out, and to my amazement, in the same ways from which we were launched the previous day, was another keel of a future 'Liberty' with the forecastle head in position. I could hardly believe my eyes, and questioned the Manager about this, and he told me that the forecastle head had come down by road from Missouri. The building of the 'Liberty' vessels was a wonderful achievement, and too much praise cannot be given to the USA for this work.

A week after launching, I went out on trials, still as the Charles A. Young, *which were in every way successful, and two days later we left the port for New York. The night before*

Yacaré, *1,022 tons, just after being launched in Holland in 1959. Together with her sister-ship* Yaguarete, *she was built as a meat lighter for service in the River Plate.*

departure, the name Charles A. Young *was obliterated and* Samspring *substituted. As we left the port, the yard gave us a great send-off, and as a gesture of goodwill I sailed from the yard with the Stars and Stripes flying where the Red Duster should have been, and with the flag of the State of Maine flying at the fore. The only time I have ever sailed under the American ensign!*

Samspring was bought by Royal Mail from the Ministry of Transport on 21 April 1947 and renamed *Beresina*, her first master on commercial service being Capt. T.W. Stevens RD RNR, who initially took her to Brazil and the River Plate. By the 1960s, Capt. Stevens was Company Commodore, commanding *Aragon*. The first master of one of those 1960s 'A' ships, Capt. Harry Sang (who took over *Amazon* from the builder's yard late in 1959), was another who travelled to America in the war to command a brand-new Liberty ship. This was *Samfaithful*, which Royal Mail bought in 1947 and renamed *Balantia*. Capt. Sang, writing his reminiscences in 1949, re-inforced Capt. Duncan's comments on the manner of the ship's construction:

No interference was permitted during the building of the vessel and not even a screw could be altered, thus a rigid timetable of day-to-day progress of construction could be maintained. The vessel was in fact built up from prefabricated parts, for example the stem plates, including chain locker, were simply welded in position as one piece. Likewise the stern frame, plates and after peak were welded in position as one piece, each section fitting exactly like a jigsaw puzzle. Accommodation was likewise welded to the deck, and bulkheads and furniture ready crated in these sections ready for carpenters to erect in position, including ready-cut lengths of electric cable.

Teviot and *Tweed* were likewise wartime standard ships, but British-built as *Empire Abbey* and *Empire Lady*. Further tonnage in South America trades in the post-war years was provided by the former MacIver ships *Gascony* and *Lombardy*.

248

This volume has covered nearly all of the ships which traded to South America for Royal Mail. A handful of others made an occasional South Atlantic crossing – they included *Esk* (1883), *Tyne* (1904), *Segura* (1906) and *Dee* (1914). Even a ship indelibly linked with the West Indies, *Culebra*, made a rare sortie to Brazil late in 1937.

Once *Amazon* and her sisters had left the fleet late in the 1960s, there was a remaining presence for a short time with three ageing cargo liners acquired from other Group companies. The first was Furness-Houlder Argentine Lines' 9,726-ton *Duquesa*, which had been built at Newcastle in 1949. Even older, dating from 1946, was Houlder Bros.' *Hornby Grange*, which RML renamed *Douro*. During 1969 Shaw Savill's large twin-screw steamer *Persic*, 13,593 tons, entered the fleet and became the third Royal Mail ship to receive the name *Derwent*. Though she was by then twenty years old she was, from a freight point of view, comparable with the 'A' ships with about 500,000 cu.ft. of insulated space, a length only about twenty feet less and a service speed, at least in her earlier days, of 17 knots.

Those three ships were the last significant traders for the Company to Brazil and the River Plate, and they had left the fleet by the early 1970s.

Mention should also be made of the meat lighters which ventured up the River Plate to collect meat cargoes from beef properties and bring them to the ships. Between 1912 and 1914 three were built by Cammell Laird at Birkenhead, the need for them caused by the advent of the 11,000-ton 'D' ships which could not venture so far upriver. The first was the 1,104-ton *Dart*, built in 1912. She remained in service until 1959, when she was sold to Rio Frio SA Mar y Comercial of Buenos Aires and renamed *Riofrio I*. She left the Register in 1964.

In 1913 *Doon* joined her, and *Devon* was completed a year later. They were slightly larger at about 1,360 tons. All three were utilised for the war effort during the First World War, and afterwards *Doon* was sold to Las Palmas Produce Co. of Buenos Aires to continue similar work and was renamed *Britanica*. In 1928 she was sold to the Union Cold Storage Co. (Blue Star Line) and remained with Blue Star until leaving the Register in 1949.

The longest career belonged to the third vessel, *Devon*. She was sold in 1959, also to Rio Frio SA Mar y Comercial, and continued her work in the River Plate until leaving the Register in 1986. The sale of *Dart* and *Devon* was occasioned by the arrival of two new lighters, *Yacaré* and *Yaguarete*; they operated well into the 1980s, though RML had disposed of them during the previous decade.

Comparison of Sizes

These eight computer drawings, generated from contemporary photographs, drawings or accommodation plans, display the size comparisons of major ships built for Royal Mail's transatlantic mail services from 1841 until mail services ended in 1969.

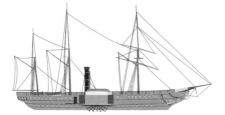

Dee *(I). 1,849 tons. Built 1841. One of fourteen similar units of the first fleet, among the largest steamers of their time, unnecessarily so for some Caribbean routes on which they operated.*

Atrato *(I). 3,467 tons. Built 1853. Replacement for (and considerably larger than)* Demerara *(I), she was RMSP's first transatlantic mail ship to be built of iron.*

Rhone. *2,738 tons. Built 1865.* Rhone *and her sister-ship* Douro *were RMSP's first transatlantic mail steamers designed specifically for the Brazil service. The West Indies was still the premier destination, which explains their smaller size.*

Orinoco *(II). 4,572 tons. Built 1886.* Orinoco *pioneered for the Company steel hulls and triple expansion engines, and had more substantial deck housing than earlier ships.*

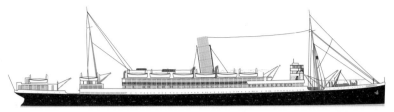

Avon (III). 11,073 tons. Built 1907. The fourth of the original 'A' ship series. They were Royal Mail's most crucial ships in terms of design and size development – the first true ocean liners.

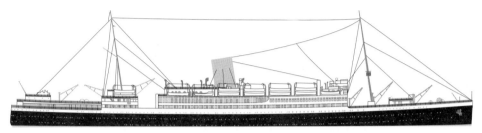

Alcantara (II). 22,209 tons. Built 1926. The largest diesel-powered ship in the world when she was built. Together with her sister-ship Asturias (II) she was over 6,000 tons larger than any previous Royal Mail ship. The picture shows her final profile, as she appeared after the Second World War.

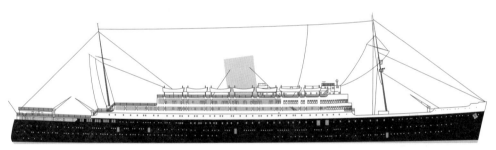

Andes (II). 25,895 tons. Built 1939. The largest passenger liner owned by Royal Mail, she was at about the maximum size which South Atlantic routes at their peak could support. By the time she entered commercial service in 1948 there was already competition from aircraft, and this escalated through the 1950s.

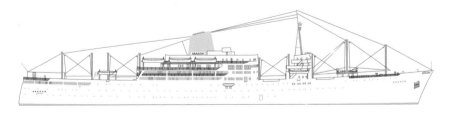

Aragon (II). 20,362 tons. Built 1959. Aragon and her sister-ships Amazon (III) and Arlanza (II) were the last passenger and mail liners built for the Company. The size reduction from Andes (II) was a reflection of the changed trading conditions described above, and their large refrigerated cargo capacity was as important as their passenger facilities.

Select Bibliography

Books

Bonsor, N.R.P, *North Atlantic Seaway*
Bushell, T.A., *Royal Mail 1839-1939*
Bushell, T.A., *Eight Bells*
Davies, P.N., *The Trade Makers* (Elder Dempster 1852-1972)
Dowden, P & G.F. Campbell, *Ships of the Royal Mail Lines*
Grant, Sir A., *Steel & Ships – The History of John Brown*
Harbron, J.D. *Communist Ships and Shipping*
Hurd, A. *Official History of the War, Vol 2: The Merchant Navy* (First World War)
Leslie, H.W., *The Royal Mail War Book*
Murray, M. *Union-Castle Chronicle 1853-1953*
Nicol, S., *Borda Landfall (unpublished)*
Parker, Capt. W.H., *Leaves from an Unwritten Log-Book*
Sawyer, L.A. & W.H. Mitchell, *The Liberty Ships*
Sawyer, L.A. & W.H. Mitchell, *British Standard Ships of World War I*
Talbot-Booth, E.C., *Merchant Ships (1943)*
Wardle, A.C., *Steam Conquers the Pacific* (PSN, 1840-1940)
Witt, H.A.J., *Bush Bishop*
Woolward, Capt. R., *Nigh on Sixty Years at Sea*
HMS *Almanzora* (record of WW1 service)
British merchant vessels lost or damaged by enemy action during Second World War (Admiralty)
Lloyd's Register (various issues)

Other Sources

Atlantic & Pacific Breezes (RML/PSN house magazine), 1959-1966
Log, The (Furness Withy Group house magazine), 1966-1971
Royal Mail News (newsletter of the Royal Mail Association), various issues 1990-2000
Sea Breezes (various issues)
Ships Monthly (various issues)
Macqueen, J – *A General plan for a mail communication by steam between Great Britain and the eastern and western parts of the world; also Canton and Sydney NSW, westward by the Pacific*
RMSP and RML annual reports and half-year reports, 1843-1936
RMSP and RML directors' minute books 1839-1909, 1932-1940
RMSP and RML ship movement list 1841-1919, 1933-1940
Officers Book: extracts of reports on captains and officers (principally 1841-1860s)
Fletcher, Capt. G.M. – personal reminiscences
Purcell-Buret, Capt. T.J.C. – personal reminiscences
Treweeks, Capt. H.H. – personal reminiscences
Berry, Capt. B.K. – personal reminiscences, photographs and scrapbook

Bushell, T.A. – *Royal Mail 1839-1939* and *Eight Bells*: author's files

Blue Peter, The (1923)

Illustrated London News – various issues 1840s-1880s

The SS Great Western *Centenary* (Port of Bristol Authority, 1938)

Orinoco (I) – description, *Household Words*, 1852

Correspondence, yellow fever in *La Plata* (I), 1867

Loss of *Douro* (I), 1882 – extract from *Hull and Eastern Counties Herald*

Agreement, RMSP purchase of PSN interest in Orient-Pacific Line, 1906

Memorandum, 1908 Marconi offer to supply wireless telegraphy on RMSP ships

Letters from James Rawes & Co. to RMSP, 1910 (Portuguese revolution)

Convoys to North Russia, 1942: Release of official documents

Address by RML Chairman on *Andes* (II), January 1948

The Shipbuilder and Marine Engine-builder, May 1949 (*Magdalena* (III))

Magdalena (III) – Proceedings of court of enquiry

Letter from W.C. Warwick to Sir Frederick Rebbeck, October 1949, re *Magdalena* (III)

RML Regulations, 1950

Aragon (II) and *Arlanza* (II) Captain's Voyage Reports

Tristan da Cunha re-settlement, 1963: supporting files

Furness, Withy acquisition of RML: Press announcement 1965

Furness Withy Group staff memorandum 13 November 1970, detailing ships to be withdrawn from service

The small non-trading craft, though not dealt with in this volume, were important parts of the Company's infrastructure. This was the 577-ton tender Atalanta, *used at Bermuda from 1923 and later at Cherbourg.*

Index

References in brackets () are image numbers on colour pages

General

RMSP and RML Ships

References to feature entries are not included – they are listed on the Contents pages.
The Index lists references outside feature pages, and ships not included as features.